A Nation
of Serfs?

A Nation of Serfs?

How Canada's Political Culture
Corrupts Canadian Values

by Mark Milke

John Wiley & Sons Canada, Ltd.

Library and Archives Canada Cataloguing in Publication Data

Milke, Mark, 1967-
    A nation of serfs?: how Canada's political culture corrupts Canadian values / Mark Milke.

Selected sections of *Serfs* previously published Calgary: Thomas & Black, 2002 under title: Tax me I'm Canadian.
Includes bibliographical references and index.
ISBN-13 978-0-470-83856-3
ISBN-10 0-470-83856-6

1. Taxation—Canada.   2. Fiscal policy—Canada.   I. Title.

HJ2449.M54 2006   336.200971   C2006-901425-6

Production Credits:
Cartoon illustrations by Adrian Raeside. Used by permission.
Cover design: Ian Koo
Interior text design: Adrian So
Front cover illustration: The Payment of the Yearly Dues (oil on panel)/
    Pieter Brueghel the Younger/The Bridgeman Art Library/Getty Images
Printer: Printcrafters

John Wiley & Sons Canada, Ltd.
6045 Freemont Blvd.
Mississauga, Ontario
L5R 4J3

Printed in Canada
1 2 3 4 5 PC 10 09 08 07 06

Contents

Foreword

It is safe to say that nothing like this book has ever appeared in Canada. News, according to the cliché, is history written on the run. *A Nation of Serfs* is an up-to-the-news reference work written on the run, and I mean that in the best sense. For anyone who follows political and economic developments in Canada, through newspapers, magazines or electronic media, nothing could be more useful than this fact-filled analytical companion to navigate the horrors of modern 21st century government.

We live in an era of great economic achievement surrounded by national and international government folly. The economic achievement is a function of the relative freedom we enjoy as individuals. It is individuals—workers, business people and even civil servants operating outside and/or despite the destructive foolishness created by governments and our politicians—who propel Canada to greater and greater heights of prosperity. No matter how intense the collectivist pressures in law and regulation, they are not yet enough to overcome the most powerful force in the world, the individual drive for personal achievement, growth and prosperity.

Mark Milke stands on guard against the relentless daily assault on the freedoms that make our country great. As the former head of the Canadian Taxpayers Federation operation in British Columbia, Mark brings first-hand experience to the task of exposing government abuse of the tax system. But he also makes remarkable and often devastating forays into scores of areas well beyond the pernicious work of politicians drunk on spending the people's money. This sweeping range is what makes *A Nation of Serfs* so useful.

Let me just draw attention to a couple of the high points in this book and some of the subject areas that make it such a functional guide to current affairs. Perhaps my favourite is the chapter (13) devoted to exploring some of Canada's true roots as a nation of freedom-loving people—a nation as attached to original principles of limited government as any in the world. For people unfamiliar with

Canadian ideological history—and all of us have been indoctrinated into ignorance at government schools—the ideas that shaped Canada at its foundation and in its early years were profoundly grounded in individual economic freedom and limited government.

The words of Sir Wilfrid Laurier, in 1894, ring loud the call of a country born in freedom. "The good Saxon word, freedom; freedom in every sense of the term, freedom of speech, freedom of action, freedom in religious life and civil life and last but not least, freedom in commercial life." I should add that Mark here has just scratched the surface of one of the great ideological scams of our time, the popular idea that Canada has always stood as a great collectivist alternative to the live-free-or-die American model. This is a wholesale lie, a deliberate false rendering of Canadian history created by collectivist radicals later in the 20th century. Readers stimulated by Chapter 13 of this book could use it as a springboard to deeper research. Two books in particular stand out: *Globalization and the Meaning of Canadian Life* by William Watson and *Canada's Founding Debates* by Janet Ajzenstat.

And that's the beauty of Mark's book. Each section and chapter contains insights and references that shed light on the subjects at hand and lay the groundwork for further excavation. Whether the subject is corporate welfare or day care policy or the funding of non-government organizations (NGOs) and foreign aid, there's plenty of material and insight to send us searching for more. Or, better still, the book itself is substantial enough on its own to act as a companion to the news of the day and as a guide through the policy chaos created daily by our governments. Now I should add that I don't agree with everything here. But that's beside the point, especially given the range of subjects covered in *A Nation of Serfs*. Only through books like this will Canadians emerge out of political serfdom and begin to reclaim the freedom-based foundations of our great country.

The 21st century can belong to Canada.

~ Terence Corcoran
Toronto

Acknowledgements

Books are never a solitary effort despite the hours spent hunched below candlelight—or these days—over a laptop. Many thanks to Terry Corcoran, Corina Dario, Andrea Mrozek, Sam Hiyate, Tasha Kheirridin, John Williamson, Don Loney, Niels Vieldhuis and Walter Robinson.

Introduction

It shall be lawful for the Queen, by and with the Advice and Consent of the Senate and House of Commons, to make Laws for the Peace, Order, and good Government of Canada.

~ Section 91, the British North America Act, 1867

Perspective on one's own country is usually gained from a trip outside of it. A light bulb went off in my head in a German pub in 2000 when an English-speaking local complained to three Canadians—about the Swiss.

I don't recall how Switzerland came up; perhaps we mentioned plans to head south. But the gist of the gentleman's comment was that the German-speaking mountaineers to the south were a bit odd—they thought of themselves too favourably. He had "concerns."

The subtext was that the Swiss were just too successful at business and at wealth creation (and presumably for a German–organization); with that came an attitude. Fair enough. Riches *can* breed arrogance. But for a visitor to Europe, there was weird irony in the complaint: it originated in a country which thought so well of itself that it unfortunately "shared its identity" with its neighbours twice in the last century. But beyond the bemusement, I saw Canada in a new light: here was a fellow in a more populated country who was unhappy about a smaller, wealthier enclave to the south. Switzerland is populated by human beings—so there's no point in romanticizing it. But I was charmed by the prospect of how Switzerland—small in comparison to Germany—was the target of envy. My question: Why shouldn't North Americans have that relationship; that is, why aren't Americans able to look north to a more prosperous nation—Canada—and be occasionally miffed by us for the right reasons?

That is a pleasurable thought but to arrive there one first has to confront the reality of the status quo. I love Canada and my region's place in it: The Rockies in winter, the alpine flowers in July, the Banff Springs Hotel with its evocation of early Dominion life, the British Columbia vineyards, lakes, fruit trees, and ski hills of my earlier years. The "but" is entirely separate from the land. It applies to how far, organizationally, we have strayed from our own ideals of peace, order, and good government.

Over the last decade, citizens were again treated to a spectacle of corrupt government—a most un-Canadian trait if Section 91 of the British North America Act is the credo to which we seriously aspire. It has been some time since we could apply the adjective *good* to the noun *government.*

Readers should consider the most recent example of how we live below our constitutional credo. The Sponsorship Scandal came with a $332 million bill (plus another $30 million for the Gomery inquiry); think about where that money could have been better used.

There are endless possibilities and all preferable to Quebec advertising agencies who hit the jackpot at our expense: 198,209 Canadians with a $20,000 income could have paid no federal income tax for one year. Sections of the Trans-Canada highway might have been upgraded, women's shelters could have hired more staff, more urban green space like Montreal's Mount Royal or Vancouver's Stanley Park might have been created. The RCMP might have used $332 million to better track con artists who steal from seniors (or to investigate rogue federal politicians and their acquaintances who do the same to the rest of us).

On the first and second ideals (peace and order), it is true we have peace; we are not substantively involved in any major war. But the reason is not always laudable. It too often stems from an isolationist reflex of the sort previous generations thought unhelpful when practiced by Americans. Similar to pre-Pearl Harbour U.S.A., Canadian foreign policy now rarely originates in a seasoned mix of long-term domestic interests and responsibilities to the world community. Instead, clichés, moral superiority, and knee-jerk reaction to the U.S. animate public debate and influence our government overmuch.

On order, Canadians are subject to more *dis*order in our urban environment than is reasonable or healthy, itself a result of a failure of citizens (and those who represent and judge them) to abide by and enforce basic norms. But while our urban centres drift towards civic behaviour which 20 years ago was thought to be the domain of American inner cities, Canadian politicians and then the courts have increasingly imposed restrictions on the one area where the opposite is healthier: freedom of expression. Too many Canadians believe social order requires conformity and a necessity to snare contrary opinions; thus our litany of speech codes, gag laws and *faux* public debates. (Oddly, despite that reality, some claim we yet have robust public deliberation.)

That lack of frank discourse is why many Canadians blithely believe we have the best health care system in the world when reality places us in the muddling middle among developed nations. That many believe universal access to health services and private involvement is oxymoronic reveals the poverty of our national discourse. In Canada, naked emperors too often go un-remarked on and sacred cows are well fed.

True, the recent election of a Conservative government in Ottawa may address some of the more obvious, recent rot with in Canada's body politic; one assumes Quebec advertising agencies will get less work for some time. It is one function of a new government to clean out the stable from the last crowd. But politics and politicians follow culture—not the other way around. The change in who commands the ship of state will actually give new life to those who: think every violent criminal deserves a soother rather than a sentence, want Canada to be less entrepreneurial and not more, and equate sensible military and security preparation and international participation against dictators as "war-mongering."

Thus, Canadians should expect a ramp-up in: shrill rhetoric from those who think any tax relief makes us American; anti-globalization activists who—through subsidies—would have governments support tottering industries at home and destroy opportunities for the poor here and abroad; the foes of civic participation who place all their faith in one institution (the courts) to the detriment of others—parliament and provincial legislatures.

In fact, just how averse some Canadians are to new ideas was demonstrated in how quickly the Conservatives ran away from private health care. It was one of their first acts of conception as a newly constituted party. Whether that tack to the status quo was necessary to become government, the fact that Stephen Harper thought it necessary to downplay any possibility of innovative private sector reform says more about many voters than it does about the policy wonk-turned-Prime Minister. Such citizens may be in the minority and worship at the false shrine of 100% government health care. But the political response showed Harper thought there was yet a significant price to be paid if he offended Canada's civil religion: the presumption that government is *good by definition* and not by demonstrative proof.

It wouldn't do to overstate the case; on corruption, Canada is not Nigeria. On crime and urban problems, we are not yet France. But relative measuring sticks are no excuse for moral drowsiness; the lowest bar is just that, not a reason to ignore the high-jump competition.

Insofar as they are useful, governments, tax dollars, and redistribution should exist for: the poor who cannot help themselves, not for the well-connected who can; re-training and relocation when a single industry town goes bust, not a business that asks for corporate welfare in two countries (and plays each nation's taxpayers off against each other); single parents and seniors on fixed incomes, not daycare for wealthy families; treatment for the heroin addict but not a light parliamentary or judicial slap for drug dealers; common sense and helpful treatment for the mentally ill, not a scattering of the same onto the streets (and into poverty) under the guise of rights.

In short, good government is akin to character—it's not instantaneous but results from an accumulation of sensible, proper choices over time. And that requires responsibility and reflection both individually and corporately: citizens can blame *some* politicians and—as of late, *some* justices for various ills—but they might reflect on their own role and choices.

In 1988, two American observers of Canada, Charles Doran and James Sewell, claimed that Canadian "take seriously their credo of peace, order and good government," and that while freedom was important to us—a debatable proposition in my view, "authority looms much larger in their system than it does in the United States ... Good government means strong government, tough government, ever-present government."

We have the *last* form of rule. The question—regardless of the political party in power—is how and why many Canadians think such pervasiveness is equivalent to *good*.

Mark Milke,
Calgary, January 2006

Chapter 1

Gomery, Gotham Grit and the Governor General: The troika of evidence for modern Canadian attitudes

We make men without chests and expect of them virtue and enterprise. We laugh at honour and are shocked to find traitors in our midst. We castrate and bid the geldings be fruitful.[1]
    ~ C.S. Lewis, *The Abolition of Man*

A Culture of Conformity: Our Reaction to the New Governor General

It is perhaps fitting that Canada's newest governor general symbolizes the weakness in modern Canadian life with regard to loyalty. There is the belief that eternal Canadian values exist that set us apart from every other country (and especially the one south of the 49th parallel); but there is the contradictory reality played out in the drama of the recent appointment of our head of state in 2005. There, Michaëlle Jean's ascension demonstrated how little loyalty need be shown to our Canada in order to serve it; loyalty can apparently be professed, in a pinch, in a press release and in a subsequent speech.

As Jean sat in Montreal's Quai des Brumes tavern in 1990 to the left of Pierre Vallières, she could never have imagined that a video clip from that night would, 15 years later, end up as fodder for a national discussion on separatism and crass career and political opportunism. Jean and her film-maker husband, Jean-Daniel Lafond, well knew that Vallières was one of the founders of the Front de Libération du Quebec (FLQ), the Quebec separatist group responsible for the murder of Quebec Cabinet minister Pierre Laporte in 1970. In any other country, that fact would have torpedoed a candidacy for head of state. Had Jean's toast of "no more dominated people!" in the company of hardline separatists, shown in her husband's documentary, occurred in the American south among erstwhile Confederate rebels, the possibility for being head of state one day would have evaporated with the last call. So too the position of prime minister over in the United Kingdom; if an English bloke were filmed in a Belfast pub with former IRA members still unhappy with English rule and raised such a cheer, the chances of obtaining the top job 15 years hence would be distinctly limited.

Vallières, as the *Toronto Star*'s Andrew Mills wrote, was responsible for the second wave of the terrorist FLQ and hoped it would be the tipping point for the revolution. "Vallières spent time in and out of jail as the FLQ set about its bombing campaign, and in the late '60s wrote the part memoir-part manifesto *Les Negres blancs d'Amerique* (*White Niggers of America*) in which he compared the Quebecois' struggle with that of America's blacks."[2]

When news of that 1990 dinner broke 15 years later, Scott Reid, then the prime minister's chief of staff, said Jean and Lafond would not issue any clarifications or statements about their past. "We have no intention about asking the future governor general, or her husband, about their former acquaintances or who they might have had dinner with 15 or 20 years ago," said Reid.[3] The staffer then asked Canadians to trust his superior, who just then happened to head a party deeply tainted by the sponsorship scandal: "When the prime minister [Paul Martin] says Madame Jean and her husband are committed Canadians, you can rest assured they are committed Canadians," intoned Reid.[4]

Ordinary Canadians who never broke bread with those who once belonged to a terrorist cell might have thought that some in the political and journalistic class had lost their collective backbone, and perhaps their minds. Some, such as the *National Post*'s Andrew Coyne, initially zeroed in on the key issue as soon as the prime minister announced the appointment in August 2005: "It could have been worse," wrote Coyne. "The Prime Minister might have appointed to Canada's highest office a citizen of another country, perhaps one who was hostile to Canada's continued existence and—what the hell, just for argument's sake—delighted in the company of terrorists."[5]

Coyne then wrote of the pivotal point: loyalty. With reference to Jean's dual French and Canadian citizenship and her 1990 toast to independence: "Is it too much to expect that the governor general of Canada should actually believe in Canada? That she should have a conspicuous record of commitment to the country, passionate and undivided?"[6]

After the prime minister's office continued to insist, akin to a Monty Python accident scene, that there was nothing to all of this and would everyone just move on, the couple released a written statement to try to defuse the controversy: "I want to tell you unequivocally that both he and I are proud to be Canadians," wrote the soon-to-be head of state. "We have the greatest respect for the institutions of our country. We are fully committed to Canada. I would not have accepted this position otherwise."[7] Jean added that she and Lafond were "equally" proud of their attachment to Quebec and—damn the critics—that they had "never belonged to a political party or the separatist movement."[8]

That was nice. But no one claimed that the soon-to-be head of state and her husband had been card-carrying members of the FLQ, the Parti Quebecois or the Bloc Quebecois. The concern was over Jean's choice of dinner companions and the toast to independence in a pub, city, province and country where everyone knew *exactly* what that meant. The concern was also over how someone who made such celebratory gestures voted in the 1995 Quebec referendum on separation when the country was almost fractured—thanks in part to the people who supped with Jean that 1990 night.

But after her installation speech as head of state, which was indeed magnificent in its call for Canadians to look beyond the English–French solitudes, the *Post*'s otherwise rational apostle of reason folded: "Madam, I surrender," Coyne wrote. "Let us forget past criticisms. Let us put aside old quarrels. Your speech has collapsed my defences. You are my Commander-in-Chief."[9]

Well, that was easy. Coyne was correct to admire the call beyond the dysfunctional, bi-polar English–French divide. He was right to note how un-Canadian the speech sounded in its affirmation of human freedom—at least un-Canadian in the post-modern, intellectually flabby, culturally hollowed-out sense, all too typical of modern intelligentsia, media and many in the political class. But it was not un-Canadian in the Macdonald–Laurier–King sense.

But then, Jean wasn't the first to say it. Others, especially in the West, said it long ago. There, the reality of massive new immigration over the past century dwarfed any lingering English–French divide; Jean's call had been spoken multiple times before, including by politicians such as Preston Manning, someone anathema to central Canada when he wrote and spoke about such issues as Reform party leader.

Then there were the columnists who looked at the Jean appointment by Prime Minister Paul Martin as just another day in the life of political games. Also post-installation, Chantel Hébert, *Hill-Times* and *Toronto Star* columnist, wrote that "for a rare time in his tenure, one of his [Martin's] Quebec gambles seems to have paid off."[10] Even the chairman of the Monarchist League of Canada, John Aimers, was happy with Jean's statements about her current allegiance to Canada. Aimers was "totally satisfied"[11] and was quoted as saying it should end the controversy and "the media feeding frenzy."[12]

It was bizarre. At the same time Martin appointed Jean, a U.S. president with majorities in both congressional branches couldn't even get his judicial nominee past the committee stage for approval. That occurred in part because the Federalist Society and others wondered about her credentials and loyalty to the conservative movement. In Canada, that Michaëlle Jean was a talented, pleasant person was not the issue; that she dined with a former FLQ member who yet romanticized Quebec separatism, made inappropriate toasts, possessed the dual citizenship of France and Canada, and was of questionable historical loyalty to Canada—was. The Monarchist League should have resolutely opposed her coronation; instead, it rolled over and into the Canadian consensus.

Not everyone played dead. The *Globe and Mail*'s Rhéal Séguin was more skeptical and did his research. On the royal consort's claim he only fought for Quebec's "cultural independence" and its "identity" but went no further, Seguin noted that Lafond had once written something more damning:

Yet his comments are in marked contrast to those he expressed in a documentary he produced accompanied by a book entitled *La manière nègre* (*The Black Way*). In the book, Mr. Lafond says: "So, a sovereign Quebec? An independent Quebec? Yes, and I applaud with both hands and I promise to be at all the St. Jean [Baptiste] parades."[13]

Still, the true believers would not be dissuaded. *Saturday Night* magazine featured a fawning piece in its Winter 2005 edition on the new governor general. In breezy *People*-like style, the writer opined that "if you want to get ahead, get appointed governor general ... the prime minister can't call an election unless you give him the green light. You get a rent-free mansion with a driver, a chef, and an extensive wine cellar."[14]

So far so good—had *Saturday Night* stuck to innocuous descriptions of useful accoutrements for a head of state. But in the culture of conformity, now that Jean was installed, it was *the critics* who were by virtue of their stance on the wrong side and disloyal. *Saturday Night* complained that to enjoy the governor general's lifestyle, "you have to pass the 'I love Canada' ideological test—a tougher exam than you might think, administered as it is by newspaper pundits, political hacks and other small-minded patriots."[15]

Normally, Canadian-ness was a virtue in the circles in which *Saturday Night* writers travelled, at least if defined as love for the CBC, or the "correct" opinions about social issues, the United Nations, George W. Bush and properly chosen objects of contempt. But turn it on one of downtown Toronto's and CBC's own, and patriotism was akin to praise for Hicksville. That a more genuine loyalty to Canada, and demonstration of the same, dwelt deeply in plenty of people from Victoria to St. John's, from business magnates who built Canada Inc., and to hockey dads who stopped at Tim Hortons on their way to their children's hockey games—and that they could object to Jean's appointment on solid patriotic, federal and Canadian grounds, was unthinkable to some.

The *Saturday Night* piece made one wish Mordecai Richler and Pierre Trudeau were still around or could have been cloned. The Politician would not have made Paul Martin's mistake; the Writer would never have given Martin's appointment such an easy pass. The old Canadian loyalty as expressed by Trudeau and others was to Canada as a country; the new Canadian loyalty was to consensus *über alles*.

The *Star's* Mills noted that the Jean and Lafond dinner companion that fateful 1990 night, Vallières, had disavowed many of his more revolutionary ideas by then and thus it would be odd if Jean held a perspective that even Vallières had (mostly) renounced. But the 2005 controversy over Jean's loyalty to Quebec or to Canada was never about the most radical means of separatism and FLQ terror; it was always about the ends of separatism: the amputation of Quebec from Canada, something the federal Liberal Party and Pierre Trudeau once fought against ferociously when he was at the helm.

That a Liberal prime minister would, 25 years after the patron saint of the Liberal Party crushed the separatists in the first Quebec referendum in 1980, appoint someone with such tenuous federalist credentials (and evidence of the opposite), revealed much about the modern Liberal Party. It was out to sea drifting on a raft far from the solid shore of Trudeau's passionate convictions on such matters.

The defence of Jean and Lafond revealed as much about the defenders as it did about the Quebecois couple. Defenders failed to grasp the central necessity of demonstrable loyalty in a modern nation—if it is to survive—to actually *have* an identity and, with it, something useful to offer the wider world.

In an October 2005 post-installation interview, Lafond attempted to extinguish the occasional flicker of doubt some Canadians might yet possess about the couple's loyalty to Canada. In his CBC/Radio-Canada interview, Lafond said the appointment to Rideau Hall did not diminish the couple's strong attachment to Quebec. "We are both Quebeckers. We are Quebeckers before being Canadians."[16] Yes, well, that was just what many Canadians suspected. It was also the problem and the indictment.

A Culture of Crime: Gotham's Grit

If the culture of conformity in Canada was typified by the why-can't-we-all-just-get-along shrug among too many pundits, politicians and the public to the nomination of Michaëlle Jean as head of state, the tut-tut, slap-on-the-wrist approach that lets drug dealers ruin our urban environments highlights the culture of crime that has arisen in Canada. It's a partial result of past Supreme Court decisions that make it tough for cops, prosecutors and lower-court justices to do their job. It's also due to a Parliament that won't pass tougher sentences for chronic drug dealers and those convicted of crimes of severe violence. Such non-actions have consequences. By the 21st century, the peaceable kingdom was no longer. According to the OECD,[17] out of 16 countries surveyed, 11 nations had better overall crimes rates (with the exception of the murder rate) than Canada, including, surprisingly, the United States.[a]

But such ills are not unique in recent history. Back in the late 1980s, *Time* magazine ran a cover story about New York City with a rotten apple imposed over the city's skyline. The piece polled New Yorkers and found the vast majority would like to leave, citing high crime rates, the graffiti-covered subway stations and cars, and the fact that public spaces were no longer public because aggressive panhandling and vagrancy had taken over streets and parks.

Add to that the city's chronic racial conflicts and hollowed-out boroughs such as the Bronx, and urban decay and high rates of crime were thought irreversible. It turned out the pessimists were wrong. But before a look at why, New York City's 1980s-era plight should be recalled by Canadians as it concerns our major cities. In 2004, a report on Vancouver's darker side published by the Vancouver Board of Trade noted that city was second in North America only to greater Miami for property crime.[18] One year later, over in Hogtown, murder hit the headlines. While not as bad as New York City at its peak, Canada's largest city did record its highest number of murders ever in the city's history, much before the year had even ended.[19]

A step back from the headlines didn't provide reassurance. A nationwide survey by Statistics Canada showed that violent crime in 2004 was stable compared to 1999—except that if attacked in 2004 you were more likely to be injured. Meanwhile, the five-year comparison showed that theft of personal property was up 24 per

a. Categories included car theft, theft from car, car vandalism, motorcycle theft, bicycle theft, burglary, attempted burglary, robbery, personal theft, sexual incidents, and assaults and threats. Countries with a better overall average were Belgium, Denmark, Finland, France, Japan, Northern Ireland, Norway, Poland, Portugal, Scotland, Spain, Switzerland and the United States. Worse rates were recorded in Australia, England and Wales, the Netherlands and Sweden.

cent with a 42 per cent rise for household property theft; vandal-ism was up by 17 per cent. And as a signal that the public thought the police and courts might be of less help than they used to be, only 34 per cent of Canadians reported crimes to police in 2004, down from 37 per cent in 1999.[20]

But if that five-year look[b] showed a picture of *violent* crime that was stable, another Statistics Canada report released earlier in 2005 provided a longer perspective. It noted that "the violent crime rate was 10 per cent lower than a decade earlier, but 35 per cent higher than 20 years ago."[21]

GOTHAM AND CANADA: SHIPS PASSING IN THE NIGHT
The parallels between major Canadian cities in the first decade of the 21st century and New York City two and three decades ago are an object lesson in the inability to learn from others' mistakes. Panhandling and graffiti, once endemic in New York, have been significantly reduced and are now less visible in comparison to Toronto, Vancouver and even Victoria. But the spray-paint epidemic in Canada's cities is only a surface symptom of the urban disorder, something attacked root and branch earlier in New York City.

One factor was the presence of a mayor determined to chal-lenge expectations and then reverse them. Rudolph Giuliani, whom most of the world came to know after the September 11, 2001, terrorist attacks, had, before he was Gotham's mayor, been a prosecutor. Among other work, he led the investigation into the 1985 hijacking of the *Achille Lauro* cruise ship and the kill-ing of New Yorker Leon Klinghoffer. Klinghoffer was an elderly Jewish man in a wheelchair who was shot and dumped in the Mediterranean Sea by Palestinian terrorists. Giuliani came to his dislike for bullies honestly, regardless of their crime or locale.

In 1989, Giuliani ran and lost in his first attempt for the may-or's chair to Democrat David Dinkins. Dinkins oozed the same

b. Those Statistics Canada self-reported statistics were somewhat at odds with an-other Statistics Canada report released earlier that year, which showed that there was a slight decline in 2004 from 2003. The difference can be explained in re-ported crimes, i.e., as the latter survey noted, fewer people were reporting crimes to police.

sort of excuses that emanate from councillors in Vancouver and Toronto and in many other Canadian cities: crime is often blamed on provincial or federal "cuts" to a budget, aggressive panhandling is either ignored or downplayed, and homeowners and businesses are given a not-so-subtle message from politicians that if they would just cough up more in taxes, all would be well. (Some, such as Toronto's David Miller and Edmonton's Stephen Mandel, thought giving cities income tax would solve their problems.[22]) The culture of blame-someone-else is nowhere so endemic as it is on city councils, the level of government often touted as the most responsive to citizens and their concerns.

So, as civic politicians in cities like Vancouver pontificate about the Iraq war and the unwanted arrival of big-box retail stores such as Wal-Mart, citizens too often put up with poor value for their tax dollars spent as they endure muggings and petty harassment when they duck out for a coffee in our urban centres. Meanwhile, public parks are surrendered as *de facto* private property to addicts or those desiring garden sex in others, Vancouver's Stanley Park being a prime example of the latter tendency.[23]

And it's not clear that all of Canada's politicians, prosecutors or courts are helping as it concerns crime and sentences. Some are distinctly *unhelpful*:

- In August 2005, a Calgary Court of Queen's Bench Justice shortened a heroin trafficker's sentence because of the trafficker's "exceptionally hard time" in prison, which included being repeatedly denied a vegetarian meal.[24]

- Dougald Miller, an Edmonton owner of an apartment building, was beaten into a vegetative coma as he attempted to escort 34-year-old Leo Teskey outside from a hallway where Miller found him sleeping. According to media reports from the trial after the November 2001 attack, Teskey ripped off part of his ear, fractured his skull, ransacked his suite, stole his television and then fled in the victim's car.

At the time of the attack, Teskey was on probation for a weapons conviction and his record included "nearly three dozen previous criminal convictions—nine for crimes of violence,"[25] including shooting a police officer in 1989. After Teskey was convicted in 1996 of a 1992 assault on his girlfriend's two-year-old son (by ripping part of his penis), the Crown finally applied to have Teskey classified as a dangerous offender—a request denied by the judge but which was finally granted nine years later, after more violence. In 2005, Teskey was finally given dangerous offender status. Miller, 64 at the time of Teskey's 2004 conviction, suffered permanent brain damage.[26]

- Parliament hasn't been particularly helpful. In 2005, three federal parties—Liberals, Bloc Quebecois and New Democrats—voted to keep the age of consent for sex at 14 years of age despite the international norm of 16.

About the same time as those parties voted, *Vancouver Province* crime columnist Joey Thompson noted that a 19-year-old Fraser Valley man seduced a 13-year-old grade-eight girl. Her mother, "Amelia C.," visited the 19-year-old and his parents, he confessed and Amelia C. informed police.

As Thompson wrote, "Police told her he's abused other youngsters but has avoided criminal charges, even though her daughter was still months shy of 14, the age at which Ottawa figures she's ready to decide for herself. Police told her Crown counsel thought a conviction would be iffy because the girl was near legal age—leaving us to conclude adults can engage in illegal sexual conduct with minors without fear of reprisal."[27]

- Dean Edmondson, who raped a 12-year-old girl on the Yellow Quill First Nation reserve in Saskatchewan in 2001, received a two-year house arrest sentence in 2003. In 2005, the Supreme Court of Canada refused to hear a review of the man's sentence requested by Saskatchewan Justice. The judge who gave the sentence "conceded the crime usually means jail time, but said the girl could have been the sexual aggressor because of an

11

abusive upbringing."[28] Even if true, it was a curious statement, as if a grown man couldn't be expected to resist the advances of a 12-year-old.

Perhaps one of the more visible tragedies of late took place in March 2005, when four RCMP officers—Leo Johnston, Anthony Gordon, Brock Myrol and Peter Schiemann—were gunned down in Mayerthorpe, Alberta, by James Roszko. The killer was first convicted of a crime (breaking and entering) in 1976. In the decades since, he faced 44 charges and was convicted of 14. (A report from Alberta Justice noted many other charges were stayed or withdrawn.)

Even if Roszko were innocent and not merely "not guilty" in a legal sense of the other charges stayed or dropped over the years, the courts did convict Roszko at other times of behaviours that were tip-offs to his potential danger: in April 1979, when he made harassing phone calls and breached his probation order, he received 45 days in total; in December 1990, Roszko uttered threats to cause death or serious bodily harm, for which he received a $200 fine; and for repeated sexual assaults on an 11-year-old boy beginning in 1983, Roszko was found guilty and sentenced to two-and-a-half years in prison in 2002.[29]

Roszko was a poster boy for the need for a three-strikes-you're-in-prison-for-a-decade law. Critics often point to excesses down south—some felon convicted a third time for a minor theft and sent to jail for years as a result—as a reason why Canada should not adopt such a tough approach. But absurd exceptions are just that and also straw man arguments. More narrow legislation, applicable to violent crimes only, could be passed by Parliament. But even if Parliament and the courts couldn't bring their sensibilities here into line with reality on the street, Canadian parents and their children shouldn't have had to share the streets, parks and their community with the likes of Roszko, someone convicted of sexual assault on a child. As of 2002, society had the right to see the last of him for good as he headed back to a penitentiary; the RCMP families and friends had the right to their husbands, brothers and sons. Only Parliament with inadequate legislation, and the courts with possible weakening after-the-fact responses on much tougher, longer sentences, stood in the way.

It would be utopian to think every human foible could ever be "solved" in totality, including gaps in legislation, enforcement and convictions. But too many Canadians suffer from the opposite belief: that cultural attitudes and legal expectations cannot be changed or, worse, should not be changed.

In milder cases, some who have taken over our streets and parks do need treatment, but that may include mandatory hospitalization in some cases; there's nothing compassionate about letting heroin addicts waste away on a street corner, Calcutta-like. Others, with multiple-violent convictions, deserve some combination of minimum sentences, dangerous offender status and/or a three-strikes-you're-out response. To show leniency to the latter is not compassionate, it's a show-trial of compassion, which sends the opposite message to the perpetrators and victims. The critics mistakenly argue that such tougher laws and minimum sentences wouldn't make any difference because they don't dissuade the violent.[30] But they will separate the chronically violent from potential victims for a much longer time.

Toronto: The Most American of Canadian Cities

If a small Alberta town became a poster child for a criminal justice system with too many cracks, Toronto has become so very American when it comes to murder. Even a columnist from the everyone-is-a-victim-there-must-be-a-root-cause *Toronto Star* noticed the Toronto-the-Good label no longer applies. Linda Diebel noted how much that city resembles the murder-plagued American capital of years past. Diebel wrote that the Children's Defense Fund named shooting violence as the leading cause of death for young people in Washington, D.C., in 1989 and came up with a number—70—"not so far off Toronto's numbers today," she wrote. "To me Toronto feels increasingly like an American city— say Washington, D.C.—about a decade ago."[31]

New York City's Giuliani faced a mix of lax and occasionally contradictory political, judicial and public attitudes in 1993, this after he beat Dinkins in the second mayoral match-up. Back then, there was the same growth in concerns from even the more liberal elements within the Big Apple. Yet they were combined with the usual clichéd solutions of ever more tax dollars and "compassion," the overused code word for societal navel-gazing. This, as opposed to rebuilding a culture of respect in the urban jungle; everyone has a right to public streets and parks.

In 1993, Giuliani tackled some seemingly insurmountable problems and did so with police chief William Bratton. They added to the one sensible thing begun by Dinkins—they hired more cops and then implemented a then creative and controversial approach to criminals: the "broken windows" theory of law enforcement.

The approach was simple, but not simplistic: When petty crime and public and private spaces are allowed to continually degrade, be it graffiti on subway cars, public urination or a broken window in a building (from which the theory gets its name), it sends out a signal that no one cares. More dangerous criminals might as well take over where petty crime left off. Meanwhile, fearing both petty harassment and crime, the public increasingly retreats from public spaces that are left to decline.

All this has been known to the Canadian political class for at least a decade and as they pursued the same failed strategies of American cities in the 1970s and 1980s. Giuliani and Bratton were helped by shifting demographics in the 1990s: young males, more likely to commit crimes than anyone else, began to decrease as a percentage of the population.

But that was only partly responsible. There was no reason for New York to see a faster decline than other cities. The city's crime decline, faster and deeper than in any other major U.S. city, was no mere lucky accident. The approach to petty and dangerous crime was instrumental in restoring a sense of decorum, of civility, a sense that New York City's public spaces were for all and that public deviance and petty crime were again beyond the pale. In addition, when the men in blue began to enforce the law for minor violations, they inevitably picked people up who turned out to be under an arrest warrant for other, more serious crimes. This factor, along with tougher federal laws and longer jail sentences, helped depress American crime rates. When chronic criminals spend more time in jail, they can't break and enter, steal a car, mug, rape or murder.

Many in Canada's political class are similar in temperament and culture to New York City, pre-Giuliani. A soft set of liberal assumptions pervades local politics. Unfortunately for such leaders, their very approach has ripened and opens up the possibility for leadership that will respond to the dissatisfaction now emerging, similar to the public discontent in New York City in 1993.

And there is some evidence Canadians have finally tired of the apathetic approach to urban disorder. In late 2005, Vancouver police finally cracked down on public injections of heroin. "People are getting tired of tripping over 18,000 needles a month,"[32] said Vancouver's Inspector John McKay, in an explanation of why the police decided to act. Predictably, in response, the Vancouver Area Network of Drug Users planned a public protest; it argued that while it supported the legal shoot-up facility, addicts were forced to inject publicly on the streets because there were waits of 10 to 45 minutes at the injection clinic.

Apparently, Canada's cities yet await their own versions of a sensible prosecutor-turned-mayor. In Toronto, in 2005, the drive-by killing of 15-year-old Jane Creba on Boxing Day by battling youth only reinforced the conceptual confusion evident in the minds of politicians. Mayor Miller blamed guns, then Prime Minister Paul Martin blamed "the consequences of exclusion,"[33] and Toronto councillor Olivia Chow blamed it on a "decade of neglect"[34] (whatever that meant) and claimed it was everyone's "collective responsibility."[35]

All seemed to miss the relevant point that one youth involved in the Boxing Day shootings and charged with eight weapons offences—though not Creba's murder—had already been prohibited from owning a gun because of past crimes. That suspect, 20-year-old André Thompson, was convicted of assault in March 2004 but received only a suspended sentence. That light wrist-tap was of little use. In October 2004, Thompson robbed a Mac's convenience store while he was supposed to be at home, under a court-ordered curfew.[36] In December 2005, shortly before the Boxing Day shootings, Thompson had been released from just a 30-day jail sentence for the 2004 robbery.[37] If Torontonians wanted to have fewer thugs with guns on the streets, it might have helped if the thugs were actually *kept off the streets*, i.e., if courts treated assaults and robberies as crimes worthy of jail time and if politicians could get beyond root-cause arguments about "exclusion" and "collective responsibility."

But if political and judicial attitudes in Toronto and Vancouver about crime revealed evidence of a deeply confused culture, unsure if it is "permissible" to even expect civilized behaviour from each other, over in Montreal a political inquiry revealed evidence of a culture of a different nature, but one also deeply flawed.

A Culture of Corruption: Memory Loss in Montreal

The Sponsorship Scandal was a bargain basement, C-film detour into the venal and cynical garden of human nature. It bloomed when arrogance combined with rationalization, which joined with power and then was strengthened by a cocktail of other people's money—ours.

A re-telling of the lurid details and financial figures is unnecessary; Justice John H. Gomery's work did that in three volumes and Auditor General Sheila Fraser covered similar terrain. However, less noticed was another phenomenon: the apparent widespread memory loss that became rampant among chief executives of advertising and sponsorship firms based in Quebec. Even the hard drive of collective memory in genetically related executives—i.e., family—seemed to have broken down with alarming regularity.

In April 2004 in testimony before the Gomery inquiry into how $332 million in taxpayer money was diverted for less-than-noble purposes, former Groupe Everest president Claude Boulay testified in front of a House of Commons committee about where the money disappeared and "corrected" the critics, including the auditor general. Boulay argued "it has been alleged wrongly that agencies pocketed $100 million in commissions and fees."[38] Boulay, who soon suffered lapses in memory, claimed the money went to production costs.

Sheila Fraser's exact words were: "Documentation was very poor and there was little evidence of analysis to support the expenditure of over $250 million. Over $100 million of that was paid to communications agencies as production fees and commissions."[c]

Note the difference between "fees"—the word used by the auditor general—and "costs," used by Boulay. Note also Fraser's second word omitted by Boulay: "commissions." When those under the glare of a public spotlight omit words and emphasize others that disguise rather than describe behaviour, the evasions reveal more than truth-telling serums ever could.

The parliamentary committee queried what those production costs and fees were for; that is, where did the money go? Boulay asserted, vaguely, that his company's responsibility was "to manage contracts. Manage the administrative aspects of files."[39] The 2004 testimonies were perhaps a troubling first sign of increased memory loss, and one year later, another advertising executive from Quebec suffered from gaps in his recall of events. Jean Lafleur testified before the judicial commission headed by Justice John Gomery and by one count, courtesy of CanWest reporter William Marsden, Lafleur declared "I can't remember" 22 times in testimony before the commission.[40] (Lafleur was president of Lafleur Communications Marketing Inc., which received more than $35 million from the federal government and Crown corporations during the 1990s.)

In early testimony, and when asked by a commission lawyer about an extra $6.9 million that his company earned in 1995 that was unaccounted for, Lafleur said: "I am not able to give you any further details of this."[41] When Justice Gomery wondered whether the money came from non-government contracts, Lafleur's response was that he did not know. But a forgotten source of income was not the only memory malady from which Lafleur suffered. He also had unclear answers on various billing methods.

Then inquiry lawyers pointed out that one of Lafleur's employees, Pierre Davidson, actually billed Lafleur's company for

---

c. It was an underestimate. Justice Gomery said $332 million was spent, with $147 million doled out in fees and commissions to communications and advertising agencies.

sub-contracted work. The sub-contract bill was worth $74,100 for design work on VIA Rail logos. But Lafleur later charged the government $202,537, a mark-up of 173 per cent, for the work of an employee who was also a sub-contractor. Lafleur's company was invoiced for 83 project hours by his employee/sub-contractor; the bill given to government for that VIA design work claimed Davidson worked 209 hours—but as an employee. Lafleur couldn't recall the details nor remember if he pressured employees to donate to the Liberal party so he could later reimburse them, this even though employees later recalled such details with clarity.

More unfortunate failures of synapses to fire yet occurred in testimony before the Gomery inquiry. One afternoon in March 2005, Lafleur's son, Eric, who through his own company supplied jackets to his father's firm, which then supplied them to the government, also suffered from memory loss.

Eric couldn't explain why the work of one of his own employees was occasionally billed to government but via his father's company. Nor could the younger Lafleur explain why his father's firm charged the government mark-ups of 100 per cent plus shipping and handling on goods originally bought from Junior, when by his own admission, the normal mark-up was 40 per cent to 60 per cent. When a commission lawyer asked about the reason behind an additional 15 per cent agency fee charged on top of an $18,000 warehousing bill, the reason "escapes us," said the lawyer. "It escapes me too,"[42] Junior replied. "I did my work on the ground with my team and delivered the goods."[43]

Yes, he certainly did, as did many others in the Sponsorship Scandal. The circle of corruption, crime and conformity in Canada was never so evident as in the existence of bogus sponsorship contracts that enriched insiders for years before anyone blew a whistle.

Chapter 2

Redistribution Run Amuck: Why B.C., Alberta and Ontario support everyone else

It is a sound principle of finance, and a still sounder principle of government, that those who have the duty of expending the revenue of a country should also be saddled with the responsibility of levying it and providing it.[1]

~ Sir Wilfrid Laurier, House of Commons Debate, February 1905

When will the federal government solve the problem of the fiscal imbalance, not only for Quebec, but for all of Canada?[2]

~ Quebec premier Jean Charest, May 2004, demanding more federal transfers

Premiers to Ottawa: "Tax Our Citizens More!"

In what has become an annual summer tradition, the country's premiers gather together every year, stomp their feet, claim there is a mysterious, hungry entity known as the "fiscal imbalance" and then demand more money from Ottawa to feed the beast.

"While respecting the jurisdiction of the government of Quebec, when will the federal government assume its responsibility in financing health care?" brayed Quebec premier jean Charest in 2004.[3] "We will take the money if it's there—naturally," said Alberta premier Klein in 2005.[4] And in an article in the *Edmonton Journal,* which reported on that same 2005 conference, the headline blared "Show us the money, premiers say."[5]

On this fiscal imbalance cry, premiers have federal allies, including the Conservative Party and New Democrats, most of the Liberal Members of Parliament and—naturally—Quebec separatists. At a *Calgary Herald* editorial board meeting I was privy to in 2005, even Bloc Quebecois leader Gilles Duceppe spun the line that the provinces—and especially Quebec—were shortchanged, a remarkable assertion given the historical approach of federal politicians to that province's chronic demands: How much and how high?

None of the demands for more money stops the premiers from another demand: that the federal government "respect their jurisdiction."[6] It seems not to occur to the provincial leaders, similar to ladies of the night, that if they wish for more respect, a means to that end might be a refusal of the easy cash. But beyond the inherent contradiction, the "fiscal imbalance" assertion, i.e., that the national government has all the tax revenue while the provinces hobble along in rags, is an urban myth. It's on par with conspiracy theories about alien spaceships and NASA's and Rockefeller's control of the world.

But before an explanation of why the premiers engage in a duplicitous spin, it's fair to note that a demand for more useless redistribution is hardly a provincial tendency. Think not only of transfer payments to have-not provinces, but transfers to remote Indian reserves. Remember the tragic story of young Aboriginals sniffing glue at Davis Inlet, a remote Labrador reserve? The government's solution was to spend $152 million to move the reserve to *another* remote area, barely less isolated than the first, as opposed to a suburb of a major city where the young people might have a chance to connect with the larger world and solid educational opportunities and employment. Then, in 2005, after headlines alerted our distant colonial capital to the awful state of infrastructure on Canada's reserves, the federal government followed up with plans for more cash for reserve buildings. This, as opposed to perhaps re-thinking the failed experiment in collective apartheid Ottawa has practised since 1867 vis-à-vis Canada's most vulnerable first peoples. This is progress?

Whether funding for native reserves far away from urban Canada, employment insurance rules that "help" people to remain in regions with little prospect of job growth, or the annual handing-over of ever-increasing amounts of cash to have-not provinces (to encourage them *not* to develop their resources or human capital), the economic illogic of large transfer payments continues unabated. Far from retreating from an ill-advised policy, in 1982 Canada's governments—provincial *and* federal—instead entrenched such absurdities in the Constitution. But, as with many apparently unfathomable addictions, this one also has roots in historical explanations.

Canada's First Transfer Payments and the Deal: 80 Cents Per Person and No Provincial Trade Barriers

Federal transfers to the provinces are as old as Confederation, but not because the founding fathers wanted it that way. Canada's founders wished to *avoid* subsidies to the provinces. The conundrum was that the Dominion government did not want to risk the prospect of provincial tariffs on each other's goods (tariffs then being the main source of revenues for governments) and in so doing create trade barriers within the new country.

Another option was to give the provinces greater revenue powers. They were given the right to collect direct taxes (i.e., on income) in order to raise revenues, but the provinces were not expected to actually use that option, given the rank unpopularity of that tax. As tax historians Milton Moore and Harvey Perry write, with the exception of Ontario, where property taxes and some local income taxes already existed, "it is evident from the speeches of the day that the founding fathers counted on the very unpopularity of direct taxation to prevent its extensive use."[7] Thus, while the provinces were given direct taxing power, they were unlikely to use it, or so went the theory, which proved mostly correct during Canada's first few decades.[a]

At the time of Confederation the provinces were given responsibility for welfare and education and not much else. Back then, those two items were not particularly burdensome and, given the sentiment of the times, were never expected to be overly costly. In fact, provincial spending was expected to decline in terms of per-capita expenditures as municipal governments grew.[8] The Dominion government was responsible for developing the country's railway system, bridges, roads, harbours and other infrastructure, and thus was given much of the needed revenue base.

Examining expenditures from the year before Confederation (1866), total government revenues across Canada amounted to $20 million, with 70 per cent ($14 million) accruing to the provinces (then colonies) while the remaining portion, 30 per cent

---

a. British Columbia was the first to introduce a provincial income tax in 1876.

($6 million) went to municipalities. Upper and Lower Canada as well as the Atlantic colonies were the biggest kids on the government block.[9]

Seven years after Confederation, the flow of revenues to the colonies/provinces decreased dramatically. In 1874, out of revenues of $33 million, two-thirds flowed to the Dominion government while the next largest jurisdiction was that of cities and towns, which garnered $8 million, or about 24 per cent of all revenues. The provinces were then a distant third with $3 million, or 9 per cent.[10] Thus, their revenues had dropped to one-fifth their pre-Confederation collections.[b]

Given that the provincial responsibilities and their related costs were forecast to decline, the possibility that provincial governments would institute income tax to raise revenue was remote. Provincial tariffs would lead to unwanted trade barriers. So the default option for the federal government was a subsidy. Thus, Ottawa chose what is best described as the first transfer payment. Subsidies were agreed upon and amounted to 80 cents for each person in each province, although there was a cap for any province with a population greater than 400,000.[c] But there were exceptions to the general rule; New Brunswick was given an extra 10-year grant, for example.[11] After that, and because of the initial reluctance of the Dominion government to dole out subsidies, the agreed-upon settlement at the time was stated to be the "full and final" settlement of all claims by the provinces upon the new Dominion government.[12]

It did not last. As other provinces joined Confederation, additional special annual grants were made, and soon "special" disbursements (annual) were made from the central government

b. Their third-place role (in terms of revenues) continued until 1947 when revenue flows to the provinces once again overtook that of municipalities for the first time since 1867.

c. Only the populations of Quebec and Ontario exceeded that number. In 1871, Quebec had almost 1.2 million inhabitants, while Ontario had more than 1.6 million. Prince Edward Island possessed 94,000 inhabitants, Nova Scotia 388,000, and New Brunswick 286,000, while 25,000 inhabited Manitoba and 36,000 lived in British Columbia. The Northwest Territories, which then also encompassed the now separate Nunavut and Yukon territories, had 48,000 people.

to Nova Scotia, Prince Edward Island and British Columbia. With those major changes accommodated within the first decade of Confederation, the subsidy program remained mostly unchanged for the next 40 years. At that point, the introduction of new provinces (Alberta and Saskatchewan joined Canada in 1905) prompted Prime Minister Wilfrid Laurier to convene a general conference in 1906 to reconsider the subsidy question. One result was the removal of the subsidy cap that limited the 80-cents-per-capita subsidy to only a province's first 400,000 people; the effect was that average subsidies increased by one-third.

This too was to be the "final" settlement but, as federal finance ministers and prime ministers would discover up to our present day, finality was an elusive end. So experimentation with other transfers, including conditional grants (for agricultural instruction) began in 1913. In the 1920s, additional federal grants were given for vocational education, highway construction, employment offices, venereal disease prevention and old-age pensions. The provinces were to be responsible for half the money spent on such programs.

The Depression, the Second World War and Post-war Arrangements

The onslaught of the Depression knocked Canadians and their governments into a tailspin. The country's gross national product reached a high of $6.2 billion in 1929 only to plunge to $3.6 billion by 1933, a fall of 57 per cent in four years.[13] The provinces and the federal government taxed heavily to stay afloat, but even that was not enough to meet the many needs that arose out of the Depression.[d] The Dominion government gave special assistance to the provinces to prevent defaults in debts and to continue the financing of essential services.[14]

Over the next 40 years, transfer payments and tax agreements between the provincial and federal governments changed several times. For example, during the Second World War, the provinces

d. For example, in unadjusted dollars, total government revenues dropped from a pre-Depression high of $932 million in 1929 to a low of $701 million in 1932. Thus, in the early 1930s deficits reached record proportions, as high as 42 per cent of all government expenditures in 1931, for example.

agreed to forego income and corporate tax revenues in exchange for compensation from the federal government. The federal government levied much of the increased tax burden and also raised taxes to prosecute the war effort. The tax increases and other more costly sacrifices were the price of war; the side consequence was that the confusion and overlapping jurisdictional authority on some taxes was removed between 1941 and 1946.

By 1947, a new tax agreement was in place where the provinces agreed to continue not to tax personal incomes in exchange for guaranteed federal payments; provinces were also restricted to a maximum 5 per cent corporation tax under the terms of the deal. (Ontario and Quebec opted out of that particular arrangement.)

Between the 1950s and 1980s, federal-provincial arrangements shifted from the immediate post-war arrangement where the federal government levied all income and business taxes and transferred an agreed-upon portion to the provinces (who stayed in the post-war arrangements) to a system where the provinces once again levied their own specific taxes. With the exception of Quebec, they did allow Ottawa to collect and process income tax.

The changing nature of federal and provincial tax agreements and policy as regards transfer payments over the past half-century would test the acumen of all but the most dedicated tax historian. For the lay reader, the most useful information for understanding federal subsidies to the provinces is an examination of current arrangements.

Ottawa's $59-Billion Pot of Gold: Equalization, Canada Health and Social Transfers, and Tax Transfers

Fast-forward to our present premiers and the claim that provinces are eternally shortchanged in confederation. The short and long answer to that assertion is exactly the same: *nonsense*. That provincial Caesars claim their governments are shortchanged without turning three shades of shame-induced scarlet proves there is an exception to every rule, and especially to Nietzsche's claim that man is the only beast with "red cheeks."

The federal government uses three main instruments to transfer money to provincial governments. When premiers and mayors talk about the fiscal imbalance between the provinces and Ottawa they have it precisely backwards: the *federal* government transfers large amounts of cash to the provincial and territorial governments (and also now to cities); it has rarely been so generous with taxpayer dollars, at least to the provinces.

The first instrument, **equalization** payments, consists of money transferred to six have-not provinces and three have-not territories.[e] As the name suggests, the money is intended to "equalize" (to some degree) per capita revenues among the provinces.

The second, **health and social transfers**, also consists of cash transfers, but is given to every province and territory.

The last part of Canada's current federal-provincial transfer system is in the form of **tax transfers**. A few have occurred throughout Canada's history, and the most recent was in 1977. The federal government gave up tax "room" and let the provinces tax citizens for the same amount instead.

The value of all the above? About $59.4 billion or $1,845 per person.[15]

THE FAKE "50-50" CLAIM

Despite that $59 billion reality, the provinces are quite adept at pretending they are Tiny Tim fiscal cripples. Witness their regular claim that Ottawa once provided 50 per cent of all health care funding and that it now only provides 16 per cent.

However, voters should be skeptical about provincial propaganda and here's why: prior to 1977, Ottawa shared half of a number of items but excluded others, such as hospitals for the mentally ill, home care and related administration costs. The result was that the federal government never actually paid more than 41 per cent of health care costs—and that was back in the 1960s when all governments had the luxury of a younger

e. Transfers can become even more confusing. For the purposes of equalization payments Saskatchewan is now, recently, a "have" province. However, when all major transfers beyond equalization are included, it is still a net beneficiary of federal largesse while B.C., Alberta and Ontario are net payers.

population compared to today. Of course, health care costs rise as people hit 65-plus.

In addition, the premiers arrive at their 16 per cent figure by contrasting what Ottawa transfers to the provinces with what they spend in total on health care *and* all other social programs. That's politically convenient if one wants to make the federal government look cheap; it's also dishonest.

So how much in federal transfers ends up in provincial health care? Finance bureaucrats—who are not running for political office—note that given the portion of provincial budgets spent on health care, it's reasonable to argue the same portion of transfer payments and equalization is also spent on health. That means the provinces use $30.5 billion transferred from Ottawa for health, or about 37 per cent of the $83 billion spent on health care by provincial governments.

But wait: add in the $5 billion spent by the federal government directly on health (natives, veterans and research) and the result is that 40 per cent of total government spending on health care in Canada ($88 billion) is financed by the federal government.[16] That's a tad more than the 16 per cent figure that emanates from the premiers each summer during their tale-of-woe recital for the television cameras. The federal share is now almost equal to the 41 per cent split in the 1960s and at a time when health care bills—a provincial responsibility as the premiers continually remind the public—were dramatically lower.

Provincial statistical spin-doctoring aside, in a perfect world Ottawa would eliminate transfer and equalization payments and—if provinces could actually prove their case on the supposed fiscal imbalance—just hand over more tax room and let provincial budgets sink or swim. That, in fact, was the intent of our country's founding fathers; they only grudgingly transferred money to the provinces because they were concerned about the twin dangers of provincial tariffs and provincial income taxes. If anyone decided to welsh on earlier deals, it was the provincial governments who all happily imposed taxes on incomes, some starting shortly after Confederation.

THE ACTUAL FISCAL IMBALANCE EXISTS *AMONG* PROVINCES: WHY B.C., ALBERTA AND ONTARIO WRITE THE CHEQUES[f]

But if the premiers ignore facts when they press federal politicians to hand them more of our tax dollars, some at least justify it on the grounds that, *à la* cod liver oil from our mothers, such transfers are good for us. The defence is that equalization helps provinces provide roughly comparable levels of services to citizens.

But as is often the case with well-intentioned policy, there are multiple unintended consequences. The first is that the tax burden on everyone is higher than it would be if more people moved from economically depressed areas to the more prosperous jurisdictions. In lieu of that, the promotion of inefficiencies doesn't come cheap. Thus, inter-provincial transfers of money punish the regions that have the most to offer in terms of economic potential, job creation and wages. It's a bit like taxing Microsoft more heavily than its competitors because Bill Gates has been so successful at developing and selling new technology and creating jobs. Such "equalization" also has another, less pleasant description: knee-capping.

This odd transfer of wealth is also why it is perverse for anyone in the have provinces of B.C., Alberta and Ontario to call for more transfer payments.[g] When such demands originate in Alberta, Ontario and B.C, they in effect demand that their own taxpayers hand over even more federal cash to Ottawa only to receive back proportionately *less* to their own provincial government later in the form of transfer payments.

---

f. There's also another fiscal imbalance in Canada: between governments and citizens. According to the OECD, government revenues collectively take up 41.7 per cent of our country's economy.

g. The federal government's position to the argument that the have provinces support the have-nots is that tax dollars come from taxpayers in *all* parts of the country. Thus, as taxpayers in every province pay federal tax, it is technically incorrect to say that the rich provinces (the haves) finance the have-nots. The claim is sort of true. But while taxpayers in have-not provinces do contribute to federal coffers, have provinces *pay much more in federal tax* than their provincial governments receive back in federal transfers. After all, that's the entire point of such transfers: to take from the supposedly rich provinces to give to the poor.

SENDING MONEY FROM VANCOUVER TO ST. JOHN'S

Over the 1961 to 2002 period, every Alberta family of four transferred the annual equivalent of $10,040 to other provinces; Ontario families "wrote cheques" of $3,032 while a B.C. family gave $1,712 annually, on average, this according to economists Robert Mansell, Ron Schlenker and John Anderson.[17] Through federal taxes and counting federal program transfers, those three provinces consistently sent net transfers to Ottawa while the seven provinces and three territories on the receiving end happily cashed the cheques.

Transfers from high-cost provinces to low-cost provinces

PROVINCE	Transfers between provinces per family of four* Annual average 1961-2002	Average house prices in major metropolitan areas **	
Newfoundland	$16,476	St. John's	146,500
Prince Edward Island	18,636	Charlottetown***	120,000
Nova Scotia	16,796	Halifax	195,600
New Brunswick	13,420	Saint John	123,000
Quebec	3,068	Montreal	218,400
Ontario	**–3,032**	Toronto	348,750
		Ottawa	255,350
		Hamilton	240,000
Manitoba	7,012	Winnipeg	140,700
Saskatchewan	5,488	Regina	130,300
		Saskatoon	149,800
Alberta	**–10,040**	Calgary	275,000
		Edmonton	202,650
British Columbia	**–1,712**	Vancouver	462,000
		Kelowna	284,500

Sources:
*Institute for Sustainable Energy, Environment, and Economy, University of Calgary, 2005
**Forecast, Re/Max Housing Market Outlook 2006
***2005 price, Century 21
Provinces with net loss after transfers in **BOLD**

The response to such facts is usually two-fold: first, denial, or second, the more general response from many across the country: such transfers are desirable because we should all "share."

Limited redistribution from the tax base to poverty-stricken fellow citizens is sensible. But only someone with a strange view of compassion can defend bribing entire populations to stay in areas beyond what local conditions would naturally support and doing so, in some cases, *at the expense of some families with less income in the have provinces*. But for some, that's the Canadian way, including cementing some transfers (equalization) in the Constitution.

Nor do such transfers make sense when the average home costs $275,000 in Calgary, $348,750 in Toronto and $462,000 in Greater Vancouver. Families in those cities could use the extra tax dollars they now send to people who live in Montreal where an average home costs $218,400, $140,700 in Winnipeg or $123,000 in Saint John.

Laurier Was Right: Transfers Promote Unaccountable Government

One last perverse effect of large transfers of taxpayer cash between governments is that most voters are never sure which government taxes and for what purpose. Multiple, large cheques that circulate among governments thickens that fog of accountability and allows political leaders to blame each other for their own hospital line-ups or new health care taxes. Accountability for taxes raised and money spent is served best by clear and direct links between the taxes a government collects and the money it spends, precisely Laurier's point in 1905.

Chapter 3

The Plucked Canadian Goose:
Taxes–how they're collected and spent,
and one historically nasty example

Canada is bound up in taxes as tight as Laocoon with snakes.[1]
   ~ Stephen Leacock, "Come out to Canada"

Don't give people 25 bucks a day to blow on beer and popcorn.[2]
   ~ Then Liberal Prime Ministerial Chief of Staff Scott Reid, on a
   Tory proposal to give parents $1,200 per child annually for
   child care expenses

It's the *Type* and *Amount* of Spending, Stupid

Only anarchists and (some) libertarians argue that government shouldn't exist. The former do it because they have a destructive impulse; the latter because they commit the mirror mistake of the far left: a belief in utopia as they define it, the means to which results from a basic misreading of human nature.

But beyond the revolutionary and the mistaken, the rest of us accept some government as a reality and argue about its scope, size and proper appetite. Those who favour an endlessly expanding state (in assumptions if not in actual rhetoric) get away with such nonsense because they're able to equate limited government with *no* government in the public mind. That conjures up a medieval image of marauding bandits roaming the countryside, beating up grandmothers and children; it's a nightmarish, Hobbesian vision of all against all.

It's also folly. "Limited" is not equivalent to "anarchy," but modern Canadians too easily accept high taxes and overbearing governments in part because of that mistaken link. Thus, to expand the sphere of freedom and flexibility for individuals, families and communities (i.e., for everyone but those in Ottawa and provincial capitals), those interested in choice must do the tough work of looking at what government does and why, and propose private or non-profit alternatives that are superior to those now offered—minus the middleman's "recycling fee" of government delivery. Most people are creatures of habit and prefer the security of the known to the new, even if existing arrangements are less-than-optimal as is the case with health care. Those who desire replacements for government intervention or delivery must make the case that their proposals are not only superior but provide better security than now exists through government services; without that, Canadians will not trade up to a newer model to replace the jalopy.

Errant Spending Case Study 1: Subsidized Day Care for Yuppies

If Canadians wish governments would spend smarter and tax less (the second is tied to the first), one-size-fits-all programs must be dumped in favour of those that actually allow families maximum choice. The best recent example of an errant Ottawa spending plan is in the area of child care.

Sociologist Reginald Bibby surveyed parents in 2004 and found that their number-one choice (other than themselves) about who should raise their children was their spouse.[3] That was followed by their parents, other relatives, home day care and then institutionalized day care. Federal-provincial policy encourages the last priority of parents but not their first—and despite the Conservative election win and a promise to hand over $1,200 per child to parents.

Parents tempted to think institutionalized day care is in their interest may wish to examine the much-touted Quebec model (where $7-a-day day care exists). It's a case study in an expensive government-directed model that leaves choice, parents and kids at the back of the policy bus.

There is the initial problem of political promises combined with questionable math. That's where initial cost estimates for new programs are always below the eventual bills. (Think of federal day care as the program equivalent of Montreal's Olympic stadium.) In the case of Quebec, day-care costs ballooned to $1.4 billion in 2004[4] from $290 million in 1998 with recent estimates nearing $1.7 billion. *Quelle surprise*, given that the government in that province A: allowed everyone to pay the same low rate of $5 per day (later $7) regardless of whether they were rich Mount Royal types or a single-mother waitress in Quebec City who makes $15,000 a year; that led to B: more people who flooded into the system, including those who could afford to pay the full cost; which then led to C: day care encouraged by *la belle province* of the government-union, high-cost variety.

Then there's the wrong-headed notion of imposing national standards, be it in child care, health, education or the environment in an attempt to foist a one-size-fits-all model on every province and territory. The provinces have jurisdiction over all of the above so the only way in which the federal government can set national standards is to offer money. But that initial carrot later hardens into a stick with which to beat provincial governments if they actually come up with an idea they think works better but displeases the federal government.

That Ottawa's politicians and mandarins want such power over provinces, parents and kids was an act of capital city hubris. It was as if the politicians and the bureaucrats solved the problem of health care line-ups, lax parliamentary and judicial attitudes towards crime, and the embarrassment of decrepit, underpaid, ill-equipped armed forces and thus thought they had the skills with which to instruct Canadians on the proper care and feeding of children. In that context, Paul Martin's belief that money must be funnelled to government-approved, union-run, punch-a-clock day-care dens was only an extension of the thinking of the policy wonks who surrounded him. And while the Tory election plan of $1,200 per child was an improvement—parents could decide whether to spend it on day care or on other caregivers, including each other—the Conservatives lacked the bravery to attack the flawed Liberal plan head-on: Conservative leader Stephen Harper pledged to create 125,000 new day-care spaces over five years at a cost of $250 million annually.[5] His first idea—the $1,200 per child—was better than his last.

As for premiers from St. John's to Victoria, that they welcomed a day-care program funded by the federal government was predictable: demands for more money from the federal government have been chronic since John A. Macdonald. Canada's premiers talk about respect for provincial jurisdictions, but that lasts only until Ottawa delivers a cheque.

But beyond the exchange of federal cash for the delivery of heretofore provincial powers, a "national" program limits the very brilliance of the Canadian confederation: the separation of responsibilities that was supposed to *encourage* provincial experimentation in child care, education, health, environment and welfare (where it does happen in the case of the latter category and to largely satisfying results).

But beyond the restrictive nature of such federal control, Ontario, Alberta and B.C. families already heavily subsidize other provinces. The federal government's new national day-care program will only increase that wealth transfer (and with all the perverse effects described in the previous chapter).

Defenders of one such inequity, the federal equalization program, argue it is necessary because governments with widely varying revenue capacities can then provide similar levels of social services. More correctly described, equalization gives have-not provinces the ability to overpay taxpayer-subsidized employees relative to the local cost of living and local wage rates. It's evident in Quebec's day-care system where pressure for unionization and lavish wage increases are intense. The true inequity is that single-income families in other provinces are the ones who pay such bills; they sacrifice, while some families with two working parents—sometimes the wealthiest in a community—benefit from the day-care subsidies.

WHY *EVERY* PARENT SHOULD PREFER CHOICE

The new national institutionalized child-care approach replicates Quebec's twisted incentives and results: high-cost unionization, exposure to a system-wide shutdown via a strike because of the same, and inflexibility in how to provide care for kids.

The Quebec model and its national imitation both restrict options for every type of parent from single moms to wealthy two-income families. A parent who now uses day care but later chooses to stay home, part-time or full-time, or prefers to avail themselves of a parent, grandparent, other relative or friend, will lose out on any money now sent to day-care centres—the invisible subsidy. If *all* the money followed the parent's choice—say, a tax deduction worth several thousand dollars a year or re-routing current day-care money in the manner of the $1,200 per child direct payment idea—care could be provided by any number of people; it could be provided in an endless array of combinations and at times that are convenient for parents. That's true choice in child care, and it doesn't exist in Ottawa's top-down version. But that's the problem with hubris: it restricts one's ideas and vision to the existing tunnel.

Errant Spending Case Study 2: How to "Help" the Unemployed and Exacerbate Labour Shortages at the Same Time

Thus far, no argument against the continual subsidies from Ottawa to the provinces for all manner of inflexible standardization (and which Confederation's founders were so wary of) has yet convinced most Canadian politicians it is time for a policy change; quite the opposite. Late in 2005, in another counterproductive wealth transfer, the federal government once again relaxed employment insurance rules in high-unemployment regions. It was the predictable signal of an election, akin to how birds flying south signal the coming winter.

In so doing, the federal government worsens the wrong incentives, especially unwise when parts of the country such as B.C. and Alberta suffer from skilled labour shortages. The new stay-at-home, put-your-feet-up-longer EI rules only compound the likelihood that underemployed workers will stay put as opposed to moving to regions where jobs go unfilled.

But even more bizarrely, just as the federal government encouraged people not to move from, say, St. John's, it wanted more workers to pack it up in Shanghai and St. Petersburg and come to Canada to help with labour shortages. Immigration is desirable and welcome both for the Canadian economy and for immigrants themselves; anything that helps a carpenter or doctor arrive here from Vladimir Putin's corrupt, autocratic Russia, Germany's incentive-destroying welfare state or China's one-party affair should be welcomed. In addition, every other Canadian has an immigrant ancestor if one goes back far enough in time.

But it's also clear that new immigrants won't solve Canada's labour woes. A recent Statistics Canada survey showed that 87 per cent of recent arrivals in the skilled worker category came here with a university degree.[6] That's positive, except that such percentages don't fill the need for skilled workers of other sorts, such as in the trades. So current immigration patterns won't help much with the dearth of carpenters, plumbers and electricians; meanwhile, the federal government gives skilled workers in high-unemployment regions another reason not to move: election-time unemployment cheques for extended periods.

Beyond employment insurance games, which work at cross-purposes to labour market needs and individuals' hopes for prosperity, there are other millions spent to persuade the unemployed to stay in uneconomic regions and for businesses to locate there in a vain attempt to sop them up. It's the equivalent of bringing the mountain to Mohammed rather than sensibly giving Mohammed a bus ticket to Calgary.

One example comes courtesy of the federal Atlantic Canada Opportunities Agency (ACOA). In 2000, the federal government announced it would spend $700 million through ACOA over five years to help the region; in 2005, another $708 million was dished out with plans for more to come.

And what will the latest instalment for Atlantic Canada buy, at least in the misguided hopes of Ottawa's central planning departments? ACOA trumpets that it will spend $50 million to "foster entrepreneurship and business expansion" and to "attract and retain skills in the region." The agency-to-fund-non-movement-of-labour will spend $175 million to develop competitive, productive, strategic industry sectors.

ACOA will also throw $300 million at what it calls "investment in innovation" but what others might describe as picking corporate winners and losers. ACOA cash will also be used to "maximize the region's ability to access national R&D funding programs." Thus, tax dollars will be used to leverage even more tax dollars.

In late 2005, Ontario had a 6.4 per cent unemployment rate, British Columbia's was 5.1 per cent, and Alberta's was 4.0 per cent; the rates in Newfoundland, Prince Edward Island, Nova Scotia and New Brunswick were 15.2 per cent, 11.1 per cent, 8.5 per cent and 11 per cent respectively. To extend benefits specifically in high-unemployment areas was the exact opposite policy of what should have been enacted. Ottawa managed to pay out more money and exacerbate a labour shortage at the same time.

AND IT DOESN'T WORK: THE TRAGEDY OF ATLANTIC CANADA

On the positive side, some bright spots have appeared to challenge the status quo thinking on the subject. One of the better analyses of the folly of such redistribution comes from the Halifax-based Atlantic Institute for Market Studies (AIMS). Its 1999 study noted how well Ireland and the New England American states have performed in comparison to Canada's Atlantic provinces.

Two decades ago, Ireland's per-capita economy was 40 per cent less than that of Canada; now it has a per-capita economy 10 per cent *higher*, and regional subsidies from the European Union are minuscule in comparison to what the Atlantic provinces receive from Canada's federal government. Moreover, such EU subsidies are never touted as the reason for Ireland's astonishing catch-up over the past two decades.

Rather, the success is credited to lower tax rates (10 per cent for businesses) and labour agreements where workers agreed to modest wage increases in return for increased investment by business. The net effect over time is that increased investment led to a booming economy and wages rose as demand for workers increased.

Not that provincial finance ministers from Atlantic Canada are ready to consider the Irish evidence. In 2001, Patricia Mella, the provincial treasurer for Prince Edward Island, told the Senate Committee that reviewed equalization that Atlantic Institute analyses and others do not take into account the "fiscal capacity" of the have-not provinces.[7]

The "fiscal capacity" argument is one often given by finance ministers for the have-not provinces; this writer heard the same from provincial finance officials in British Columbia in pre-budget discussions. Essentially, the fiscal capacity argument amounts to the claim that some provinces are richer than others.

But the argument ignores the choices available to governments. When the British Columbia government almost shut down the mining industry in the 1990s through a variety of measures—some intentional, some not—the fiscal capacity of that province was indeed restricted. When Newfoundland's then-Liberal government under Brian Tobin refused—for years—to allow the development of Voisey's Bay for political reasons (the company that owned it did not promise enough Newfoundland jobs), the fiscal capacity of that province was likewise limited.

Worldwide, there are multiple examples of countries with little in the way of natural resources that have prospered. Japan, Hong Kong, Singapore, Taiwan and South Korea are now prosperous to a degree unimagined 60 years ago.[a] Some countries rich in natural resources, such as Venezuela and Congo, exist at a level far below their potential.[8]

Some academic evidence suggests that natural resources are not naturally a help to countries rich in resources as they tend to rely on such natural wealth instead of concentrating on economic fundamentals such as trade and investment and post-secondary education opportunities. Economist Thorvaldur Gylfason explains:

Abundant natural resources may imbue people with a false sense of security and lead governments to lose sight of the need for good and growth-friendly economic management, including free trade, bureaucratic efficiency, and institutional quality. Put differently, abundant natural capital may crowd out social capital, by which is meant the infrastructure and institutions of a society in a broad sense: its culture, cohesion, law, system of justice, rules and customs and so on, including trust. Incentives to create wealth through good

a. For an excellent analysis of how and why nations prosper, see *The World Economy: A Millennial Perspective* by Angus Maddison. The OECD economist traces economic history since AD 1000 and analyses the reasons why some countries prosper and notes the remarkable progress of many formerly poor countries since just the 1950s.

policies and institutions may wane because of the relatively effort-
less ability to extract wealth from the soil or the sea. Manna from
heaven can be a mixed blessing.[9]

Far from a help to Prince Edward Island, Nova Scotia, Newfoundland
and New Brunswick, transfer payments and other similar policies created a perverse situation where economic development
is discouraged.

Ottawa's Orwellian apologists can use all the feel-good euphemisms they like. But their stay-at-home programs are costly,
inefficient and persuade people not to think about new opportunities. And those policies now exacerbate labour shortages in the
rest of the country. It's possible that one day Atlantic Canada will
thrive and provide prosperity for those who choose to stay and
even attract back many native sons and daughters, but it won't
happen under current federal policies.

The Fuel for the Folly: Canada's Various Taxes

But those examples of Ottawa's tragically misdirected efforts are
possible because of the taxes delivered to the various levels of government. Here's a review of their depth and breadth.

Personal income tax. Corporate income tax. Property tax.
Goods and services tax. Provincial sales tax. Tobacco tax. Permit
tax. Hotel tax. Employment Insurance tax. Canada Pension Plan
tax. Royalty tax. Air conditioning tax. Airport security tax. Natural
resource tax. Business tax. Toll taxes. Airport departure tax. Airport
navigation tax. Duty taxes. Tire tax. Environmental tax. Fuel tax.
School tax. Licence tax. Gun permit tax. User fee taxes. Tape
tax. Excise tax. Personal surtax. Corporate capital tax. Personal
capital gains tax. Financial institutions tax. Provincial payroll tax.
Alcohol tax. Liquor mark-up tax. Customs tax. Import tax.

And now governments even tax you for the withdrawal of
your own money at an Automatic Teller Machine (ATM).

And that's the short list. Add up all the taxes and they equal
33.9 per cent of the economy.[10]

But that's not the whole story. Add up all the *expenditures* by every level of government, and it equals 41.1 per cent of the economy.[11]

Add up all the *revenues* governments in Canada collect and the size of government in Canada equals 41.7 per cent of the economy.[12]

The difference in the percentages results from, for example, Crown corporations. They don't collect taxes but charge fees for their services. If such extensions of government were categorized as a ministry instead of a Crown, their "taking" and "spending" would be counted in government budgets as regular revenues and expenditures.

SEE THE TAX RELIEF? TRY AGAIN WITH THE MICROSCOPE

There has been some tax relief recently, though Canadians might be forgiven for missing it. As of 2003, the latest year for which this comprehensive comparison is available, personal tax payments account for 20.2 per cent of the average Canadian family's expenses; that was down from 21.5 per cent in 1998. But in both examples, personal tax was the number-one expense and trumped food, clothing or shelter.

Average household spending, total expediture $51,000

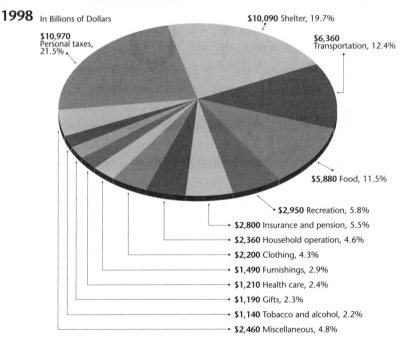

1998 In Billions of Dollars

$10,090 Shelter, 19.7%

$10,970 Personal taxes, 21.5%

$6,360 Transportation, 12.4%

$5,880 Food, 11.5%

$2,950 Recreation, 5.8%
$2,800 Insurance and pension, 5.5%
$2,360 Household operation, 4.6%
$2,200 Clothing, 4.3%
$1,490 Furnishings, 2.9%
$1,210 Health care, 2.4%
$1,190 Gifts, 2.3%
$1,140 Tobacco and alcohol, 2.2%
$2,460 Miscellaneous, 4.8%

Average household spending, total expediture $61,150

2003 In Billions of Dollars

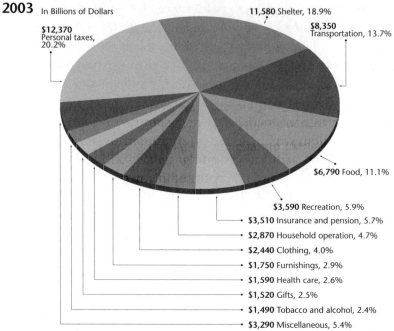

11,580 Shelter, 18.9%

$12,370 Personal taxes, 20.2%

$8,350 Transportation, 13.7%

$6,790 Food, 11.1%

$3,590 Recreation, 5.9%
$3,510 Insurance and pension, 5.7%
$2,870 Household operation, 4.7%
$2,440 Clothing, 4.0%
$1,750 Furnishings, 2.9%
$1,590 Health care, 2.6%
$1,520 Gifts, 2.5%
$1,490 Tobacco and alcohol, 2.4%
$3,290 Miscellaneous, 5.4%

Source: Statistics Canada, Average household expenditure and budget share. Totals may not add exactly due to rounding.

Marginal efforts all around

The marginal reduction in marginal rates is the result of marginal efforts at tax relief by all levels of government, or outright hikes by lower levels such as city hall. That, and the fact that while Ottawa and some provinces reduced income taxes, newcomers reversed direction and slapped on additional levies, taxes and health care "fees." In the case of Ottawa, overall payroll taxes jumped between the 1990s and the early 21st century because of drastic increases in Canada Pension Plan taxes to make up for many previous decades when earlier contributors didn't pay in enough to properly finance their own retirement.

One of the more oversold tax increases was the falsely labelled "$103-billion tax cut" then-federal finance minister Paul Martin talked about in Budget 2000. But that $103 billion was the estimated tax reductions in *total* between 1997 and 2004. However, even that wasn't an accurate number after subtracting the falsely claimed tax relief and accounting for never-mentioned tax hikes. And just prior to Christmas 2005, Martin and Finance Minister Ralph Goodale were at it again, this time promising $30 billion in tax relief even though part of it was due to inflation adjustments in tax brackets—hardly a tax cut—and much of the rest was delayed until 2010.[13]

By 2005, the actual annual reduction in personal taxes was about $12.4 billion, better than an overall hike in taxes. But the much-vaunted relief of 2000 and 2005 amounted to just 5.4 per cent of expected federal revenues in 2005.[14]

Canada's nastiest tax: The "Chinese head tax"

If modern Canadians complain about taxation—understandable given Adscam, HRDC, David Dingwall expense accounts at the Royal Canadian Mint and billion-dollar gun registry overruns—some history might at least put such irritants in perspective. Canadians of Chinese ancestry can match any modern complaint about taxes and then some, thanks to a mostly forgotten entry fee imposed on the basis of race.

Back in 1885, after the completion of the Canadian Pacific Railway across Canada, and to British Columbia where that portion was built mainly by Chinese labourers, thousands of whom died in the process, the Canadian government passed the *Canadian Immigration Act.*

The Act stipulated that most Chinese immigrants must pay a "capitation tax" before being granted the right to disembark. Certain occupational groups such as merchants and clergy were exempted (and later, teachers) but the "Chinese head tax," as it is more commonly known, was set at $50 in 1885, raised to $100 in 1890, and to $500 in 1903. Given the exemptions, it was mostly labourers who paid the head tax.

To understand how costly that was to workers of that period, a labourer in 1885 worked an average of 60 hours a week for an annual salary of $290. By 1905 when the average annual earnings of a production worker in Canada was $375, the tax bill was $500.[15] So, depending on the year, the head tax was equivalent to between two months' and 16 months' worth of an average labourer's salary, though that assumes Chinese workers were paid equivalent to white Canadians, not a safe assumption given the era.

The effect of the federal legislation was to restrict the flow of Chinese immigrants—not to exclude them entirely. But even that restriction was not enough for some. At the time, British Columbia labour leaders and politicians lobbied repeatedly for the full exclusion of the Chinese, sentiments they claimed were grounded in "concern" over competition for jobs. Perhaps, but stark racism was clearly also a factor. From the 1885 inception of the Act until 1923, more than 82,000 Chinese paid the tax, which contributed $18 million to federal coffers. A worse law—the *Chinese Exclusion Act*—which completely banned the entry of Chinese immigrants, then replaced the earlier 1885 legislation.

In addition to the federal imposition, the B.C. government also instituted a "Chinese tax" that collected over $7.7 million. The money was not insubstantial, either for those forced to pay it or for the government that collected it. At its revenue peak in British Columbia, the provincial levy brought in over $1.7 million in 1913—or about 18 per cent of the total $9.6 million in provincial revenues that year. The provincial "Chinese tax" was the third largest revenue source behind mainly timber royalties (31 per cent) and the sale of timber and land (24 per cent).[16]

In addition to the discrimination, the head taxes were tragic in other ways. The demographics of the Chinese who entered Canada (mostly male) meant there were limited opportunities for marriage given the relatively few single Chinese women (and the almost complete absence of interracial marriage). The high cost of the head tax also meant that many who were already married could not afford to send for their spouses.

Various Chinese associations have long pressed for redress and repayment through the courts and through Parliament, but the legal claim was rejected by the Ontario Superior Court in 2001 on the grounds that the 1982 Constitution could not be applied retroactively. The judge did note that there was certainly no question about the inherent racism of the 1885 legislation.[17]

Parliament could refund the tax to Chinese descendants, something Prime Minister Stephen Harper pledged during the 2006 election, but this brings up a dilemma for today's taxpayers. To refund a voluntary tax, even one as offensive as the Chinese head tax which began in 1885 and ended eight decades ago, could open a Pandora's box of penalties for modern workers. Today's taxpayers are then required to compensate many for the sins of politicians of generations ago. And many of today's immigrants would pay for the policies enacted long before they or their ancestors arrived in Canada, some with equally tragic histories from the countries they fled.

Regardless of the legal and philosophical arguments for and against reimbursement, the Chinese head tax should be recalled as Canada's most unfortunate and egregious levy. And, given the Chinese contribution to the country's first transcontinental railroad, it was also, tragically, Canada's nastiest and most ungrateful tax.

The Boring Data Stuff
(Just in case you want to know anything about your tax dollars)

Where the money comes from: Revenues—all levels of government

Types of taxes	Revenue (billions of $)	Amount %
Income	205.1	38.7%
Sales	104.1	19.6%
Property	46.8	8.8%
Other	17.7	3.3%
Health insurance	3.1	0.6%
Pension	67.6	12.7%
Govt sales of goods and services	41.1	7.8%
Investment income	38.5	7.3%
Own-source revenues (user fees, etc.)	6.6	1.2%
TOTAL	**531.0**	100.0%

Type	Spending (billions of $)	Amount %
Government services	16.7	3.2%
Protection of property and persons	42.0	8.1%
Transportation and communication	21.4	4.1%
Health	96.2	18.5%
Social services	154.8	29.9%
Education	76.5	14.8%
Conservation and business subsidies	19.4	3.7%
Environment	13.3	2.6%
Recreation and culture	13.5	2.6%
Labour, employment, and immigration	3.4	0.6%
Housing	3.9	0.7%
Foreign affairs and international aid	5.1	1.0%
Regional planning, dev't and subsidies	2.5	0.5%
Research	2.0	0.4%
Debt charges	46.5	9.0%
Other	1.4	0.3%
TOTAL	**518.0**	100.0%

Source: Statistics Canada, Catalogue no. 68-213-SIE, p. 14. revenue sources and expenditure functions, consolidated governments, Canada.

Chapter 4

Business Pork

*One of Canada's greatest success stories but also one of the largest re-
cipients of government assistance.*
> ~ Then-Opposition Leader Stephen Harper, in 2004, on
> Bombardier, and on his plan to end subsidies to business
> worth $4 billion annually.[1]

*If we say to this chip manufacturer, "You get $100 million or you get a
special loan or a loan guarantee," what do we say to other, smaller companies who received absolutely nothing, who established businesses on
their own hook without any government assistance?*
> ~ Alberta premier Ralph Klein, in 1999, declining to reverse
> the Alberta government's opposition to corporate welfare.[2]

Trough-Seeking Inc.

If there is any group in the country more confused about what it
wants from government than corporate Canada, they have yet to
show up on the public radar screen. Many corporate CEOs preach
the virtues of low taxes, free trade and open competition. They correctly argue that high taxation, whether personal or business, serves
as a drag on economic growth and its benefits: more jobs, better opportunities and improved living standards. And when it comes to
government intervention in the economy, the country's best-known
business lobby groups, such as Canadian Council of Chief Executives
(CCCE), the Canadian Chamber of Commerce and the Canadian
Manufacturers & Exporters decry "inflated spending levels."[3]

But such groups and their public advocacy are undercut by
their very members who, in the past and now, continue to receive direct taxpayer cash from government, a policy known
politely as "business assistance" and more frankly as "corporate welfare." The examples are not difficult to find. Prominent
among the membership of the Council of Chief Executives are
businesses legendary for their attendance at the public trough.
They include aerospace giants Pratt & Whitney—Canada's worst
offender, more so than even Bombardier (also a CCCE member),

which is often incorrectly identified as the top corporate welfare recipient.

Corporate welfare harms competitors who must fight against government-(taxpayer-)financed companies. It slows the economy at large through the transfer of tax dollars from productive companies and individuals to less productive sectors. And taxpayers and consumers must make do with higher prices, higher taxes, less competition and a lower standard of living than otherwise would be the case.

Business associations and corporations who wink at corporate welfare undercut credibility they might otherwise possess on government spending and taxation. The public observes some businesses at the trough and wrongly concludes that a healthy dose of state favouritism for some corporations may actually help the economy. If business wants to know why it has the Rodney Dangerfield problem of so little respect, the addiction to corporate welfare is a key reason.

The Excuse of History

One excuse for taxpayer assistance to business is that it has always existed. The federal government financed the Canadian Pacific Railway, some companies received hefty subsidies to build it and lucky as well as unscrupulous land speculators made a killing. By one estimate, the CPR's cost was $150 million (about $4.5 billion today) and 59 per cent of that was paid by taxpayers.[4] But that was the late 19th century; it would indeed have been fanciful to expect a private company to build a railway line across 3,000 miles just to reach 25,000 people in British Columbia.

To assume that what *might* have been necessary for the development of an agrarian colony in the late 19th century is still useful for urban Canada 140 years later, is to live—apologies to Aristotle—the unexamined policy life.

So how do Canada's companies and the politicians presently justify the subsidies? On the grounds that they're good for us; call it the nanny approach to economic policy. In some cases, as with small business or start-ups, capital access *is* a problem. But much corporate welfare in Canada is sent to the country's top firms with market capitalizations and revenue in the billions of dollars.

CANADA'S BIGGEST WELFARE RECIPIENT: NOT BOMBARDIER

Canada's largest corporate welfare recipient, Pratt & Whitney, was authorized to receive more than $176 million in straight grant money from the federal department of industry (Industry Canada) between 1982 and 1997, another $773 million in conditionally "repayable" contributions over the same time frame, and in 2005 received another $207-million authorization from the same department. Pratt & Whitney, a division of United Technologies Corporation, with a market capitalization of US$37 billion, hardly qualifies as a charity case.[a]

And if tax dollars for some of the planet's largest companies are not enough to dispel the myth that such subsidies are about start-up capital or small business, the same agencies that write cheques to aerospace companies also hand over money to the favourite corporate sport: golf.

Exhibit A is Newfoundland's Gander Golf Club; it once received almost $1 million from Atlantic Canada Opportunities Agency (ACOA), another federal agency. ACOA also handed out $20 million to other golf courses, fly-fishing societies, tennis clubs, snowmobile associations and sailing clubs.

Two Ways to Define Corporate Welfare

In very broad terms, corporate welfare could include industry-specific tax credits. For example, the film industry is the favoured recipient of generous tax credit programs federally and in some provinces. The usual justification is to attract an industry that might not otherwise set up shop in a province. But such rationalizations are weak, given that provincial tax credit programs do

a. Under the federal *Access to Information Act*, it is possible to discover how much money is authorized for disbursal to companies. But it is not usually possible to determine how much a specific company repaid. In the case of Industry Canada, grants and contributions are straight handouts. There is no repayment required. In the case of conditionally repayable contributions, full repayment may occur, or only partial repayment, or none at all. Conditional contributions are tied to projected sales.

little more than shift film production from one province to another.[b] That makes sense for a local politician's re-election campaign, but it is less than compelling in a wider national or international context. Governments should concentrate on tax rates and tax credit programs that actually create wealth in the long term all over the planet. With film tax credits, they instead merely shift a highly mobile industry such as film from one province to another in search of another government willing to help finance the newest Hollywood production.

However, while discriminatory tax credits are not the smartest of policies—they artificially shift investment decisions—a tighter, more defensible definition of corporate welfare is anything that helps a *specific* business or industry vis-à-vis other businesses or industries as opposed to neutral government policy, where a government does not intervene or choose between specific companies or businesses.[c]

Corporate welfare is never as useful as proponents claim. And this becomes clear when observed from a national and then international perspective. Consider the transfer of tax dollars from have to have-not provinces. When the latter lure specific businesses from the wealthier jurisdictions, they do so with the very money given to them by those provinces. A more sensible approach is for provinces to compete on land costs, labour rates and tax levels without business-specific "bribes."

EVERYBODY DOES *NOT* DO IT
As ill advised as corporate welfare is economically, so long as governments offer money, companies respond. It's in their interest to

b. In late 2004, the film industry lobbied both Ontario and British Columbia for higher tax credits and used the exact same arguments in both provinces in discussions with government and publicly. The result was Ontario increased its tax credit; B.C. followed soon thereafter and put the game back to square one. The film industry was no doubt cheery, but it allowed them to escape the sort of taxes imposed on business in general and under the most dubious of justifications.

c. For example, when a government gives $1 million to "Widget Maker A," it automatically puts "Widget Maker B" at a competitive disadvantage; that's not a neutral action. If the government raises or reduces taxes on *all* businesses, such an action may be desirable or undesirable, depending on one's view, but it is a neutral action towards any specific company or sector.

do so. If a competitor receives a grant or contribution from government, most companies argue they too must take subsidies or they will be at a competitive disadvantage. There is a solution to that game: cut off the flow of money to all.

In Canada, two provinces recognized the case against corporate welfare and (mostly) restricted the practice. Taxpayers in Alberta lost over $2.3 billion in grants, loans and loan guarantees to Alberta-based businesses in the 1980s and 1990s due to policies enacted under previous Conservative governments.[5] Thus, in 1996, the Alberta government of Ralph Klein ended taxpayer assistance for companies with its *Business Financial Assistance Limitation Statutes Act.* It requires any assistance over $1 million to be voted on in the provincial legislature, i.e., in full public view.[d] British Columbia passed similar legislation in 2002.

The Art of Pork: Federal Largesse

Despite the example of two provinces that refuse to subsidize most business, the federal government has so far refused to change its policy. The excuse of history (i.e., the Canadian Pacific Railway) is one reason. The Department of Regional Industrial Expansion under Pierre Trudeau was broken up and simply reformulated into new corporate welfare departments (named regional development agencies) in the 1980s under the Mulroney Tories, and continued under the Liberal government. Despite the stated purpose of these agencies to create economic growth, they more often simply redistribute wealth, that of tax dollars from one tax-paying business and productive sector to another that is presumably less so.

Another reason is political; all federal parties support the practice, including the Conservative Party, which has become mute on the issue. In the 1990s the Reform Party and its successor, the Alliance, mostly opposed the practice of business subsidies, which was largely a reflection of western sentiment, especially in B.C. and Alberta, where the public had written off many soured government

d. There are exceptions. Alberta did loan money to Canadian Airlines in the mid-1990s even though it had a then-informal policy against business assistance; it still provides loans of less than $1 million to small business. B.C.'s 2002 legislation does not cover business loans to Aboriginal businesses.

loans to business. Since the merger of the Progressive Conservative Party and the Alliance in 2003, opposition to corporate welfare was later dropped at the behest of Conservative members of Parliament from Ontario.

INDUSTRY MINISTER DISSIMULATION

Just as the Conservatives dropped their principled opposition to the economically counterproductive trough-seeking by corporate Canada, more evidence came to light that the federal government's welfare dispensary of choice—and handmaiden to the then Liberal government, which the Conservatives should have been less than happy about—Industry Canada, handed out cash to the usual suspects, many of whom bent the rules.

Worse, it's not as if successive ministers were unaware of the rot. In April 2002, then-Industry minister Allan Rock dismissed concerns from the Canadian Taxpayers Federation about how corporate welfare was being handled in his department. Specifically, Rock downplayed concerns about a program called Technology Partnerships Canada (TPC), which handed out hundreds of millions every year in "investments," i.e., conditionally repayable loans to business.

In 2002, Rock told Vancouver's *Georgia Straight* newspaper that the "auditor general has twice taken a very close look at Technology Partnerships," and then neglected to mention what the auditor found, thus leaving the impression that all was fine or anything amiss had been corrected. Rock also questioned the accuracy of Canadian Taxpayers Federation's research. But as both previous and later audits from Rock's own department and others showed, the CTF research was bang-on, even at the very moment that Rock assured taxpayers Industry Canada was properly handling its massive business loan portfolio.

In fact, Auditor General Sheila Fraser slapped Industry Canada and its Technology Partnerships program and noted that "Project and results monitoring could be improved."[6] Also, she noted that "TPC does not yet systematically monitor project results," and "there is no explanation of the basis for an extent of sharing risks and rewards with firms."[7] That was in 1999, three years *before* Rock claimed all was well at Industry Canada.

One year after Rock came to Vancouver and dismissed concerns about how money was doled out, an internal 2003 audit of Technology Partnerships Canada noted the following after a few perfunctory compliments:

> *Opportunities exist to strengthen project file documentation and ensure that technical advisors have the business backgrounds and/or business related experience needed to minimize the risk that items, of a critical financial nature, are not appropriately considered in the due diligence and monitoring processes.*[8]

Translation: The auditors were not sure everyone who handed out taxpayer cash had the expertise to understand what they were looking at.

Another excerpt from that 2003 audit noted that "documentation in a number of files was incomplete and/or non-standardized, especially surrounding due diligence. This increases the risk of TPC not being able to demonstrate the level of due diligence performed on funding proposals and the rationale for decisions made."[9] Translation: Bureaucrats make decisions without due diligence and several files reveal this and/or are missing critical documentation.

TARGETS A PROBLEM? POOF! NO MORE TARGETS!

In September 2005, a new industry minister, David Emerson, finally came clean—sort of—and confessed to taxpayers that his department's money-losing corporate welfare programs were, well, money-losing corporate welfare programs but also that the nine-year-old Technology Partnerships Canada had come off the accountability rails. Those were not his exact words, but when he replaced Technology Partnerships Canada with the new (!) and improved (!) Transformative Technologies Program, everyone understood the message.

To obviate the problem of missed targets the new industry minister hit on a new strategy: scrap them. Thus, the department announced the measure of success for the "new" business loans program was no longer cost recovery but "sharing the risks of innovation."[10] The lower expectations meant taxpayers could assume that a recoup of their investment would indeed lag in Ottawa's priorities. Thus, hundreds of millions of dollars would be cashiered from the "new" corporate welfare program annually without so much as a fig leaf of justification when dollars did not return.

In the future, how much taxpayers will recoup is unclear. But past handouts might provide a clue as to how much will be transferred out of the public treasury and to whom: in the 18 months that preceded the no-need-for-repayment-goals announcement by Industry Canada—and to use just three examples—Industry Canada cut cheques to Rolls-Royce ($30 million), Raytheon ($4 million) and Pratt & Whitney ($207 million).

Emerson was likely sincere about the clean-up; that's why Prime Minister Paul Martin recruited him from a successful private-sector career. But the changed priorities were comparable to a teacher announcing to her students that exam marks would no longer count towards a final grade. Instead, it was the effort, the "shared effort" of teacher and students that would be the measure of success. The lowered standards would allow future industry ministers to claim that the public had been warned; indeed, they had.

As for the Conservatives M.P.s from Ontario who pushed for a don't-ask, don't-tell party position on corporate welfare, it was an unwise tactical move that saw them forego credit for years of firmer opposition to business subsidies—just as the public saw evidence of more of their opponent's incompetence on that very issue.

TRANSPARENCY WHEN CONVENIENT: POST-MORTEM ON THE *LATEST* SCANDAL

After years of secrecy, Industry Canada finally deigned to give taxpayers some results about taxpayer money under their stewardship. Truth is, they could hardly avoid it. Years of digging by the Canadian Taxpayers Federation and then the *Ottawa Citizen* kept revealing uncomfortable facts about the department.[11] The *Citizen* researcher who dug out the latest sorry statistics about the TPC noted that the department had been "deceitful and misleading" and had concealed records about the true nature of the program.[12]

Here's what's known now: Technology Partnerships Canada loaned out $2.1 billion from its 1996 inception and has recouped $115 million or 5.5 per cent. Significantly more is expected to be paid back over time. As of late 2005, the department claimed that only three loans, totalling $904,000, were write-offs, and that no grants were handed out (though that ignores the opportunity cost of lost interest, or a reduction in the federal debt and missed savings on interest payments there).[13]

However, the government's long-term record on every other corporate welfare file contained similar claims. Also, because Industry Canada needed to re-jig corporate welfare yet again and with an explicit downgrade of cost recovery, it begs the question if Technology Partnerships was on track to be different from past corporate welfare crashes or, as is more likely, if more write-offs were already in the pipeline. And then there was the issue of TPC's almost $17-million annual administrative budget, which would be transferred to the new-and-improved agency; it's not just lost interest and write-offs that swallow tax dollars.

SCAMMED AGAIN

Shortly after the announcement of the re-jigged corporate welfare agency in September 2005, yet another Industry Canada audit was made public. It found almost one in three companies investigated in the TPC program to date (11 out of 32) was in violation of its agreements with Ottawa; it appeared $6 million has been paid out in improper commission to agents who hooked companies up to Ottawa's corporate welfare gurney.[14]

The government declined to name the 11 in violation. As usual, transparency would come only if someone could obtain leaked documents. Past transparency arrived only *after* information that reporters and the Canadian Taxpayers Federation had already squeezed out of an unwilling department. Thanks to the media, the public did find out, however, that former Liberal cabinet minister David Dingwall received an illegal $350,000 commission for lobbying on behalf of an Ontario pharmaceutical company, a commission the company was forced to return when it became public knowledge.[15]

The Evidence against Corporate Welfare

In 2005, a spokesman for Industry Canada claimed that returns in the TPC program compared favourably to those of a private-equity firm.[16] Given that angel investors don't reveal their private successes or dogs, it's hard to know. What is known is that the Canadian Chartered Bankers Association reported that the average business loan loss provision was 0.3 per cent. In other words, Canada's major lenders expect 99.7 per cent of their business loans to be repaid.[17]

Compare that to any government loan programs and guarantees. Compare it specifically to Canada Economic Development Quebec, which wrote off 33 per cent of its 1989-2001 loan portfolio: a write-off ratio 110 times that of Canada's chartered banks and, in the case of CED-Q, all done with our tax dollars.

Governments are not adept at picking winners, but losers are excellent at picking governments. A more sensible stance for governments is to build a level playing field between businesses and sectors. That means lower personal and business taxes, an internationally competitive regulatory framework (yes, we'll have to convince some protectionist-minded American senators) with an aggressive anti-subsidy stance at the World Trade Organization.

The core problem with corporate welfare is that it doesn't work. Some politicians and many labour leaders love local subsidies—except when other countries outbid our nation—but there is no solid evidence that such programs actually promote economic development.[18] Even supporters recognize that the lack of supporting evidence imperils the future of these programs.[19] The overwhelming body of evidence is that direct government incentives to retain, attract or expand business do not significantly influence the location or growth of economic activity.

Professor Terry Buss of Suffolk University reviewed more than 100 targeted industry studies and concluded that corporate welfare programs in the United States are based on poor data, unsound evaluative methods and faulty economic reasoning.[20]

The reason corporate welfare exists is not economic but political: it gives the illusion that members of Parliament, provincial politicians and local mayors are "doing something" to help create jobs. Politicians cut ribbons at aerospace factories or automotive plants and the headlines read: "Hundreds of jobs created because of federal/provincial investment." But what the cameras and headlines don't capture is the shuttering of a plant down the road, across a provincial or national border, and the equivalent employment losses there. In terms of job creation, corporate welfare is a wash; it kills as many as it creates. And it does so after first diverting tax dollars through consultants, lobbyists and then the government bureaucracies that deliver the cheques.

THE PAST RECORD OF CORPORATE WELFARE

Federally, the major distributors of corporate welfare include Western Economic Diversification (WED) in the four western provinces, Canada Economic Development (CED) in Quebec, Atlantic Canada Opportunities Agency (ACOA) for the Atlantic provinces, and one for northern Ontario—FedNor. In addition to those Crown corporations, the federal department of Industry gives out grants, contributions (grants by another name), loans and loan guarantees.

Over the last decade in Alberta, British Columbia and federally, and to a lesser extent in the eight remaining provinces, the Canadian Taxpayers Federation has obtained a large amount of data on corporate welfare. Here is a summary of some results, based on Access to Information requests and, in very rare cases, publicly available information.

Atlantic Canada Opportunities Agency
$1.8 billion in free money over a decade

Time frame:
• 1989-1999

Amount disbursed or authorized:
• $2.577 billion, in the four Atlantic provinces

Number of disbursements:
- 22,867

Amount given in *grants or contributions* (i.e., non-repayable):
- More than 72 per cent, or *$1.85 billion, in the form of non-repayable grants and contributions.*

Loan write-offs for the 1989-1999 time period:
- ACOA loaned out $591 million during this period and *wrote off an amount equivalent to 34 per cent* of the amount loaned during this time period, or *$205 million.*

Repayment records:
- The government has not yet made such information available.

Other noteworthy facts:
- In the case of ACOA, 4.2 per cent of all funding recipients accounted for $1.498 billion or 58 per cent of all funds received. In straight figures, 475 (out of 11,297) recipients received $1.498 billion.

Canada Economic Development (in Quebec)
Free money for Quebec: $1.4 billion over 12 years

Time frame:
- 1989-2001

Amount disbursed or authorized:
- $1.778 billion

Number of disbursements:
- 8,964

Amount given in *straight grants or contributions* (i.e., non-repayable):
- More than 81 per cent, *or $1.4 billion, in the form of non-repayable grants and contributions.*

Loan write-offs for the 1991-2001 time period
• Since 1991, CED-Q has written off 378 loans worth over *$118 million*. This is more than *33 per cent* of the value of CED-Q's total loan portfolio between 1989 and 2001.

Loan repayment records:
• Information withheld by government.

Other noteworthy facts:
• In the case of CED-Q, $817 million was doled out to small, medium and large Quebec businesses either in the form of contributions, subsidies or "repayable contributions." They include a who's who of corporate Canada, including SR Telecom, Johnson & Johnson, Intranets, the Royal Bank, Banque National, Ingersoll-Rand Canada and Siemens. Associations, unions and chambers of commerce and other organizations received more than $154 million in funds. The fashion industry received more than $10 million.

Western Economic Diversification (WED)
$1.25 billion in free money over 13 years
Time frame:
• 1987-2000

Amount disbursed or authorized:
• $2.003 billion to the four western provinces

Number of disbursements:
• 13,776

Amount given in *straight grants or contributions* (i.e., non-repayable):
• *More than 62.7 per cent, or $1.25 billion, in the form of non-repayable grants and contributions,* though $34 million was for flood relief—a justifiable expenditure.

Loan write-offs for the 1987-2000 time period:
- *$65.9 million—or 8.8 per cent* of a loan portfolio value of more than $746 million—was written off by 2000.

Loan repayments 1988-2000:
- WED loaned out over $132 million in *conditionally* repayable contributions, but has only received $4.5 million in repayments or a 3.4 per cent rate of return on these royalty or level-of-sale agreements.

- WED loaned $4.5 billion in repayable contributions and has received back $351 million or 7.8 per cent.

Industry Canada
$5.8 billion in free money since 1982

Time frame:
- 1982-1997

Amount disbursed or authorized:
- $11.279 billion across Canada

Number of disbursements:
- 32,969

Amount given in *straight grants, contributions and interest contributions (i.e., non-repayable)*:
- $5.796 billion

Loan repayment records:
- As of 2001, *21 per cent of the money* expended by Industry Canada for 1,773 different projects between 1982 and 2001 *was repaid.*

Loan write-offs/repayments for the 1987-2000 time period:
- Information withheld by government.

Other noteworthy facts:
- More than18 per cent ($2.1 billion) of the $11.279 billion was authorized through various forms of assistance to *five* companies:

Pratt & Whitney ($949 million), De Havilland ($425 million), Bombardier/Candour ($245 million), Le Groupe MIL Inc. ($244 million) and Air Ontario ($241 million). More than 49 per cent ($5.6 billion) of the $11.279 billion was authorized to 75 of some of Canada's largest companies.

Technology Partnerships Canada

Technology Partnerships Canada was Industry Canada's successor to past, failed programs within Industry Canada (most notably the Defence Industry Productivity Program) that were criticized in the past by the auditor general and others. As of 2005, Technology Partnerships Canada authorized $3.0 billion and spent $2.1 billion. Repayment thus far is 2.6 per cent.

The repayment record for the *similar* previous program, the Defence Industry Productivity Program (DIPP), was and is poor. By 2001, 19 years after the DIPP program began and five years after DIPP ended, *repayments amounted to only 18 per cent* ($393 million out of $2.159 billion in expenditures) for 654 loans, loan guarantees and conditionally repayable loans that dated back to 1982.

Time frame:
• April 1996-October 2005

Amount authorized/spent:
• $3.01 billion authorized/$2.1 billion spent

Number of disbursements:
• 702

Loan repayments:
• Repayments as of March 2005 amounted to just under $55.5 million, or just over 2 per cent of the $2.1 billion disbursed. (Approximately another $900 million was authorized as of October 2005 but not yet disbursed.)

Loan write-offs for the 1996-2005 time period:
• Three worth $904,000, according to Industry Canada.

Chapter 5

The Last Canadian Monopoly:
Government unions and the public sector

JIM SINCLAIR: If anyone opened up the purse and gave away money it was Mr. Campbell. He gave away $20,000 and $25,000 in tax cuts to the richest people in the province.

NATIONAL POST: That was their money to start with.

SINCLAIR: No, it wasn't their money. It was all of our money.[1]

~ B.C. Federation of Labour president Jim Sinclair, in 2002, arguing against tax relief

Taxpayer Casualties

Whenever governments and unions go to war, taxpayers are the first casualties. Governments with negotiators and lawyers square off against public-sector unions with lawyers and negotiators; the public pays the bill for both. In such battles, governments rarely win and sometimes it is not clear that they intend to. Canadians are too often squeezed between politicians unwilling to stand up to labour and government union leaders who happily want taxpayer spigots kept open no matter the cost to other Canadians.

Unions are more than desirable and useful; they serve as a counterbalance against the possible concentration of power in any business and prevent all the chips from being held by executives with none left for workers. But an abusive overdose on power is not a temptation reserved exclusively for corporate bosses or elected officials; unions placed in a monopoly position also succumb to the potent combination of human nature + power. It is especially tempting when government unions have a *de facto* monopoly in health care and education, two of the more critical services citizens require.

In Canada, the result of a strong government union movement[a] is that average Canadians are hit in the pocketbook by

a. In Canada, overall unionization is at 30.6 per cent. However, only 20 per cent of the private sector is unionized compared to 61.4 per cent of the public sector. (Statistics Canada, "Perspectives on Labour and Income," April 2005, Vol. 6, No. 4. p. 6.)

government unions in at least three distinct ways: first, the above-market higher pay and benefits for most government jobs, the cost of which is borne by the private sector; second, monopoly control, which allows government unions to disrupt the most basic of human needs—education and health services; and third: the power of organized labour, which, in addition to extracting advantages for itself at the cost to all parties, also lobbies actively against competition, competitive bidding and tax relief.

Pocketbook Hit 1: The Public Sector's Pay Advantage

A comprehensive study produced by the Canadian Policy Research Networks (which is itself funded in large measure by the federal government) noted that public-sector salaries were on average 11.6 per cent *higher* than those of the private sector.

After the authors accounted for unionization (much higher in the public sector than in the private sector), the public-sector salaries were still higher by 7.6 per cent. That was *after* the authors accounted for variables such as age, education and other factors that might explain the higher average wages paid to the government employees.

The study, based on Labour Market Survey data from Statistics Canada, was limited in one important respect: the data did not include some health care workers as "public" but instead classified them as private. As the authors wrote:

> *The narrow definition of the Labour Force Survey definition of the public sector does mean that some organizations in the broader public sectors of health, education, and transportation, communication, and utilities that are funded and controlled but not owned by the government are considered here as in the private sector....*
> *The public-private wage gap here may thereby be biased downwards and could be considered* a conservative estimate of the gap for that reason.[2] *[emphasis mine]*

So, the 11 per cent (or 7.6 per cent after unionization factors are looked at) is a *low* estimate of the wage advantage public-sector employees have over private-sector employees.

65

But note carefully the language on unionization. Unionization is an *explanation* for higher average wages in the public sector vis-à-vis the private sector; it's not the same as a *justification* for higher average public-sector pay. Expressed differently, high unionization rates in government help *explain* the pay advantage government workers receive, but it is still the lower-paid private sector that pays the bill. (If the private sector did not put the money into the public treasury to begin with, public-sector workers would not be paid.) One can argue that private-sector workers should be paid more, but no magic wand magically brings about such outcomes. That government workers are more unionized is merely a technical explanation of the preferential difference, not a justification.[b]

A 2003 study from the Canadian Federation of Independent Business, which used census data, found that federal wage levels were 15.1 per cent higher in the public sector when compared with the private sector. The difference was 9.1 per cent provincially and 11.4 per cent locally. Add in benefits and the government advantage over the private sector was 23.2 per cent federally, 14.8 per cent provincially and 14.2 per cent locally.[3]

The Public Sector Pay and Benefits Advantage

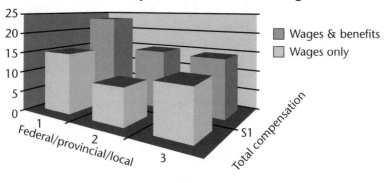

b. Even if the private sector had the same union density as the public sector, the public sector would likely be paid more unless governments bargain more robustly with public sector unions. Why? Private-sector unionized firms almost always face competition from other private companies, both union and non-union. Rarely is there competition in the public sector to provide service. One group of unionized employees does not, as a rule, compete with another potential group of public-sector employees in a different union for the right to provide services to the public.

And the advantage continues. A 2004 study by Human Resources and Development Canada on more than 616,000 workers concluded that the previous year's wage increase in the public sector was almost double that of the private sector, 2.9 per cent compared to 1.5 per cent.[4]

Pocketbook Hit 2: How Government Monopolies Hurt Kids

If governments owned grocery stores, farms and the supply chain, the Public Service Alliance of Canada would staff the tills, the Canadian Union of Public Employees would collect the crops, and both would drive the trucks that deliver the meat, vegetables, fruits and other foodstuffs. The unions and the Council of Canadians would decry the encroachment of privately owned food stores, including neighbourhood convenience stores, but especially entirely private big-box superstores. Shirley Douglas and her famous-actor son, Kiefer Sutherland, would hold press conferences denouncing Alberta for disparaging the memory of Tommy Douglas. Maude Barlow would write book after book about how food was such a precious resource that only government (and by extension, government unions) should be allowed to handle it. And a food poisoning scandal in Walkerton, Ontario, would be blamed on the private sector even when the testing company did its job (finding evidence of salmonella) while two government employees neglected to perform theirs.

If the above seems fanciful rhetoric, it is only because Canadians—quite properly—cannot conceive of giving government monopoly control over their food supply in the manner they blithely accept when it comes to matters as critical as health care and water.

But in health and education, massive government involvement —and, by extension, massive government *union* involvement—is assumed a normal state of affairs. Therein also lie the best examples of the damage public-sector monopolies can inflict, with two of the more recent examples originating in British Columbia.

In 2004, the Hospital Employees Union, which provides cleaning and food services in B.C.'s hospitals, engaged in an illegal strike to protest government legislation that rolled back salaries and provided for competitive bidding; wages were reduced but were still above the private sector. In proper context, the government action took place after a decade of ever-rising and artificially inflated wage increases put in motion by the previous New Democrat government. The union had a point: no one likes wages rolled back. But the government also had theirs: above-market wages diverted health care dollars from other staff and services: doctors and nurses as well as needed equipment and infrastructure.

The end result of the week-long strike was a significant reduction of service in B.C.'s hospital system. That meant the cancellation of operations for a nine-year-old Campbell River boy in need of heart surgery, two Kelowna women who needed breast cancer surgery, a three-year-old boy who waited months to have a growth removed at B.C. Children's Hospital and another 79 children who also had their surgeries cancelled at that facility; 514 MRIs and 1,852 CT scans were also scrapped along with thousands of other cancellations.[5]

Powerful monopolies are inured to most suffering and the victims in this case—patients—were at the mercy of a system-wide shutdown by those who had patients in just such a vise-grip. In contrast, if the HEU strike had occurred in the food industry, consumers would simply have crossed the street to another store.

In 2005, another government-union dispute and another illegal strike took place. In October, B.C.'s 42,000 teachers struck for two weeks, this after the B.C. Liberal government imposed a contract, something the previous NDP government had also done on several occasions.

The practical result was that teachers not in favour of the action were forced to choose between two weeks' salary to cover their mortgage payments or cross the picket line and face colleagues they would work with for years after the strike. Parents had to stay home, or, if that wasn't an option, pay for daily care for their younger children. Students likely enjoyed the two-week vacation, but at the price of falling behind in their studies.

The B.C. Teachers' Federation was twice ordered back to work by a judge, but their defiance of the courts revealed a double-standard in the labour movement at large: had businesses refused to comply with labour legislation, despite court orders to do so, union presidents would have called for severe penalties and perhaps jail for executives until corporations came to heel. But when one of their own hit the bricks and was under two court orders to comply with provincial legislation, other teachers' unions from across the country came to B.C. to show support.

The surface issues in the dispute concerned wages and class size, but the underlying wrangling was really over choice, though not in the manner assumed by B.C.'s unions: whether to work or not. Canada's labour movement consistently lobbies for monopoly control over education and health care and yet complains when governments give it to them at the cost of not being allowed to strike. It would be tempting for the public to be unsympathetic to teachers but that would miss the obvious remedy.

To cut the Gordian knot of the monopoly service providers in health and education that now exists, independent schools should receive 100 per cent of the per-pupil funding that public schools now receive; that would end the possibility for the near-total closure of all schools when some teachers wish to strike, a legal right they should have in a non-monopoly environment. Similarly, in health care, universality need not be sacrificed in the pursuit of quality; the only change needed is in the constricted pipeline of who can deliver the health services. Open up health care delivery and insurance to private, non-profit as well as existing government providers, and system-wide shutdowns because of labour disputes will be history.

A variety of private-sector companies safely deliver bottled water and food to the public every day; it's not only basic human needs such as health care and education that are far too critical to be left to strike-prone monopolies.

Pocketbook Hit 3: Government Unions Dislike Competition; They Also Lobby against Tax Relief

The reason why government unions argue against tax relief is not difficult to discern: taxes allow public-sector employees to be paid and thus the assumption is that higher taxes equal ever-higher pay, better benefits and job security. That the assumption breaks down when too-high levies begin to impede economic growth and slow it for all—even for those fond of burgeoning government revenues—is not a point government unions have yet considered.

Nevertheless, the attempt to keep taxes where they are, if not raise them, is undertaken every year by public-sector unions, the umbrella organizations that represent them, such as the Canadian Labour Congress, and the many advocacy groups and think-tanks that serve as fronts for government labour. As for competition, the bumper-sticker joke that one shouldn't steal because the government hates competition is especially true as it applies to public-sector unions. For them, competition is a threat akin to Dracula during a full moon; their preferred method of dealing with such an entity is to drive a stake through its heart.

On taxes and competition, the friends of high taxes have never been shy about their opposition to tax relief or competition:

"We won't accept privatization and impoverishment—that's what it comes down to."[6]
> ~ Arthur Sanborn, president of the Montreal Central Council of the Confederation des syndicats nationaux, in December 2003, protesting changes to Quebec's labour laws.

"They're hiding behind the courts and it's not going to work and it's making a big mess out of the education system."
> ~ British Columbia Federation of Labour president Jim Sinclair in October 2005, after a B.C. court ordered teachers engaged in an illegal strike back to work.[7]

"I call this economic terrorism."[8]

> ~ Dave Coles—Communications, Energy, and Paperworkers
> Union, on British Columbia government budget cuts,
> October 2001.

"They want to dismantle every vestige of civilized society."[9]

> ~ Fred Muzin, president of the Hospital Employees Union, at
> the same protest.

*"Um, but you know, when I stand back and I look at it, uh, no Canadian
has ever uh, died 'cause of uh, anthrax, at least uh, you know, not delib-
erately. Umm, very few Canadians have ever died in a terrorist attack.*

*"But thousands of Canadians die every year as a result of homeless-
ness and poverty and hunger and pollution and the lack of adequate
environmental uh, safeguards, uh, of our water systems and, and food
systems, etcetera. And the budget had ... essentially, nothing on all of
those."*[10]

> ~ Seth Klein (brother of Naomi), director of the union- and
> government-funded Canadian Centre for Policy Alternatives,
> three months after 9/11, on the federal budget update, mon-
> ey for the military, and on relative priorities.

*"I won't deny the fact there are a lot of union workers that are seduced
by this notion that somehow this surplus will result in tax breaks for
ordinary people."*[11]

> ~ Ken Georgetti, president of the Canadian Labour Congress
> on tax cuts promised in the 2000 election by the Liberals
> and the Alliance parties.

Chapter 6

moregovernmentfunding.org
How taxpayers subsidize special-interest
groups that love big government

Toronto feminist Beth Symes received a [government] grant to challenge the limit on tax-deductible child-care expenses. At the time her case was heard by the Supreme Court, Syme's annual family income was $200,000.[1]

~ Ted Morton and Rainier Knopf in *The Charter Revolution and the Court Party*

Everyone into the Pool!

Most Canadians might think that government policy is at least partially determined by interest groups and lobbyists who fight it out in the public square *mano a mano*. A tax-and-spend group saddles up against a limited government lobby and duals it out in front of politicians in scenes reminiscent of *Gladiator*. In other policy areas, a pro-choice group may cross swords with pro-lifers, business groups hash it out with labour, gay liberation groups with Baptists. In this view of politics, such groups pick up their rhetorical weapons, studies, soundbites and whatever else is within reach, and after they fight it out for a season, politicians and bureaucrats wisely decide on the policies and legislation for the next year, or 20.

Truth is, Canada's governments long ago stopped being neutral in public policy fights. To extend the *Gladiator* example, many politicians and the multi-billion-dollar departments they control are more likely to load up their favourite "non-governmental" organization with taxpayer cash and other weapons of choice such as access to themselves, influential bureaucrats and political staff who write the regulations and laws. Meanwhile, groups not in political favour might as well wrap a ball-and-chain around their ankles.

That this is a distortion of the democratic process is obvious to any honest observer who has had the misfortune to closely observe it. (It is also why German chancellor Otto von Bismarck said laws are like sausages; it is better not to see them being made.) Sure, politicians and bureaucrats will have their biases and some will make up their minds long before cross-country hearings are held on an issue. But when governments use tax dollars to fund advocacy groups, government is no longer on the receiving end of various pleas and demands from the public. Instead, the government as an institution becomes a megaphone-amplified voice, a major player in the public square—one that carries with it all the resources, funding and power that a state possesses, which is substantial. With such power, most other voices—the ones *not* favoured by government—are shunted to the side.

Any attempt to provide a complete breakdown of government funding for special interests is destined for an exercise in frustration. When it comes to interest groups at the public trough, a comprehensive list of subsidy-seeking (and receiving) groups would fill several telephone books. Every government—federal, provincial and municipal, and government-owned businesses—dishes out cash to non-profits, registered charities, labour unions and chambers of commerce. Social, political and legal advocacy groups are all funded to wage public campaigns on behalf of their favourite cause.

Often, many groups have a vested interest in government intervention because they are dependent on government (taxpayer) money for their budgets. And the fact that such groups rely so heavily on government funds reveals that their public base of support is indeed narrow. Were it not so thin, they would raise money directly from the public. From environmental groups to teachers' unions to lobby groups that want government to be more involved in various aspects of Canadians' lives, many special interests have a vested interest in high taxes precisely because government revenues flow directly to their bottom line.

The Battle in Seattle and the Granola Gang in Genoa

One illustration of how taxpayers fund advocacy against their own best interests and that of the poorest citizens on the planet is this: government funding of anti-globalization groups and their protests and others associated with such events.

The anti-globalization protesters who travel the world from Seattle to Genoa to Caracas are sincere—and misinformed; they

75

would cut Third World countries off at the economic knees and limit the ability of the poor to improve their lot. The anti-free-trade movement—now dressed up "fair trade" drag—is another version of provincial-minded protectionism. With apologies to Churchill, never have so many protested so often for so wrong a method to relieve poverty around the world. Access to rich countries' markets will lift developing nations into better conditions; in contrast, an expansion of protectionist policy under any guise will only guarantee more misery.

But if many Canadians assume as much about the protesters vis-à-vis free markets, they are likely unaware that much of the anti-globalization fervour is taxpayer-funded. When professional protesters show up at every trade summit, much of the ensuing circus is financed by tax dollars, either indirectly or directly.

Remember the 1999 "Battle in Seattle"? The British Columbia Teachers' Federation sent 100 union activists to that melee. That union's take from taxpayers was $4.6 million in grants and contributions from the British Columbia government between 1992 and 2001 and another $700,000 in contracts the then-New Democrat government arranged with the teachers' union.[2]

And then there was Quebec City in 2001. The Canadian Teachers' Federation helped along anti-free-trade festivities there, and that union has received $579,000 from the federal department of Multiculturalism since 1996.[3] Besides such indirect taxpayer funding for the anti-globalization crowd, politicians also feed them direct cash. Quebec City anti-free-trade activists were given $300,000 by the federal government and $200,000 from Quebec to hold their own so-called People's Summit.

But if education unions are at the taxpayer trough and feed anti-free-trade sentiment, they are not alone, as sponsors of a 2002 anti-G8 gathering in Calgary illustrated. Participants at that anti-G8 fiesta included the Canadian Labour Congress, itself a recipient of $304,480 based on an analysis of just *two* federal departments, Canadian Heritage and Environment.[4]

On the environment side, tracking taxpayer funding for every anti-globalization group is near impossible; there are multiple agencies from all governments that disburse grants to environmental lobbyists. But here are several examples from those present at the 2002 Calgary protests: the Canadian Environmental Network, whose website offered to help protesters deliver their message to the "corporate media," took $481,250 in 2001 from the federal government, which takes taxes from, among others, corporations.[5]

Environment Canada gave the Sierra Club more than $175,000 in grants and contributions to that lobby's British Columbia and Alberta branches in 2000 and 2001. (The Sierra Club also received more than $213,000 from the B.C. government when the New Democrats were in charge.)

The unions, environmentalists and social activists will argue that no indirect taxpayer cash goes to their anti-globalization fiestas. At other times, chambers of commerce and business lobbies argue that some of the money they receive goes to conferences. Both are weak defences. Business groups ought to hold their conferences without government sponsorship on principle. On a practical level, many of those same groups call for lower taxes and then undercut their call by taking government cash.

Regardless of which favourite cause a lobby group spends money on—an anti-free-trade rally or a Kyoto newspaper ad—the tax dollars that flow from governments allow such groups to engage in more advocacy than they otherwise could if forced to rely only on the public or union dues.

How Governments Fund Their Very Own Lobby Groups

To use an example from the environmental movement, while some money goes to environmental projects worth doing by someone, taxpayer cash also ends up funding day-to-day advocacy. There's nothing wrong with advocacy, nor with a single-issue group or a single view. The group, issue or view may be the correct one to have in light of a particular problem—environmental, economic or otherwise.

But the problem arises when a group avails itself of taxpayer funding *and* promotes one side. For example, the Alberta-based

Pembina Institute, critical of Alberta Premier Ralph Klein for his Kyoto protocol stance, received at least $291,371 in 2000 and 2001 from Ottawa to push what amounted to the federal government's view on that treaty.[6] How it received the money is no surprise; it was on friendly terms with former federal Environment minister David Anderson, with whom it once held a very public black-tie dinner.[7] Anderson was a fan of the institute's approach to global warming and vice-versa.[a]

Over the next two years, Pembina received more than $1.4 million in fees for service contracts, of which government contracts constitute a chunk, though the institute's annual report doesn't list the breakdown. But some of it originates with government as Pembina lists the following as partners and clients: Alberta Environment, Alberta Municipal Affairs, B.C. Hydro, B.C. Ministry of Energy and Mines, Department of Foreign Affairs and Trade, Environment Canada, the National Energy Board and Natural Resources Canada.

Then there is the Sierra Club, which, according to its own financial statements, received $574,431 in 2003 and $758,608 in 2004 in what it labels government contracts.

When such cash arrives via a government contract and not a grant, the response will be that just as Staples isn't subsidized when it provides paper clips to a federal department, neither is Pembina or Sierra when it provides consulting services. Fair enough, except that it's one thing to receive taxpayer grants to plant trees, and quite another to get in on the government consulting bandwagon to help push an agenda. It's also why government consulting by advocacy groups has such a tortured history. Such organizations lobby politicians with the very funds they receive from government; that allows for oversized influence. Such merry-go-round coziness between government and advocacy groups distorts public policy choices much in the same way corporate welfare distorts economic choices.

a. It was a sure bet that Pembina would never invite the author of the *Skeptical Environmentalist*, Bjorn Lomborg, to speak. Lomborg also argues that global warming is real and at least partly caused by humans; he just thinks governments should spend money to help people adjust to the change instead of attempting to fight it.

While such lobby groups receive government funds, it is easier to take positions that may kill off development. That's not bad if a company might poison the water; it's not so positive if the group has its facts wrong or has debatable solutions to a problem, which almost every organization does. When governments fund non-governmental organizations that also do advocacy work, it allows them to publish, lobby and agitate for policies regardless of whether enough people would actually support the efforts of such a group. It's a perfect way to insulate the organization from real-world effects and inculcate radicalism.

A provincial example of this occurred in British Columbia. Throughout the 1990s, the New Democratic government funded the Canadian Centre for Policy Alternatives (CCPA), an organization (with offices across the country) that, not coincidentally, constantly presses for higher taxes and more spending.

To say that a fair majority of Canadians would disagree with the Centre's policies is an understatement. The CCPA, which has tax-deductible status, is solidly in favour of higher taxes and more government intervention in the economy including, oddly, corporate welfare. (Curiously, its call for higher taxes, if implemented, would negatively affect high-income workers on the auto assembly line who are probably unaware their labour bosses at the Canadian Auto Workers Union *also* fund the group.)

In British Columbia, the New Democratic government in power between 1991 and 2001 gave the CCPA at least $610,231 over a decade.[8] And $400,000 of that was doled out in the last three months of the NDP's mandate in 2001. Access to Information requests to government reveal that in some cases the CCPA gave 50 copies of each study they produced to government ministries or Crowns. That enabled the Centre to pretend it performed contract work or sold goods and services to the government. What it did was charge several hundred dollars per report for 20-page opinion pieces produced by the Centre that were available free on its website and that other organizations regularly give to governments for free; i.e., their advice in the form of studies and pre-budget submissions. It was a covert and dishonest way for the then-NDP government to subsidize a lobby group that would routinely call for higher taxes and more spending—a lobby group that was then a convenient and well-funded ally.

And by granting $400,000 in the last three months of office in 2001, when it knew it faced certain defeat at the polls, New Democrats bought—at taxpayer expense—an ideologically similar lobby group that could be guaranteed to be critical of the expected (and eventual) new B.C. Liberal government. One "contract" given to the group by the NDP government was for studies to be conducted through to 2005, which, not coincidentally, was the time frame up to the next election. It was political advocacy bought and paid for by taxpayers who were unaware that their tax dollars were used to fund views and positions with which they might disagree.

Even after the B.C. NDP left office in 2001, governments elsewhere funded the CCPA: charity records show $600,208 in funding for 2002. Late that year, the organization received another pleasant announcement: the provincial NDP government announced the federal government would give the group a grant of $900,000,[9] presumably so the think-tank could write glowing reports on what a swell job the Manitoba NDP and federal government were doing on public policy (or just to prop up the CCPA's revenues). Unsurprisingly, in 2005, the think-tank/advocacy group demanded higher wages for government workers, no tax relief for business and no tax cuts for the average worker; instead, the government-funded lobby recommended "alternative" tax cuts in the form of higher government spending, a rather Orwellian redefinition of "tax relief" and a transparent manipulation of language.

Ottawa and SWC

In a federal example of how state funding is used generously to promote one view of contentious issues, it is hard to find a better example than Status of Women Canada (SWC). Status of Women Canada, an agency within the federal department of Canadian Heritage, receives more than $23 million every year[10] and more than $10.8 million of that is given out in the form of grants and contributions.[b]

Included in the recent department grants list is the Canadian Feminist Alliance Action for $194,988; the National Association of Women and the Law ($262,250); Feminists for Just and Equitable Public Policy ($110,712); the "52% Coalition," which noted that it wanted to make "women's issues" a priority in the British Columbia election ($18,000); and the Ad Hoc Group Raising Awareness of Lesbian Lives ($20,000).

Those are but a few examples and, as with environmental lobbies and Environment Canada, Canadian Heritage and its Status of Women agency nurtures a symbiotic relationship with women's groups; of course, the ones that share the department's bias receive the vast majority of funds. For example, the conservative group REAL Women received just $89,346 over its two-decade history, while in the 1980s the National Action Committee on the Status of Women received more than $3.7 million.[11] Moreover, REAL Women lost all government funding as of 1999. And while the National Action Committee on the Status of Women had its funding reduced slightly, most feminist groups have not, as a review of the almost $11 million in annual grants from Canadian Heritage makes clear.

Not all of SWC's grant funding goes to lobby groups; money also flows to a few agencies that run women's shelters, grants with which any sensible Canadian could agree. But that funding has become the minority of disbursements in a much larger sea of activist funding for groups that promote one view of abortion, gender and racial quotas, and other issues on which Canadians are genuinely and sincerely divided.

When such groups claim to speak for women, it is safe to assume that they speak for women who think as *they* do on their favourite issues. On the tendency of radical feminists to be anti-free-trade and anti-free-market, it is unlikely that such groups speak for

b. Readers should not confuse the National Action Committee on the Status of Women—an advocacy group—with the Status of Women Canada, a branch of the department of Canadian Heritage. It is worth noting, though, little difference can be detected between the lobby group and the agency itself in terms of positions.

the average businesswoman, *National Post* columnist Diane Francis, *Globe and Mail* columnist Margaret Wente, or *Toronto Sun* money editor Linda Leatherdale, none of whom are shrinking capitalist violets. On social issues, government-funded advocacy groups are also not likely to speak for REAL Women founder Gwen Landolt, or a Catholic pro-life mother with seven children, or a stay-at-home, culturally conservative Baptist mom opposed to state-funded day-care who wants a better tax exemption for *her* choices.

Some groups on the conservative side of the ledger refuse to apply or take government money; others, such as REAL Women, were opposed on principle to government funding for their organization, but have applied and received some funds on the justification that the government refused to stop funding their opponents. Regardless, most people could find something they agree with in almost every advocacy group, so Canadian Heritage ought to do taxpayers and honest public debate a favour—and cut them *all* off.

The Court Challenges Program

The politicization of government funding has extended far beyond the grants given by one corner of Canadian Heritage. There is the example of the Court Challenges Program (CCP), originally set up in 1977 by Pierre Trudeau's government in response to the election of the Parti Québécois (PQ). It was set up to provide funding for English speakers in Quebec and francophones outside of that province to challenge laws they thought discriminated against them despite Canada's official two-language policy. Quebec's Bill 101, which limits English on signs in that province, was the most obvious example. Rather than challenge the PQ government directly, the Trudeau government opted to wait for citizens to challenge laws (with help from the CCP) and then intervene; it was thought this would be a smarter political strategy vis-à-vis the Quebec government.[c]

c. More extensive details of the Court Challenges Program can be found in *Friends of the Court: The Privileging of Interest Group Litigants in Canada* by Ian Brodie and *The Charter Revolution and the Court Party* by F.L. Morton and Rainier Knopf.

Over the years, those wanting to advance their agenda in the courts on issues that might receive a cold shoulder in democratically elected legislatures have often used the Court Challenges Program. Using arguments from Section 15 (the equality clause) of the Constitution, and money from the Court Challenges Program, many groups bring cases to court or seek intervener status in cases they believe will advance their agenda. The budget of the Court Challenges Program has also expanded dramatically, from several hundred thousand dollars per year in the mid-1980s to $4.4 million at present.[12]

Thus, arguments over what constitutes discrimination against gays and lesbians are conducted in court and funded largely through the taxpayer-funded Court Challenges Program. The feminist organization Women's Legal Education and Action Fund (LEAF) and Equality for Gays and Lesbians Everywhere (EGALE) have been in the forefront of such legal and constitutional challenges and many of their court fights have been funded in part by the Court Challenges Program. Calgary political science professors Ted Morton and Rainier Knopf explain:

The Court Challenges Program has been a funding bonanza for LEAF and other equality seeking groups on the left. In addition to funding almost every other language rights case that has made it to the Supreme Court, the CCP has directly funded the litigants in a number of leading equality rights cases, including Canadian Council of Churches *(challenging limits on third-party interventions),* Schachter *(authorizing judges to impose affirmative remedies), and* Sauve *and* Belczowski *(affirming prisoners' voting rights).... Janine Brodie, one of Canada's leading feminist scholars, has bluntly referred to the CCP as providing the "financial underpinning for LEAF."*[13]

After its founding in the mid-1980s, LEAF received a $1-million grant from the Ontario government. Professor Ian Brodie from the University of Western Ontario estimates that about half of its current annual budget is government largesse, with most of the rest from large tax-deductible foundations.

As with many activist organizations that favour government intervention by default in one manner or another and also claim to speak for the "public interest," such organizations are dependent on government for a large portion of their revenues and not the public they claim to represent. And then there is the inevitable conflict of interest when government agencies (or those created with public funds) pick partisans to determine who should receive taxpayer assistance. One of the founders of LEAF, Shelagh Day, now sits on the Court Challenges Program, the same program that has given money to LEAF in the past and presumably still does. Canadians of all views can and should challenge laws they believe to be unconstitutional. The problem is that taxpayers fund one view, often the most strident.

DOES THE TAXPAYER-FUNDED COURT CHALLENGES PROGRAM FUND CHALLENGES TO CHILD PORNOGRAPHY LAWS?

One final note about the Court Challenges Program; despite the $4.4 million in taxpayer money it disburses to sympathetic allies every year, the public is no longer allowed to know who receives the money. Morton explains why:

> On 24 October 1995, the Liberals made good on the [election] promise, announcing the formation of a new CCP as an independent, limited corporation with an annual federal grant of $2.75 million. This independent corporate status means that Ottawa cannot shut down the CPP in the future.... The reorganization of the CCP was guided by the premise that "The program must belong to those groups likely to use it."[14]

As a result of its new independent status, taxpayers fund it but they will never know where their money goes. The CCP will not publish the names of organizations or challenges that it funds, nor is such information available through Access to Information requests. In 2001, Beyond Borders, a Winnipeg group that fights child prostitution and pornography, was denied funding by the Court Challenges Program to intervene in the child pornography case involving Vancouver's John Sharpe and his challenge to Canada's child pornography laws. The CCP refused to disclose whether it funded Sharpe's constitutional challenge.[15]

THIS LOBBY GROUP BROUGHT TO YOU COURTESY OF OTTAWA

Many groups active politically and in the courts would likely disappear or be severely restricted in the activities they pursue were it not for their tax-deductible charitable numbers or their government funding. Canadians have wide and divergent views on a number of issues, especially those most controversial.

But it would not matter if Canadians were 100 per cent in favour or opposed on any particular issue. A healthy democracy needs dissent and must preserve room for the same. When governments fund one side of an issue in advocacy work or in the courts, they in effect stifle dissent by virtue of the "megaphone effect." Groups with a funding pipeline from government hire a plethora of lobbyists, researchers and spokespeople to influence the public debate in a manner they could not if they were actually dependent on a membership base reflective of the public at large.

WHY TAXPAYER FUNDING IS WRONG AND UNDEMOCRATIC

First, subsidies to special-interest lobbies take scarce tax dollars

Every time governments write a cheque, they make a choice on behalf of those who pay the bill. Whether the citizen is an English-language teacher helping immigrant children or a blue-collar worker on the assembly line in southern Ontario, most taxes are paid by middle-income Canadians because that's where most Canadians are: in the middle-income tax brackets. Yes, the poor and rich pay taxes as well, but the poor are largely (and properly) exempt from most taxes and the rich are few in Canada, so the tax burden falls on the middle-income earners.

Thus, when governments cut a cheque they do so largely at the expense of middle Canada. When governments give money to a lobby group, the pool of cash available for more worthy causes shrinks. And whether the tax rate is low, high or whether a country is rich or poor, there will always and should always be a limit to the amount of money a government can spend. In addition, the impact of special-interest group funding on taxpayers is not limited only to the grants and contributions such organizations receive. Taxpayers are also affected by what those groups advocate for: in many cases, special interests put pressure on government for ever-higher per capita spending and its corollary: higher taxes.

Second, subsidies for political or legal advocacy distort the democratic process

One core assumption of the Canadian Constitution and of our democratic tradition is the limitation of the power of the state to compel citizens to act in ways they do not wish to. We assume people are free to do whatever they wish unless actions are expressly and explicitly forbidden in law.

This assumption also implies that there are limits to the possibility of collective action by Parliament. For example, assume some people desire to restrict others' freedom of speech or the right to vote; Parliament cannot simply and collectively remove such rights. There is the historical assumption, tradition, and—since 1982—the Constitution, which limit the collective action of parliamentarians, or anyone else, to remove anyone's rights or force one to do that which he or she does not wish to do. (There are exceptions to this; few rights are absolute. But the exception is not the rule.)

Within the context of taxpayer funding for special-interest groups, governments ought not only to respect the rights of individuals, but when it comes to collective action (which is what legislatures and parliaments are about), governments ought to, at the very least, listen first. None of this prevents politicians or parties from expressing views or even leading public opinion, but citizens deserve a government and civil service that, as an institution, is neutral. Without that, elected representatives interested in what a section of the public actually thinks cannot know if the views that a lobby group trumpets are legitimately held by a wide swath of Canadians, or are simply a parroting back of what some politicians and mandarins wish to hear—and fund.

Third, government subsidies compel people to support groups and political positions they might disagree with

Funds given by politicians to lobby groups do not originate magically within the public treasury; they are compelled by government and delivered to government coffers by taxation.

Citizens might be tempted to overlook their forced donation of funds to organizations because on occasion they may agree with some of the organizations that receive such funds, but that is shortsighted.

Government unions may like to receive taxpayer cash, but are they thrilled to know that chambers of commerce also receive money? Between 1989 and 1999, the federal Crown corporation Atlantic Canada Opportunities Agency (ACOA) gave $5,032,728 to chambers of commerce, boards of trade and business associations in Atlantic Canada. Included on the list were the St. John's Board of Trade ($435,212), the Nova Scotia Chamber of Commerce ($161,546), and the Atlantic Chamber of Commerce ($1,247,473), to name but a few.[16] Environmentalists may love their time at the ministry of Environment, but do they also appreciate it when the Canadian Association of Petroleum Producers receives $427,837 of non-repayable contributions from a federal Crown corporation, Western Economic Diversification?[17]

As an institution separate from politicians and political parties, politicians and bureaucrats should not use government and taxpayer dollars as their own personal fiefdom and slush fund and give tax dollars to groups they favour. To do so is a distortion of the political process; for those who do not agree with the agendas of the groups that receive their tax dollars, it is tantamount to theft. The entire process reeks of the Sponsorship Scandal: those with connections receive the cash.

How to Dry Up Government Funding for Special Interests

It is one thing to know that governments fund all manner of advocacy groups that then are involved in the public, political and legal debates of our country. But how do ordinary citizens cut off such illegitimate funding flows? Here are a few steps to follow.

One: Refuse to donate to organizations that take government money.

Canadians have many different views on many controversial issues. Some are pro-choice or pro-life. Some favour gun control and others are against gun registration. Some Canadians may favour unlimited development; others desire a human-free Eden. Some groups do legitimate contract work for government, but even then it can be used as a way to covertly fund advocacy work. If you suspect that the latter is happening, tell groups you favour that you will write them a cheque when and if they refuse to accept any government money.

Help government-funded groups kick the subsidy habit and strike a blow for a more robust democracy at the same time.

Two: If you suspect a group has abused its charitable number by lobbying too often, or if it openly supports a political party, report it to the Canada Revenue Agency.

Over the past several years, the Canada Revenue Agency has stripped the charitable tax number from a number of organizations that have engaged in political action and lobbying above the allowed limits (defined as no more than 10 percent of its budget to be spent on political activities). Greenpeace and the Friends of Clayoquot Sound both had their charitable tax-deductible status revoked after they engaged in too much political lobbying as opposed to charitable and educational activity. Both groups can still function as non-profits, but cannot give tax receipts for donations. That is fair; groups must choose whether they want to have the luxury of a tax-deductible number, and stick to education, research and charitable work—or whether they want to lobby.

Contact the Charities Directorate at CRA at:
www.cra-arc.gc.ca/agency/directions/charities-e.html

Three: Contact the media and your Member of Parliament or member of your provincial legislature.
Tell them you want your tax dollars to go to programs and services, not to political lobbyists. Tell them you want fair debates in the public square.

Chapter 7

Pummelling the Poor: Why subsidies
hurt the vulnerable at home and abroad

The current global agricultural subsidy regime in developed countries involves a massive annual taxpayer transfer of well over $300 billion. This is six times the amount of all the aid sent to developing countries. It is neither economically sensible nor morally defensible, particularly when typically 80% of those transfers go to 20% of the richest producers and only a small fraction of the subsidy trickles down to the farmer on the land.[1]

~Mark Vaile, Australia's minister for trade, April 2003

If major exporters made a credible commitment to throttle supplies until prices increased ... the commitment to decisive action might be enough to get prices rising.[2]

~ Canada's National Farmers Union in their 2005 proposal to the federal government

Barriers and Subsidies: How to Keep the Poor Down

Regular viewers of the Cable News Network (CNN) will recall the regular complaints of anchor Lou Dobbs about outsourcing American jobs. For a period, he listed the names of U.S. companies that hired people overseas. This, it is assumed, was done to shame corporations into stopping such horrible practices. It would be useful to imagine what would have happened if Great Britain had taken the same position in the early 1700s as regards North America. Using the logic of Dobbs and other protectionists, the colonial mother would have put fur traders, farmers and others out of work on the grounds that such jobs interfered with workers in Mother England, and insofar as fur traders went, their working conditions were not even at the level of the factories in the British Isles. Such trappers and traders endured blistering cold, wild animals and infrequent lunch breaks, especially if wild game was tough to find on a particular day.

There was some irony in the Dobbs position; he once hosted CNN's *Moneyline*, a show that featured interviews with talking heads from the financial sector. When high-tech stocks crashed in

2000, the last thing viewers wanted was a nightly reminder of how much money they'd lost. CNN's bean counters could read ratings books and Dobbs' format changed shortly thereafter.

But the old Lou was preferable to the new demagogic and provincial one, i.e., the rant against foreign countries for attracting "American" jobs—as if any country held a patent on specific jobs or industries. The Dobbs thesis, only slightly exaggerated, is that outsourcing is an evil that will see us all begging in the manner many now do on the streets of Calcutta. But that apocalyptic vision of trade and outsourcing ignores the very example of India before the 1990s. Pre-reform, India practised for decades what the provincially minded around the world today advocate: protectionism (or "fair trade" in the lingo of today's protectionists). India subsidized its own industries and kept the borders firmly shut to foreign competition. The result was stagnation, monopoly control by domestic corporations, lousy job opportunities for most Indians, anemic wage growth and continued widespread poverty. It has only been in the last 15 years that "opportunity" and "India" are no longer oxymoronic.[3]

The renewed calls for protection also ignore the reality of how trade allows other countries to advance and join the developed world. As *New York Times* columnist Nicholas Kristof wrote in 2004, he'd like to see the protectionist-minded folk discuss their restrictive trade policy with people like Nhep Chanda, "a 17-year-old girl who is one of hundreds of Cambodians who toil all day, every day, picking through the dump for plastic bags, metal cans and bits of food. The stench clogs the nostrils, and parts of the dump are burning, producing acrid smoke that blinds the eyes."[4]

The scavengers are chased by swarms of flies and biting insects, their hands are caked with filth, and those who are barefoot cut their feet on glass. Some are small children

Nhep Chanda averages 75 cents a day for her efforts. For her, the idea of being exploited in a garment factory—working only six days a week, inside instead of in the broiling sun, for up to $2 a day—is a dream.[5]

Kristof didn't excuse labour or environmental abuses—no one should—but those issues are not soluble by a retro 1930s economic policy. Protectionism is not a policy friend of workers; it limits them to employment with only domestic companies, the same corporations that often have political connections and thus can skip regulations on the environment and labour, especially in corrupt countries.

In Canada, the C.D. Howe Institute's Danielle Goldfarb once noted that a Canadian who dines out instead of at home is engaged in that dreaded form of exploitive commerce: outsourcing. Someone else cuts up, roasts and serves the meal—for a fee. The policy wonk noted that all trade is essentially outsourced production. If General Motors doesn't manufacture certain parts in its own factories (which it often does not) and contracts with someone else, that's outsourcing.

That shouldn't be scary, but it becomes so the moment the artificial barrier known as a border is in play. Then, the Maude Barlows and Naomi Kleins of the planet decry trade in a manner they don't when workers in Mississauga provide a furniture piece to a factory in Burlington. Union leaders chirp in, as when government-subsidized B.C. Ferries attempted to buy ships offshore (which it finally did). But trade critics give little thought to the long-term implications when they force any company to "buy locally," i.e., the negative rebound Canada would suffer if such protectionist sentiment caught on in other countries and our trade-dependent economy and jobs suffered as a result.

Predictably, the same unions and leaders rightly decry protectionism when practised against Canada, for example, by U.S. politicians on softwood lumber. In a 2005 *National Post* column, Canadian Labour Congress president Ken Georgetti tried to have his free trade-provided labour cake and yet oppose it too: Georgetti (properly) slammed the Americans for ignoring the NAFTA tribunal rulings on softwood lumber, but then he called for an "alternative"[6] to NAFTA. Conveniently, his version would allow Canadian politicians to do the very thing he decried in Americans: arbitrarily decide when free trade was politically useful, and when not.

Given the short horizon of politicians interested in being re-elected, and pressure from organizations such as the CLC, it wouldn't take long before even greater taxpayer subsidies and protectionist measures would be granted to industries where Georgetti's members just happened to be present. It was—as with too many Canadian labour boss ideas—shortsighted.

Admittedly, it does not help when Canada's largest trading partner is itself contradictory. There is growing protectionist sentiment south of the border; the first half of the new decade has not been friendly to freedom of movement for goods and services. U.S. Senator Joseph Lieberman identified the growing protectionist sentiment when he noted 33 state and 13 federal proposals to try to prevent companies from hiring overseas. U.S. President George Bush weakened the rhetorical case in 2001 when he slapped tariffs on steel imports to satisfy domestic pressure. The Democratic Party flip-flopped and mostly opposed a free trade agreement with the Americas; it was an unfortunate reversal of former U.S. President Bill Clinton's principled and deliverable commitment to free trade in the 1990s. And, most notably, there is the refusal by the U.S. Department of Commerce to repay $5 billion in illegal tariffs on Canadian lumber exports after Canada won successive victories under NAFTA tribunals.

American and Canadian politicians, union leaders, self-interested parties and bureaucrats play a dangerous game of Russian roulette with prosperity when they load up the revolver with protectionist bullets and begin to fire; the victims are the poorest at home and abroad.

Agricultural Subsidies: Why Canadians Pay Too Much for Milk

One obvious example of such victim-creating behaviour is in the agricultural sector. The cliché that if you give a man a fish he can eat for a day, but if you teach a man to fish he can eat for a lifetime is apt. When developed countries make food from poorer nations less attractive to our consumers (by subsidizing our own farmers and producers, or through trade barriers), those same countries are condemned to rely more on aid and less on trade—which costs them *and us* more. That's unwise and unfair for all concerned, whether it is first-world consumers who pay more for their food or a farmer in Ghana who wants to sell fruit to Paris grocery stores. It's also led to the weird anomaly where cows in the European Union receive $2 apiece in subsidies while many Africans survive on $1 per day.[7]

In Canada, chronic government subsidies and "marketing" boards—better described as "monopoly" boards—punish Canada's poorest with higher prices while taxpayers endure misallocated dollars that could be better spent elsewhere. Canadians shell out more than $9.7 billion annually in producer and consumer support to the agricultural industry. That includes billions paid out in higher prices because of government-created agencies, which restrict supply and competition (milk marketing boards, for example).[a]

That, combined with limited access for competitors from the United States, forces Canadian consumers to pay more for milk, cheese and eggs. And while Canada's wealthiest will never care if four litres of milk costs $3 or $2, or a carton of eggs sets them back $2.50 instead of $1.79, a single mom with three kids or a retired couple on a pension do care that prices are artificially kept high. Canada no longer applies tariffs to foreign-made stereos or beer; consumers can buy those non-essentials at market prices. But not a dozen eggs.

Internationally, aid agencies realize that agricultural subsidies are public enemies one, two and three for the world's poor. It's why U.K.-based Oxfam released a report in 2004 that focused on how trade barriers and subsidies hurt developing countries. Oxfam reported that while trade barriers yet exist between developed countries, rich countries pick on the poor countries in an even worse fashion. Developing countries that try to export to rich

---

a. In newspaper ads, a coalition of groups that represents interests in the managed food sector—dairy, poultry and egg farmers—claimed that Canada does not block imports because Canada allows imports that make up 4 per cent of the market for dairy products consumed in Canada, compared to 2.75 per cent allowed into the U.S. market. That hardly qualifies as an open market on either side of the border.

nations face trade barriers *four times* those that exist between wealthy countries. "Goods produced by the poorest people face the highest import barriers of all,"[8] noted Oxfam in 2003.

Shirts produced by Bangladeshi women enter the US market at a tax rate some 20 times higher than that imposed on goods imported from Britain. Vietnam—a country with 23 million people in poverty—pays more in US customs duties than the Netherlands, despite accounting for a far smaller share of imports.

To add insult to financial injury, rich countries impose higher taxes on processed goods than on raw materials. This hampers efforts by developing countries to add value locally and diversify out of poverty. Eliminating import restrictions on textiles and garments alone could generate as many as 27 million jobs in developing countries, many of them for women workers.[9]

Unfortunately, because of the off-again, on-again call for fewer subsidies, the inconsistency doesn't help. "This nation has got to eat," George Bush said in 2002 as he supported a multi-year U.S. $170-billion farm subsidy bill pending before Congress. Oddly, Bush then argued that "our farmers and ranchers are the most efficient producers in the world ... we're really good at it."[10] That raised this question: if American farmers were so "good at it," i.e., so efficient, why did they need $170 billion in subsidies?

In Canada, the same hypocrisy plays out, though the politicians are not so crass. In May 2004, Canada's finance minister properly criticized Americans and Europeans for their lavish agricultural subsidies. Ralph Goodale identified the effect developed-world subsidized pork (in every sense of that word) has on the Third World: "Those subsidies are devastating in terms of agricultural development and survival in Africa."[11] He was correct, though he spoke the words in London, England, where he consulted with British and South Africans on those issues—not back home in Saskatchewan where such comments might have helped advance the argument but would find him impaled at the end of a pitchfork.

Yet such rhetoric hasn't stopped the flow of subsidies or the vested interests that want to extend such devastations yet further. In late 2005, the lobby group representing Canada's dairy, poultry and egg farmers blitzed Canadian newspapers with advertisements during World Trade Organization talks in Hong Kong. Farmsandfood.ca used all the right images and arguments in their ads: idyllic pastoral shots of a family and the note that Canadians like farmers, that it's desirable to produce enough food to satisfy Canada's needs. The group also used the usual euphemisms: "supply management," "import controls pillar," "production discipline pillar" and "producing pricing pillar," and claimed that taxpayers don't pay a cent for the activities of marketing boards.

But perfect family-type advertorials and Orwellian approaches to language cannot disguise the fact that while taxpayers don't have to pay through their taxes for marketing board decisions (though they do pay for the operations of the boards), Canadians as consumers pay at the grocery store when they pull out their wallets. As for Orwell, "supply management" is better described as government-sponsored controls on supply and thus prices—precisely why some agricultural interests are so supportive of the "managed" approach: it shields them from domestic and international competition. Airlines and automotive companies would love it if the federal and provincial governments applied such controls to their industries: a domestic market captive and ready to be plucked by the captains of industry.

Another agricultural interest didn't just desire the status quo; they wanted supply and price controls extended. In its submissions, the Saskatoon-based National Farmers Union wanted the federal government to guarantee 95 per cent of the cost of production and persuade other countries (along with Canada) to take land out of production to reduce the supply of grain, other crops and meat (to force up prices). The NFU also wanted price controls on manufacturers who supply equipment to farmers, more food under government control, an end to "corporate" farming, for the federal government to again subsidize the transportation costs for grain, to end international free trade agreements and to "control supermarket and processor power."[12] Well, the *chutzpah* was refreshing.

In a revealing statement, the NFU put it this way: "If major exporters made a credible commitment to throttle supplies until prices increased, it is likely no actual land set-aside or payment would be necessary—simply the commitment to decisive action might be enough to get prices rising."[13] Yes, and if used car salesman or real estate agents were allowed to collude in the manner now similar to what governments mandate/permit in the agricultural sector, commissions on selling cars and homes would also skyrocket.

One way to look at the interest groups is to imagine they emerged from an interplanetary expedition or from a time capsule after too many Tommy Douglas love-fests in the mid-20th century. The accurate description for their proposals, especially those of the Farmers Union, is that they're similar to Stalin's prescription for the Ukraine in the 1930s: an end to price signals, which would lead to inadequate infrastructure, then plunged production, and then vastly higher prices for the poor-quality food that remains.

The NFU is clear about one thing, however: competition and choice keep prices in check. That the family farm has declined and many have a tough go of it is not pleasant, but that's also been the story of every enterprise since the beginning of the industrial revolution. The free movement of goods leads to more productivity with fewer people in many sectors, farming included.[b] But the benefit of that two-century move to more efficiency has been a continual drop in real prices for food and better nutrition and living

---

b. The NFU also missed another obvious economic truth and benefit of such rationalization: when some goods and services become cheaper, money is available elsewhere to create employment and incomes in other sectors; a policy that artificially redirects money to one sector harms that dynamic wealth- and job-creating process. Sometimes, reforms within a sector can also spur it on to new growth in more niche markets. In my hometown, Kelowna, B.C., predictions about the end of the wine industry were apocalyptic when tariff barriers on foreign wine were lifted as part of the 1988 Free Trade Agreement. After initial restructuring, the Okanagan wine industry re-planted with better varieties and re-focused. The result today is a thriving, award-winning wine industry unthinkable two decades ago when it produced mostly plonk.

standards.[c] True, farms have increased in size and some are run by "corporations"—be they an innovative, risk-taking farmer who expands, or a Californian entity listed on a stock exchange. That's not pastoral or romantic. But it is better for everyone's standard of living, food supply and health, especially for the world's poor. The industrial revolution cannot be reversed nor should anyone wish that it could.

SUBSIDY QUEENS

Canada's billions in subsidies, while not as great a portion of our economy or as large on a per-person basis as many other countries, are still costly. As a percentage of GDP, our farm support amounts to 0.7 per cent while the U.S. registers in at 0.9 per cent. The European Union, which has a nasty habit of being manipulated by agricultural interests (especially French farmers) while its leaders talk about the tragedy of world poverty, spends 1.2 per cent of the economy subsidizing the countryside.[14] It does so at the expense of poorer farmers in Africa who try to get their products to London, Paris, Brussels and Rome. Canada and the U.S. do the same at the expense of farmers in Mexico and Central America.

THE $1,218 FOOD TAX

If those statistical measurements seem insignificant, consider the dollar figures. The European Union agricultural subsidies amount to $198 billion annually; Canada's subsidies are over $9.7 billion, while the U.S. throws $131 billion at everything from cotton farmers to corn growers. OECD countries alone spend $455 CDN billion (US$378 billion)[15] on the agricultural industry every year—and that dwarfs other objectionable corporate welfare including that in the automotive and aerospace sectors. On an annual per-person basis, every Canadian pays over $304.50 more for groceries than they would without such tariffs and subsidies in place, or $1,218 for a family of four.

c. For more details, see: Stephen Moore and Julian L. Simon, *It's Getting Better All the Time* and Julian Simon, *The State of Humanity*, CATO, 2000.

There has been progress. Trade barriers and subsidies have been lowered. Producer support dropped from 37 per cent of farm receipts in 1986-88 to 30 per cent in 2002-04, though the OECD notes that level was reached in 1995-97 and has been stuck there ever since.[16]

End a Subsidy, Save a Child in Africa

A recent World Bank report on global poverty noted that the number of people living in extreme poverty, defined as living on less than one dollar a day, dropped by 400 million people over the past two decades, though 1.1 billion still live on one dollar a day.

And the decline has been uneven. In contrast to Asia, where there has been a substantial drop in poverty rates over the past 20 years, 314 million people in sub-Saharan Africa still survive on the dollar-a-day income, almost double the number 20 years ago. To ameliorate this, the World Bank suggests increased spending on education, health and nutrition in poorer countries. That's sensible, but such countries must still rely on the generosity of foreign governments and private donors; it still leaves poor countries in the position of eating for a day, but not being able to fish for a lifetime.

The Bank's other suggestion, continued trade liberalization, is also critical. (Toss in the rule of law, property rights and anti-corruption measures in combination with reduced trade barriers and the lessening of farm subsidies, and one can hope that a World Bank report in 20 years shows a reduction in African poverty in the manner recently reported in east Asia.)

There is nothing compassionate about a policy of sheltered domestic industries. It is unethical to kneecap developing countries such as Kenya where the per capita economy is only 1/25th that of the United States.

There is also the interest of domestic taxpayers to consider. When U.K.-based Oxfam details subsidies, it notes where some of its own countries' domestic cash ends: in the bank accounts of prominent members of the British aristocracy: the dukes of Westminster (£448,000), Marlborough (£511,000) and Bedford (£366,000), the Earl of Plymouth (£459,000), and the Marquess of Cholmondely (£306,000).[17]

The National Farmers Union claims that Canada's farms would not survive open markets. Not true. New Zealand cut most farm subsidies in the mid-1980s, and as that country's Federated Farmers claims, its experience "thoroughly debunked the myth that the farming sector cannot prosper without government subsidies."[18]

It's one thing to temporarily subsidize Canadian ranchers because of an unfair border closure or to provide transition money to a farmer or grower because the federal government has suddenly changed trade rules; a stop-gap measure is akin to unemployment insurance: it's temporary help and not expected to be permanent. But it's another for Canada to artificially inflate dairy prices at the expense of all or for the French to subsidize cows to the detriment of African producers. Canadian, American and European politicians should hasten an end to such cash-flows: it would benefit home-country consumers, free taxpayers and help the world's poorest farmers and citizens.

Agricultural subsidies as a % of GDP (OECD 2004 figures)

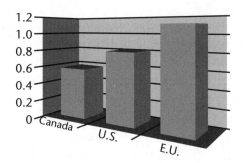

Source: OECD, includes producer and consumer supports

Myths about "Foreign Control"

If any country should favour wide-open borders, competition, and international trade, it should be Canada. We are heavily dependent on trade, especially with the United States, where 87 per cent of our exports end up.[19] It's in Canada's interest to have rules-based agreements with other countries to keep doors open for our goods and services.

Contrary to popular myth, "foreigners" don't control most of our companies, we do. Foreign-controlled corporations in Canada held $1 trillion worth of assets in Canada in 2003, the latest year for which statistics are available. That represents just 22.3 per cent of total corporate assets and it was a decline from 22.7 per cent in the previous year.[20]

Similarly, Canadians "control" more in other economies than non-Canadians control in ours. We have $445.1 billion invested abroad while foreigners have only $365.7 billion invested in our country.[21] (Some might see that as a $79.4 billion advantage in our favour, but it can be argued otherwise: if foreigners invested more in Canada that would be a sign we're an attractive place to risk money, build plants and create jobs.)

In addition, Statistics Canada noted that foreign-owned companies were more likely to have head offices in Canada than Canadian-owned companies. In the 1990s, there were five domestic firms with head offices in Canada for every 1,000 without; for foreign firms, the ratio was 116 for every 1,000 without. And foreign-controlled firms also employed more people in head offices, 25 per cent more on average than Canadian-controlled firms.[22]

Perhaps Canadians should wish for *more* foreign-owned firms and factories. In a review of the 1980s and 1990s, the statistics agency notes that foreign-controlled plants accounted for roughly two-thirds of labour productivity growth in Canadian manufacturing. Statistics Canada noted that foreign-controlled plants are more productive than domestic-controlled factories "because foreign-controlled plants and firms are also more innovative, more technologically advanced, and more likely to perform research and development."[23]

And contrary to the belief that foreign-owned firms would flee south to the U.S. after the 1988 Free Trade Agreement and then to Mexico after the 1993 North American Free Trade Agreement, foreign investment and ownership increased actually.

Concerns too had been expressed in some quarters that the contribution of foreign firms to the Canadian economy would decline during the 1990s if firms moved production to the larger U.S. market, as well as to the lower-cost Mexican market, in the wake of the two free trade agreements. Yet, between 1987 and 1999, the share of foreign-controlled plants in total output in the manufacturing sector increased from 40.5% to 52.2%.[24]

The snubbing of a NAFTA final arbitration panel by the Americans on the softwood lumber issue was and is a critical mistake, but Canadians, most of whom are now robust free-trade supporters, shouldn't listen to the siren song protectionists who want a return of 1930s-style protectionism and higher taxpayer subsidies. Without trade-friendly policies around the world, Canadians—be they in farming, manufacturing, sales, high-tech or ranching—have the most to lose.

Who "controls" Canada?

Issue	Foreigners	Canadians
Corporate assets	22.3%	77.7%
Investment	$365.7 billion in Canada	$445.1 billion in other countries

Source: Statistics Canada

Chapter 8

Myth: Higher taxes are compassionate
Fact: More redistribution won't pay the bills

They imagine that our flourishing state in England is owing to that bank-paper and not the bank-paper to the flourishing condition of our commerce.
  ~ Edmund Burke, *Reflections on the Revolution in France*[1]

I have two choices; I can distribute poverty, or I can distribute wealth.
  ~ Deng Xiaoping[2]

Values and Morality: Compassion and Caring

Since at least the French Revolution and up to the present day in Venezuela and neo-Castroite Hugo Chavez, advocates of state intervention for its own sake often believe—or say they believe— their cause is noble and just. During the past century, the belief that just a little (or a lot) more redistribution was necessary was a constant theme for Canadian and international adherents of state intervention. In politics, what matters to some, apparently, is the language and talk of prosperity, liberation and justice, no matter how little of it is ever produced under regimes that set out to "equalize" wealth; they rarely stop to ask if wringing the chicken's neck might prevent future golden eggs.

But one need not look at extreme arguments for state interventionism from the 20th century to wonder why lovers of state become giddy when the prospect of more taxes and higher spending arises. In Canada, the tax-and-spend crowd continually assumes that large government is equal to compassion and that its corollary, high taxes, is conducive to and responsible for a sense of community. Examine the rhetoric from those who think state power is somehow inherently friendly to those most vulnerable, and the assumption is that values such as compassion are somehow state-derived.

Thus, columnist Charles Gordon asserted in 1999 that "Canada's tax hell" is a "myth" and argues that "while government spending does contribute to high taxation, it also pays for a way of life that most Canadians value."[3] He implicitly made the link between a large government and the values that many Canadians believe to be distinctly Canadian, or at least, are primarily the do-main of heavily taxed countries.[a]

Bill Phipps, former moderator of the United Church of Canada, also assumed this link when he famously said, "as you fill out your tax return, you should be joyful," referencing the various activities government performs with tax dollars.[4]

Hugh Segal, who is smart enough to know better, also mis-cast the debate over taxes and civilization as one of greed *versus* good government instead of what it was and *is*—a deliberation over the proper means to desirable ends. The-then Progressive Conservative backroom adviser ignored the context of a late 20th-century Canadian state and seemed to assume every government decision in the last 100 years was beneficial or benign.[5] He also equated the existence of current government involvement as a sacrosanct relic, not to be questioned—or at least not by anyone with an existing reputation skeptical of government. Thus, in his 1997 book on neo-conservatism, Segal set up the familiar straw men to knock down, but never actually answered specific policy critiques of when and how government involvement went too far in the last century. Nor did he consider that he might revise his thinking about the proper role for Canadian government *in toto* in the context of a peacetime state that was four times larger, relative to GDP, than it had been one century ago. Segal simply ignored the evidence that *some* taxes, *some* tax levels and *some* govern-ment intervention destroys wealth[b]—and thus, critically, jobs and

a. The notion that highly taxed states have better social indicators on lifespan, health care and environmental indicators is false. There is a difference between developing economies and *moderately* taxed states on such measurements, but there is no difference between moderately and highly taxed states. Some coun-tries with less government involvement as a percentage of their economy have better indicators than Canada. For more on this comparison, see Chapter 14, "Thank the USA."

b. For example, the failed and wasteful nationalization experiments by Canadian and other governments were never touched on by Segal. Governments that owned airlines and oil companies wasted large amounts of revenues that might have been better used elsewhere or not taken from citizens at all. Moreover, such failed policy was properly a major target of reform for conservatives and libertarians who had specific policy remedies. Instead of dealing with real issues, Segal offered one general remark about privatization in his 1997 book and was skeptical at that.

livelihoods for those on the margins of society—and thus undermines the very compassionate society the Gordons, Phippses and Segals of the world—and the rest of us—desire to have.[c]

The core orientation in all three men's arguments is one of faith: government must be inherently good and critiques only serve to disturb the choir. The core assumption in that religiosity is that any call for a re-examination of this or that tax, or tax level, or this or that program, must *ipso facto* be opposite of compassion in both motivation and in result if implemented.

As with any statement there is the question of balance. But intensely believed or not, it is a chronic fault to think that any ill can be solved if enough tax dollars and smart people are mixed together in one room. In that category fall modern intellectuals, those who spent too much time in politics and thus naturally assume government largesse as a remedy to ills and never a barrier to community, and some religious folk like Phipps who mistake the Sermon on the Mount for specific instructions on government economic policy.

Others make the predictable mistake of believing that every social problem has, at root, an economic cause. *But the proper diagnosis matters because without it the improper cure is proposed.* The cause of a social problem is not economic—it's *social*. A sensible approach to social policy starts with those nearest to those in need—family and friends—to find out what might be done closest to home. Instead, advocates of cure-all government solutions start

c. Ironically, neo-conservatives such as Irving Kristol (who popularized the "neo-conservative" term) accepted the post-1930s welfare state in general and Franklin Roosevelt's New Deal in particular. In the 1990s, some just thought that even such a "deal" could go too far. Segal attacked neo-conservatives when in fact he probably should have debated libertarians, except that in so doing he would still have had to deal with actual policy prescriptions and not straw men, which is unfortunately what he spent most of his book creating and battling. Segal criticized those who critiqued the post-war consensus without ever stopping to ask what part of that critique might be valid. Segal valued consensus for consensus's sake. Segal fancied himself a traditional conservative in the manner of Winston Churchill and Edmund Burke, but it is difficult to conceive of either Churchill or Burke ever approving of the vast size of government that arrived in the last half of the 20th century. Churchill in particular was no fan of socialism. Segal's conservatism is the conservatism of the status quo: once government does something, it apparently should rarely if ever be questioned lest someone, somewhere, be upset.

at the macro level and work backwards. That's akin to phoning the car manufacturer to ask why the car won't start without first checking that the gas tank is full.

Results, Anyone?

"People before profits," "communities before corporations" and other slogans are the buzzwords of the new redistributionists. The words are attractive and compelling; after all, who would *not* prefer their local butcher, baker or candlestick maker to large faceless corporations? And who would *not* think that people are always, intrinsically, of more value than mere lucre?

But slogans are of little help in determining government policy about the proper level of tax rates and redistribution. While some wrongly assume that only those who agree with government-as-agent-of-redistribution are compassionate, the reality is that many Canadians are no less concerned for the poor and about other social ills; they just refuse to buy into the simplistic notion that every private problem has a taxpayer-funded solution.

Instead, there are remedies that governments can and do promote to better effect. The federal government *could* hector citizens to save for their retirement or tax even more than they do to fund the Canada Pension Plan. Instead, the use of the markets combined with tax breaks—tax-deductible Registered Retirement Savings Plans—has spurred more Canadians to voluntarily save more for their own retirement. It has also made capital available for companies, which helps wealth creation and employment creation.

If the placards and slogans are useless as regards policy, they are even sillier as regards one's attitude towards business. When does a successful small business cross the line between the much-loved little guy and become the mythical and hated "corporation," the supposed fount of all evil? When Starbucks was a lone Seattle coffee outlet in the early 1970s, some of the same people who might now protest free trade and throw a brick through its window would have patronized it three decades ago and lavished praise on its "local" ambience. But let the world find pleasure in the same brew and expand to a couple of thousand locations? At what point did a successful small company cross the line? When it opened store number five, 78 or 356?

There is no easily discernible dividing line between the small business David and corporate Goliath, and any attempt to define one only reveals the economic and intellectual hollowness of what is essentially a political slogan, not an economic analysis based on objective facts. Large companies (unionized or not) pay much better salaries than does small business and also provide better benefit packages, usually because they can afford to. But the anti-business/anti-globalization crowd in Canada, represented by Naomi Klein *et al.*, is not likely to throw a rock through the minimum-wage local coffee shop or overpriced corner store; that's reserved for McDonald's and Starbucks.

The illogic of slogans aside, there is another reason why the "high taxes = compassion" crowd usurps the language of compassion to push redistribution for its own sake, and beyond those who are merely the sincerely mistaken: Canada's tax-and-spend crowd resorts to "values-talk" because they often have nothing original or useful to say on policy.

Given the kind of incentives created when redistribution is emphasized at the expense of opportunity and wealth creation, the real-world record of rampant redistribution is a failure. Whether it is Cuba, which plunged from the fourth-richest state per capita in Latin America four decades ago to the fourth-poorest today, or the contrasting examples of Singapore, Hong Kong and Taiwan over the last half-century versus China (which began to take wealth creation seriously only two decades ago), there are multiple examples where the overconcentration on redistribution failed, continually.[d]

Thus, those who resort to values-talk about the "unjust" and "unequal" distribution of income do so because their own real-world policies have failed to produce much in the way of *new* wealth. In British Columbia, after-inflation per-person income

---

d. Some argue that Cuba's economic policies are not as much at fault for its poverty as the American embargo. This is a fascinating line of defence. In essence, the defenders of Fidel Castro's Cuba argue that its poverty has been caused by a lack of trade, an argument with which Milton Friedman would agree. Rhetorical excess makes for unintended bedfellows.

dropped in the 1990s when anti-wealth creation policies were enacted by that province's government, a regime that focused overmuch on redistribution. In 1992, British Columbians earned $500 more on average than other Canadians; after just seven years of anti-wealth creation policies, inhabitants of that province earned $700 *less* on average than other Canadians. That occurred in a decade when the rest of the country and much of the world experienced some of their best economic years since the 1920s.[6]

ENVY IN VIRTUOUS DRAG

When governments make such mistakes there can often be more "equality," if by that one means less distance from the top income earners to those at the bottom. That kind of equality, though, is usually based on greater poverty for most. It is curious that proponents prefer a poorer society where there is less difference between high- and low-income earners to one where everyone is better off but the difference between incomes is greater. Such a motivation is envy dressed up in the drag of virtue.

The worst off under extreme schemes of anti-wealth creation are the most vulnerable in society. Such policies result in lower investment, fewer jobs and thus less competition for workers, which in turn puts downward pressure on wages, among other negative effects. Whenever economic growth is downgraded by a ruling elite, it is the people on the margins—society's poorest—who pay the price. It is they who will be the first to lose their jobs, not CEOs of corporations or armchair critics of free markets. The much-quoted quip that a rising (economic) tide lifts all boats is as true as ever; its opposite truth is that a receding ocean certainly does leave people more "equal," but stranded on the shore and without much hope for upward movement, an equality of poverty.[e] Merely

e. A good example of the success of redistributionist rhetoric at the expense of the poor is in the constant anti-"big-box" tirades, most recently against Wal-Mart in Vancouver in 2005. Those big-box stores are admittedly ugly, but they are most helpful for competition and thus for the poorest Canadians. The wealthy will never care about the cost of bread, butter and sugar, but the poor do. That's why cutthroat competition between grocery stores is so very positive for lower-income Canadians who spend most of their income on the necessities of life. Those who oppose such open competition argue against the real benefits that it brings, especially to those with marginal incomes.

dividing existing wealth cannot create more of it—an absolute necessity in a world with a growing population. Such schemes are anything but virtuous.

Community Is Voluntary and Spontaneous, Not Coerced

The idea that only government fosters cooperation or community, or in fact is the primary motivation of such, is nonsense. The entire insurance industry is predicated on the desire of people to minimize the risk to their wellbeing, and that, without much government involvement other than the proper regulatory safeguards. People cooperatively pool their resources to guard against the after-effects of tragedy (bankruptcy and loss of income) and they do so voluntarily.

In addition, the claim that community and a healthy civic life are the result of government ignores the historical and present-day record. Charitable societies and activities, churches and synagogues, amateur sports teams, bird watchers and bowlers and countless other voluntary associations, are all the result of voluntary choices made by people who join together without coercion for a spiritual, charitable, social or other purpose. Volunteerism is part of civic duty and responsibility. If anything, governments run the risk of damaging such "little platoons" of civilized life (as Edmund Burke called such voluntary efforts) when governments take over activities formerly carried out by volunteers and charitable organizations.

Those who assume that government should be a critical "partner" with such little platoons (beyond necessary state roles such as preserving the rule of law and others) mistakenly assume that much in life is political, and has or should have a political link. That is both erroneous and narrow; many people live their lives with their families and friends far removed from politics. That, far from being unhealthy as some suggest, is the most positive thing one can say about a society; that people are free to live without concern that a government will politicize every area of their lives.

Life and Money

The last argument often drawn from the rhetorical chest of redistribution is that money cannot solve every problem. Very true, but then no one, not Milton Friedman, Michael Walker or Stephen Harper has ever claimed otherwise.

Free markets allow people to use their creativity and ingenuity to solve problems, while preserving diverse choices—nothing less and nothing more. Those who read into that process a claim that it will "solve" a particular problem, never mind all societal ills, miss the central point: markets allow more choice than would be experienced in restricted economies and in that choice-based environment, ingenuity and creativity flourish more readily and may solve *some* problems. Markets expand choices in goods, services, jobs and thus ultimately in lifestyles. What people *do* with such choices is up to them.

Dollars cannot solve all ills but those most likely to fling that charge are the ones most often guilty of such an assumption. Those who argue money cannot solve every problem, only to use the levers of the state to extract as much wealth as possible from citizens, are engaged in a dance with their own rhetoric. Thus, in a vain and ironic effort, the redistributionist attempts to demonstrate that money *can* solve every problem—so long as *government* spends it. But they were right the first time: wealth should never be the sum total of life; nor should it be assumed to be the answer for every need just because it is government that has the largest bank account.

Who pays federal tax

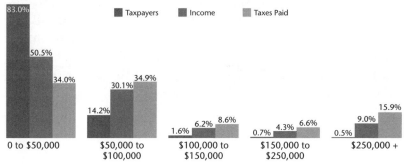

Sources: Tax Statistics on Individuals, Canada Customs and Revenue Service, 2002 edition (2000 tax year) (unedited)

Redistribution For Dummies!
(A refresher course for the rest of us)

As long as there are taxes, there will be redistribution of income; that is what taxes do. But too much of a focus on income redistribution as opposed to wealth creation can obscure the real benefits of an expanding economy. Consider these three examples.

Case study one: The rich 10 per cent pay more than 52 per cent of federal income tax

The claim that Canadians, any Canadian, should be taxed more is curious. As a percentage of GDP, taxes have rarely been so high, even with the recent reductions, and that exception was in wartime.

Canada's taxes are certainly "progressive," if by that it is meant that a Canadian pays more as she moves up the income scale. For example, with federal income taxes, Canadians who earn less than $23,000 constitute 50 percent of all tax filers; their income is equal to 16.9 per cent of all income reported, and their share of federal taxes payable is 4.4 per cent. Thus, the 40 per cent of Canadians who earn between $23,000 and $64,500 (the middle-income earners) account for 47.4 per cent of the income reported and pay 43 per cent of federal tax. In contrast, those who earn more than $64,500 (10 per cent of all tax filers and with 35.7 per cent of the income) are responsible for paying 52.6 per cent of federal income tax.

When former Conservative finance minister Michael Wilson once remarked that Canada needed more millionaires, it is this distribution of income-to-taxes-paid that he had in mind. Those who want more taxes paid by Canadians should wish for more millionaires—and favour policies that create them.

Case study two: Grow the economy like an Asian tiger or "redistribute" like Fidel?

In "Country A," the average taxable income is $10,000 and the average tax rate per person is 45 per cent, or $4,500.

In "Country B," the average taxable income is $25,000 but the average tax rate per person is 25 per cent, or $6,250 per person. In this latter case, the government's take per person is higher *even though the tax rate is lower*.

Country A could increase its tax rates in an attempt to garner the same amount of revenue per person as Country B, or it could attempt to grow the economy over time. Growing the economy may include a number of measures ranging from tax reductions to labour market changes or attracting more foreign investment.

Has this ever happened? Yes. Quite often over the past half-century.

For example, shortly before Canadian soldiers fought a war on the Korean peninsula, the average Korean's "share" of their national economy was worth $770 (all figures adjusted for inflation to 1990 dollars). In comparison, Canada's per person economy in 1950 amounted to almost 10 times that at $7,437 (again, in 1990 inflation-adjusted dollars). And while Korea's economy was small, other have-not countries in 1950 were similarly tiny. The average per capita share of GDP in the Congo, for example, was not much better, at $1,289.

Fast forward to 1998 and South Koreans were prosperous to a degree unimaginable half a century before. Per capita income grew, in real terms, 17-fold since 1950 to stand at more than $13,317 in 1998—or about two-thirds of the $20,000 per person income in Canada in that year. Alas, during the same 50 years, the Congolese did not see even a doubling in their wealth. Fifty years on, the per person economy of the Congo was worth just $2,239.

And there are examples of countries that went in reverse. Cuba, the fourth-richest out of 15 countries in Latin America in 1950, with a per capita GDP of $3,390 that year, dropped to $2,164 by 1998 and was by then the fourth-*poorest* country.[7]

Case study three: Raise taxes for the rich (those with incomes over $60,000) or increase incomes by 6 per cent?
Arguments are sometimes made that if we just "taxed the rich" more, much more money would be available for government services or for redistribution to the poor.

But to use federal tax as an example, suppose that government did tax all income from everyone who earns over $60,000. The federal government would take in an additional $50 billion in revenue. (And that assumes that such an additional tax would have zero effect on people's behaviour and thus economic output—not a serious or credible assumption, but assume it for the example.)

Imagine that the $50 billion was given to everyone whose income is less than $60,000; thus, every Canadian who earns less than $60,000 would get a cheque for about $2,600 every year. The same $2,600 increase in below-$60,000 incomes could also be accomplished by a 5.8 per cent rise in income for everyone.[8]

Governments are always faced with the choice of growing the economy or merely redistributing the existing tax base; the nations that grow in all areas focus on wealth creation even as they debate how to divvy up current tax revenues.

Chapter 9

Myth: Governments are not as corrupt
as Enron

Fact: Enron, meet Adscam

If the headlines show us anything, it is that the greed and cooked books of the corporate world are no substitute for public services.[1]
    ~ Jack Layton, candidate for federal New Democrat leader, on the Enron scandal, in 2002.

The Auditor General is obviously dismayed to learn that Public Works and Government Services Canada agreed to pay fees and commissions to communications agencies for their services in transferring funds from one department or agency of the Government to another, with little in the way of work or services required other than the transmission of a cheque.[2]
    ~ Auditor General Sheila Fraser, as cited by Justice John Gomery in his report on the sponsorship program scandal, in 2005.

The Politicians Get Lucky

If there was ever a case of a misplaced superiority complex, it came in the triumphal crowing over revelations of accounting shenanigans and fraud in the business world. Shortly after the Enron–WorldCom corporate scandals broke in the United States, Jack Layton, then running to become federal New Democratic Party leader, asserted that "the greed and cooked books of the corporate world are no substitute for public services."[3] Canadian Labour Congress president Ken Georgetti predicted the CEO scandals would revive the moribund labour movement.[4] Some in the media also chirped in. In a column entitled "Activist government becomes relevant again," *Ottawa Citizen* columnist Susan Delacourt observed that "It is suddenly the job of the public sector to restore the confidence eroded by the private sector."[5]

Closer observers noticed that even in the Ronald Reagan–Alex P. Keaton era, the most that could be said about Western governments, including Canada's, was that they finally stopped a few of the more glaring and unwise interventions from earlier decades—say, running airline, oil and telephone companies. Other than that, judging by the taxes, regulations and multiple other interventions, government activism never caught a flu, much less died; thus, a pronouncement about its glorious resurrection was unnecessary.

But the revelation in late 2001 that Enron overstated (and fudged) more than US$500 million in earnings, along with multiple restatements from other companies, gave politicians an excuse to bash business and trumpet the superiority of government. It was back to the good old days of the early 20th century when politicians could make rhetorical hay and cross swords with pinstriped corporate fat-cats. Some politicians almost drooled for a replay of those years or the ones surrounding the 1929 stock market crash and the Great Depression.

The Layton–Georgetti–Delacourt crowd were pleased as the scandals seemed to vindicate a revival of an old-time faith in *a priori* public-sector superiority. The "new" justification was simplistic but attractive: greed was discovered again in corporate boardrooms and the public should be shocked—*shocked!*—that excesses could be found where the possibility for great material gain exists.

But public or private, the common factor was the involvement of flawed human beings with all the potential for scandalous behaviour that such flaws imply. Moreover, Layton skipped over the experience of fellow New Democrats in British Columbia. There, the Auditor General and other professional civil servants ripped apart the accounting practices, estimates and budget controls of the NDP when that party had its run of the public treasury. The claim of a higher, more moral public-sector caste was a myth.

If one wanted to expand the definition of good governance beyond the obvious (not cooking the books) to not burning up taxpayer dollars, there were excellent historical Canadian examples of massive ineptitude: the government corruption that surrounded the building of the Canadian Pacific Railway is perhaps the most well-known example. Then there was the nationalization of Petro-Canada, perhaps Canada's largest government waste of taxpayer dollars. In 1991, Peter Foster estimated the portion of Canada's debt associated with that failed political experiment at $14 billion.[6] Even after a subtraction of paid-back proceeds from

Petro-Can's later privatization, the inflation-adjusted loss by 2005 was still $12.1 billion.[7] It's not as if Pierre Trudeau, Jack Austin and Maurice Strong ever woke up in a cold sweat, worried they'd one day wear prison stripes for their role in *that* boondoggle.

QUICK! TO THE HEAD OF THE PARADE!

That the embarrassment and prosecution of fraudulent CEOs and their accountants was deserved was self-evident. That the shake-out and fudge-factory accounting shutdowns were necessary is a given, though it was cold comfort for the ripped-off shareholders and employees of the defunct firms.

From Wall Street to Bay Street to Main Street and the smallest of investors, calls for reform and for heads to roll proceeded apace with vicious market sentiment strafing the crooks and number-crunching swindlers. On the biggest scandal, Enron (and its US$63.4 billion in assets) was forced into bankruptcy within six months of the first critical article in the business press about its accounting practices. WorldCom, with US$103.8 billion in listed assets, filed for Chapter 11-bankruptcy protection within one month after it admitted earnings were overstated by US$3.8 billion.[8] Tyco, Bristol-Myers Squibb and Merck had historical results that looked quite impressive—until equity markets became suspicious about their numbers; then, shares in those companies dropped 50 per cent in six months.[9]

Once companies' books were shredded by outside analysts, market reaction was swift, damning and irreversible. By the time the politicians raced to the head of the "reform business ethics" parade, it had already been underway for some time. The initial questions about Enron's books originated with *Barron's* and other Wall Street analysts and publications, not with Washington, D.C.; and it never came from a Canadian federal government—which would shortly have its own multiple Enron-like shenanigans to answer for.

The Canadian Political Pot Calling the Corporate Kettle, Um, Black

The reaction of investors in specific, and markets in general, to shoddy corporate accounting was in sharp contrast to what some politicians have done over decades and the rarity with which they have faced similar chastisement. In recent memory, any casual observer could come up with several examples of improper government accounting. The acronyms and names are now as familiar to Canadians as those of their children, the latter of which are arguably far better behaved than some who ran federal agencies over the past decade such as Human Resources Development Canada (HRDC) or the gun registry, or those in charge of government sponsorship programs.

The key difference between government fraud and mismanagement on a national or international scale is that retribution for incompetence and outright fraud is dealt with swiftly once known in the business sector. In Canadian politics, as well as international affairs *à la* the oil-for-food scandal at the United Nations, politicians mismanage files for years before they might be held to account by the electorate. Even then, voters may well take a pass, or not have the opportunity, as is the case with the U.N.

Unlike stock markets, shareholders and prosecutors who execute errant companies and chief executives and financial officers with the zeal of French revolutionaries in 1789, voters and Canadian courts have rarely shown such diligence with errant politicians, appointed politicos and civil servants.

That might be because a four-year lag exists between what elected officials can get away with and when they have to account for it. Perhaps it's because Canada is yet too small and judges are too sympathetic to people they chummed with in universities and law schools; perhaps the voting public is too cynical and thus accepts lower standards in political life than they would from a CEO. Whatever the reason, Canadian practitioners of lower ethics can massage numbers and divert cash in the comforting assurance that they will rarely be held to account by voters or the courts.

121

"Punishment" in the private sector *v.* the public sector

Private sector

"OFFENCE"	CAST OF CHARACTERS	PUNISHMENT
Made no distinction between company money and his own; stole US$170 million from Tyco.[10]	Dennis Kozlowski, chief executive officer of Tyco International	Sentenced to eight to 25 years in jail; ordered to repay US$97 million in restitution and $70 million in fines.
Pled guilty to mail fraud.[11]	David Radler, former Hollinger executive	Plea-bargain of 29 months in prison and a US$250,000 fine.
Convicted of $11 billion in accounting fraud.[12]	Bernie Ebbers, WorldCom Inc. chief executive officer	Sentenced to 25 years in prison.
Convicted of two counts of conspiracy.[13]	Former Enron chief financial officer Andrew Fastow	Sentenced to 10 years in jail.

Public sector

"OFFENCE"	CAST OF CHARACTERS	PUNISHMENT
Pled guilty to 15 counts of fraud in connection with the $355-million federal sponsorship scandal.[14]	Paul Coffin, former advertising executive and first person to be charged and convicted in connection with Quebec sponsorship scandal	*Conditional* sentence of two years less a day (i.e., no actual jail time to serve); agreed to repay $1.56 million and must speak to business students about ethics.[15]
Lost $12.1 billion in taxpayer funds through Petro-Canada nationalization.	Pierre Trudeau, Jack Austin, Maurice Strong, John Ralston Saul	None.
Stole at least $1 million in charity money for political ends. [16]	B.C. NDP Cabinet minister Dave Stupich; New Democratic organizer and "bagman"	Sentenced to two years less a day of *house* arrest and 200 hours of community service.

"OFFENCE"	CAST OF CHARACTERS	PUNISHMENT
Interference in civil service calculation of provincial budget revenues estimates; revenues estimates boosted by $800 million. [17]	B.C. NDP premier Glen Clark, finance minister Elizabeth Cull, senior advisor Tom Gunton[18]	None, although the NDP did lose power five years after the "fudge-it" budget scandal.
Involved in using taxpayer money to fund events and projects for partisan purposes.[19]	Alfonse Gagliano, former Liberal Cabinet minister	Given ambassador's job in Denmark; later dismissed from post.
Pled guilty to theft of a $64,500 ring. [20]	Svend Robinson	Given a conditional discharge, one year's probation and 100 hours of community service.
Accepted $1.14 million in sponsorship money as part of a wider $355 million sponsorship scandal.	Liberal Party of Canada	Liberal leader and Prime Minister Paul Martin said party will repay the $1.14 million.[21] No offer made to reimburse public treasury for $30-million-plus cost of Gomery Inquiry.

Enronitis in Provincial Governments: Selected Examples

It would take a whole book to list the malfeasance, missing, questionable grants, and outright pork-barrelling practised by some governments, to say nothing of the tortuous accounting often practised under the public radar (and sometimes in full view). Here are just some examples of the issues raised by the corporate accounting scandals, and parallels in Canada's political world, shortly before and after the Enron scandal broke in 2001.

Issue: Optimistic and unsupportable revenue projections
Case study: British Columbia's 1996 "fudge-it" budget

In 1996, the governing New Democrats pumped optimistic assumptions into their pre-election budget. The NDP government predicted substantial growth in revenues while private-sector analysts forecast a downturn in the same. Much of the budget optimism resulted after the ascension of Glen Clark to the helm of the NDP and the premier's office earlier that year. Mysteriously, after Clark took control, budget forecasts were revised upward despite all inside and outside advice that such forecasts were wildly inaccurate. The truth came out only after the election and due to relentless digging through Access to Information requests by the *Vancouver Sun*, which revealed consistent internal civil service advice and conclusions starkly opposite to what the premier, finance minister and political staffers had publicly claimed. After the scandal hit the front pages and the six o'clock news, it took three years before a government commission reported on how to provide more transparent and "fudge-proof" government books. It was another full year after before the NDP government accepted *some* of the recommendations. It also took a similar length of time before the province's auditor general reported on the mess, which was damning when it finally appeared:

> *Crucial information was missing from the budget forecasts and for all of these reasons, prescribing arbitrary optimism to improve the budget forecast had no merit.*[22]

Unlike Enron or WorldCom, where those responsible were sacked and charged within months, the B.C. budget books took years to clean up and those responsible for the overly optimistic and false forecasts remained in power for almost five years.

Issue: Poor bookkeeping or flouting the rules/poor corporate control
Case study: Prince Edward Island's Business Development Inc.

Prince Edward Island, as is the case with most provinces with the exception of Alberta (as of 1996) and British Columbia (as of 2002), gives financial assistance to business. Its Crown agency that performs this task, PEI Business Development Inc. (BDI), is in the business of disbursing grants, contributions, equity investments, loans and loan guarantees, and owns eight subsidiaries with expenditures of approximately $50 million. The goal is to attract economic investment.

In 2002, the province's auditor general looked into grants and contributions at BDI that totalled $26 million during the fiscal year 2001/02 and found the following:[23]

Despite the amount of money involved, the Board of BDI met only three times between 1999 (the inception of the Crown agency) and March 2001. (The Board began to meet regularly subsequent to the Auditor General's initial report on the matter.)[24]

On corporate control: "The Board did not have a role in the strategic planning process nor did it approve the corporate plan. In addition, authorization was received from Treasury Board for BDI to purchase a building for approximately $2.5 million and relocate its offices but there is no record in the Board minutes where authorization was requested or provided for this major undertaking."[25]

The Board was to approve any assistance over $1 million. In practice, any assistance above that was approved by the provincial Cabinet and without first being recommended by the Board of Directors.[26]

Most grant programs (there are 12) have eligibility criteria and guidelines, but two of the largest programs—the Infrastructure Program and the Sectoral Development Fund—do not have any criteria or eligibility requirements. The Infrastructure Fund disbursed $8.5 million in 2001 and the Sectoral Development Fund gave out $3.5 million.

In 2001, $26 million in grants was disbursed; many of the grants were given on the justification of job creation. Said the auditor general: "We noted however, that for the projects we examined, involving $26 million in grants, we saw no evidence of specific verification of jobs created."[27]

Issue: Poor governance and missing documentation
Case study: Manitoba government

In 2001, looking back over five years, the Manitoba auditor general had this to say about some of his work:

> *Too often during the past five years, our audit work was hampered by inadequacies in, or absence of, documentation supporting key decisions. It is important to keep in mind that this is not just an audit issue. It is fundamentally a threat to the effective operation of our democratic accountability processes.*[28]

Issue: Restricting auditor access to key financial documents
Case study: Ontario Ministry of Transportation

In 2001, the Ontario auditor general reported that his employees were not given proper access to key files. The auditor general's comments:

> *For the first time since being appointed Provincial Auditor, I have to report an instance where my office did not receive all the information and explanations we required. During our value-for-money audit of the Ministry of Transportation's Road User Safety Program, contrary to Section 10 of the* Audit Act, *the then-senior management of the Ministry hindered the audit process by not giving my staff full access to pertinent files, not providing all information requested, and deleting parts of pertinent documents they provided. As well, certain restrictions were placed on my ministry staff such that they may have been inhibited from speaking freely with my staff.*[29]

Issue: Large off-book transactions
Case study: Saskatchewan budgets

In 2002, more than 40 per cent of Saskatchewan's budget was not accounted for in the main set of books, the provincial budget. The most cogent analysis of this situation was in an editorial entitled "Look south, Eric" in the *Saskatoon Star Phoenix* about finance minister Eric Cline and premier Lorne Calvert:

*Saskatchewan residents are shareholders who don't have an op-
tion to dump their equity in the enterprise operated by Cline and
CEO Lorne Calvert. However, what people who are becoming pain-
fully aware of the consequence of fudged books can do is to dump
the executives at the first chance. It's something "Enron Eric" and
"WorldCom Calvert" should bear in mind as they tout the province's "balanced" books.*[30]

Enronitis in the Federal Government

Accounting practices and standards vary widely across the provinces, as well as the degree of accountability and transparency
and the time frame in which offending departments/governments
comply with auditors' recommendations. As for the federal government, it is, alas, too easy to find questionable accounting of the
type that would make Arthur Andersen executives blush.

Here are some examples of accounting irregularities and/or questionable tracking and reporting of public money from federal
auditor general reports:

General comment on erosion of parliamentary control over finances:

*Canadians have the right to control how public funds are collected
and used, and ultimately it is the members of Parliament we elect
who carry out this control on our behalf. That is why I am concerned
about recent examples of the erosion of parliamentary control, involving billions of dollars of revenue and expenditure.*[31]

*On poor management of $16-billion worth of annual grant and contri-
bution programs:*

*In 1998, we reported that two decades of audits of grant and con-
tribution programs had sent a consistent message: there are serious
and chronic problems in the way they are managed. A lack of
diligence in designing programs, assessing applications, and monitoring recipients' performance meant that public funds were placed
at risk.... The Treasury Board Secretariat recently released a revised*

and improved policy framework for managing these types of pro-grams. But the attention paid to grants and contributions has not yet been translated into overall improvement in the way they are managed across the federal government.[32]

On the $7 billion allocated to foundations—largely out of the public's and Parliament's view and control—and the possibility that the government is spending money now to make later budget balance sheets look better:

Since 1997, the government has created a number of new orga-nizations to support, for example, research and development, students in post-secondary education, and Aboriginal healing. It has allocated more than $7 billion to nine of these foundations and recorded the amount as spending by the federal government. Most of the funds, however, are still in the foundations' bank ac-counts and investments.

While the foundations will support worthy causes, I am con-cerned that a prime motivator for funding them in advance is the accounting impact on the government's bottom line: showing larger expenditures today and smaller ones tomorrow reduces the size of current surpluses. I am also concerned that Parliament has only limited means of holding the government to account for the public policy functions performed by these foundations.[33]

The Sponsorship Scandal For Dummies
(And a Modest Proposal for Permanent Remedies)

A guide to the political and bureaucratic misuse of Crown corporations

Back when Canada Post was a tax-supported agency under the federal government, it required $1.3 billion in subsidies be-tween just 1982 and 1987 to keep it afloat. VIA Rail, still a tax drain on the federal treasury, sopped up more than $1.6 billion in operating subsidies between 1996 and 2004, the latest year for which figures are available. Canadians could be forgiven if they thought that these Crown corporations, which collectively cost taxpayers $2.9 billion, might be careful not to spend an unnecessary penny: After all, if the two Crowns wished to repay taxpayers for their earlier generosity it would be some time before they would recoup a full return.

Regrettably, those two Crowns and another—the Business Development Bank of Canada—were all knee-deep in the now widely known Quebec sponsorship scandal when the federal Liberal government used agencies and Crowns to spend $355 million. Some $100 million of that amount ended up in the pockets of Quebec advertising agencies, and some of that money found its way back to the Liberal Party itself ($1.14 million).

Here's a brief summary of the three Crowns, with highlights from the 2004 auditor general's report and the particular Crown's relationship to taxpayers.

VIA Rail v. the auditor general: The $112,500 commission

In her late 2003 report, federal Auditor General Sheila Fraser noted that VIA Rail was used as handmaiden of the federal government to deliver $910,000 to a television series production company—(L'Information Essentielle), in order to finance a television production on the life of hockey great Maurice Richard. The aim of the federal agency (Public Works and Government Services Canada) was for VIA to advance the money to the production company until the department's sponsorship program received more parliamentary appropriations for the funds. [34]

VIA did so, but delivered the money through a Quebec communications firm (Lafleur) without a contract, via fictitious invoices and in so doing contravened the *Financial Administration Act*. Through a series of convoluted transactions, the ad agency's commission was $112,500, which as the auditor general noted, was "for simply delivering a cheque."[35]

The "dummies" version of the above: taxpayer-subsidized VIA Rail cut cheques for a television series of questionable advertising benefit to the Crown, used fake invoices and no contracts to do it, and allowed a Quebec communications company to reap a commission for which even lawyers would have to work long hours. VIA Rail also used Lafleur Communications to help produce a magazine, although Lafleur did "no work whatsoever"[36] for its $30,754 commission, according to Justice Gomery.

The case for privatization: VIA Rail is a substantial drain on government coffers, uses its subsidies to compete for passengers with private-sector airline and bus companies, and took in more than $1.6 billion in operating subsidies between 1996 and 2004.[37] The federal government properly exited the commercial rail business over a decade ago when it sold Canadian National Railway, it dispensed with running an airline when it privatized Air Canada, and the federal government has never subsidized passenger bus service. There is no compelling reason why taxpayers should continue to subsidize rail travel or own a train company.

The Business Development Bank of Canada v. the auditor general

In 1998, the Business Development Bank agreed to sponsor a television series on the millennium with a contribution of $250,000 to L'Information Essentielle; it agreed to the deal without a written contract. Justice Gomery notes that aside from the lack of a contract, the sponsorship was a legitimate part of BDC's advertising and marketing program. That money was paid in 1998. The $250,000 was part of a *larger* amount— $1.7 million—that the government would eventually pay to L'Information Essentielle for the television program but through communications agencies and the BDC.

The trouble started in 2000, after the program had already been aired. The BDC received a cheque for $125,000, which it then, after internal disagreements on the propriety of doing so, cashed and then wrote a cheque to L'Information Essentielle. Two communications agencies benefited from this and other "flow-throughs" to the tune of $37,500 in commissions.[38] The auditor general's comment: "There was no analysis or rationale to explain why [the government] chose to pay L'Information Essentielle through a Crown corporation or a communications agency."[39] She also noted that "The BDC officers approving the payment appear to have gone beyond the financial authority delegated to them."[40]

The "dummies" version of the above: The BDC has long argued it is not a slush fund in the manner of the Atlantic Canada Opportunities Agency or various corporate welfare agencies within Industry Canada. That said, prior to 1998, BDC used to receive as much as $27 million annually from Parliament. In the sponsorship scandal, Justice Gomery recognized that the internal conduct of the bank was not blameworthy;[41] however, as with other Crowns involved, it was available to serve as a conduit, however unintentionally.

The case for privatization: Since the bank is now required to be self-sustaining, there is little reason for government ownership, which could be used by future unscrupulous politicians or civil servants to go "beyond the financial authorities delegated to them" to advance funds in a questionable manner and to debatable ends.

Canada Post v. the auditor general

In her 2003 tour through the unfortunate file cabinets of misbehaving Crowns, the auditor general noted that Canada Post sent $1.625 million to L'Information Essentielle between 1998 and 2000 for a Maurice Richard series, and, as seemed all too natural in the sponsorship scandal, did so without a signed contract.[42] The money was for Canada Post's participation in the Maurice Richard television project. The AG expressed concern about a lack of proper documentation.[43]

The "dummies" version of the above: As with other federal money directed to the Richard television series, there was no business case, no contract and Canada Post informed the auditor general it received good value for its money and that it had done a cost-benefit analysis. The auditor noted that Canada Post "provided no evidence of this."[44]

Case for privatization: Many Canadians recall the strikes that once plagued the mail carrier and the generous taxpayer subsidies it once required. Between 1982 and 1987—never mind the years before that—Canada Post was given almost $1.3 billion in taxpayer cash. As with BDC, Canada Post is now self-sufficient, though a significant loss was forecast for 2006.[45] Given the reality that in recent years the post office has been in the black, a private Canada Post (with regulatory oversight as concerns its rates) is not only feasible but desirable. An added benefit is that critical cost-benefit analyses might no longer disappear.

Summary: Cut the conduits

Whether the Crown in question is the past subsidy-receiving Canada Post or Business Development Bank, or the still-in-the-red VIA Rail, there is an excellent business and taxpayer case to be made for subjecting all the Crowns to competition: first, from the Canadian National Railway to provincial telephone companies, new efficiencies and improved service levels were the result of privatization experiments in Canada and abroad; second, setting these particular Crowns free would stop the flow of subsidies where they presently exist; it would prevent those who are already subsidy-free from returning for taxpayer support one day; third, privatization would forever sever the political-bureaucratic axis that allowed them to be used as a political conduit for illicit taxpayer cash transfers including the use of fake invoices and fake contracts.

The sponsorship scandal is an excellent case study on why several federal Crowns should be tossed into the private sector. Without such an action, opposition parties can pledge to clean up the system, but neither that nor additional investigations and audits—useful as they are as a post-mortem—will reduce the likelihood of similar scandals 10, 20 or 50 years down the road.

Chapter 10

Putting Free Speech in Shackles: How (some) MPs and judges killed free speech but not self-created child pornography

It is time to remember that the first thing we belong to is humanity. And humanity is separated from the animal world by thought and speech and they should naturally be free. If they are fettered, we go back to being animals.
~ Alexander Solzhenitsyn[1]

While the right to political expression lies at the core of the guarantee of free expression and warrants a high degree of constitutional protection, there is nevertheless a danger that political advertising may manipulate or oppress the voter.
~ Justices Iacobucci, Bastarache, Arbour, LeBel, Deschamps and Fish in February 2004 in Harper v. Canada. The Supreme Court ruled in favour of a federal law that allowed political parties to spend 83 times more than individual Canadian citizens (or citizens' groups) on political advertising during elections.

A Short History of Gag Laws

There are few signs that better reveal a politician's true opinion of her constituents than whether or not she acts to muzzle them. Tragically, then, not only do most politicians happily pass gag laws that practically prevent anyone but themselves from voicing an opinion during elections, they then force citizens to finance political parties.[a] And now a majority on the Supreme Court has happily endorsed the restrictions—not on the skimpiest of evidence that free speech during elections is harmful, but *contrary* to the evidence and to the interests of an informed citizenry.

The restriction on free speech is relatively recent. For over a century since Confederation, no federal government enacted restrictions on election-time dialogue.[2] That lasted until 1974 when

a. The exception to this was the Reform Party and its successor, the Canadian Alliance. The Progressive Conservatives reversed their earlier position and voted against the 1997 incarnation of the gag law. Given Conservative leader Stephen Harper's past court battles and attempts to strike down the restrictive election legislation while he was president of the National Citizens Coalition, his new government, presumably, is opposed to speech restrictions during elections.

Pierre Trudeau's Liberals introduced amendments to the country's *Elections Act*, which also regulated political party finances. While the 1974 law technically banned citizens' groups, unions and others from election advertising, the law made an exception that "allowed" Canadians to advance support (or not) for issues of public policy.

By 1983, federal political parties figured their generosity on free speech was at an end. With just 40 minutes of debate, parliamentarians removed the right to free expression, i.e., the ability of citizens solely or together to advertise during an election. All three parties—Liberals, Progressive Conservatives and New Democrats—voted to restrict election-time advertising to politicians. A Tory MP in 1983 was frank about the purpose of the law: it would, he said, make elections "easier to police."[3] It was as if citizens were somehow a clear and present danger.

The comment betrayed an elitist view of the source of political power and legitimacy: that power emanates from rulers who, should they choose, may deign to share it. That it came from a Conservative who should understand the problem with concentrated power revealed the intellectual rot within Canadian conservatism in the early 1980s.

Not all Canadians agreed with the top-down consensus. David Sommerville, then head of the National Citizens Coalition, challenged the law in court, had it quashed, and thus for the 1984 and 1988 elections, freedom of speech was in play.

GAG-FREE ELECTIONS = SUBSTANTIVE DEBATES

The result was that in 1988 the most memorable election in recent Canadian history was fought over an actual issue as opposed to the usual uninformative political party pulp. If Brian Mulroney and the Tories were re-elected, a free trade agreement with the United States was to be signed; thus, would-be MPs, business and labour groups and voters themselves argued about free trade in newspapers, on talk shows and in coffee shops. By one estimate, advocacy groups that supported free trade spent $4 million on advertising.[4] That figure was equivalent to roughly 40 per cent of what the major parties spent on advertising that year. Anti-free-trade groups spent $1.7 million.[5]

Those in favour of election-time spending restrictions routinely argue that the unequal spending in 1988 meant pro-free-trade groups influenced the election more than anti-free-trade groups. But on examination, it was a baseless claim: the two anti-free-trade parties (the Liberals and New Democrats) *won a majority of the votes,* which, as one journalist noted, could have been interpreted to mean that "a majority voted for the side that spent *less* on third-party advertising."[6] It was as least as plausible as the reverse interpretation.

The Empire Strikes Back: The Lortie Commission

Not that the facts would stand in the way of more restrictions: barely three years after a robust, issues-based campaign, the federally appointed Lortie Commission urged Ottawa to again impose restrictions on so-called third parties. This time, the proposal was for a $1,000 limit (just over *three dollars* per riding) on election expenses for third parties.

The 1992 recommendations were predictable; the $17-million commission (the Royal Commission on Electoral Reform and Party Financing) was composed of like-minded commissioners who preferred restrictions on free expression. And there was no mystery as to why: if you're in power or connected with those who are the status quo is fine, even if existing policy might be deleterious for the country at large. For those with influence and tempted by power (which inflates one's perception of his or her place in the world), the temptation to silence potential critics is constant. Add to that an actual vacuum of ideas, where, if all one can offer in terms of policy are vague homilies and meaningless assertions, then fresh thinking on defence, taxation, social policy and other policy areas represent a real threat. Better to smother voices before they can be heard. Thus, Lortie's recommendations served precisely such an end; they were an attack on ideas.

That the commissioners who drafted the report were touchy about their status and ready to defend their turf became evident in a later interview with a witness who appeared before the Lortie Commission. Economist Dr. Filip Palda appeared before the committee only to be berated for two hours and told by committee members, "politicians are not respected, they are under attack and need protection."[7] The same committee later lectured media witnesses and threatened to impose new rules on what reporters could write about during elections. As further evidence that the committee was power-tripping, 80 per cent of the committee's sessions were held in private (*in camera*), with no records kept of their deliberations.[8]

Unsurprisingly, fresh thinking was not on the menu when the committee emerged to give its recommendations; instead, party hacks and bureaucrats helped deliver the politically desired result.

As further evidence that open debate was not high on the list of priorities in 1992, out of six major objectives listed by the 1992 Royal Commission on Electoral Reform and Party Financing, *not one* mentioned freedom of speech. The commission was more concerned with "strengthening political parties as primary political organizations."[9] Translation: pesky citizens' groups should hit the road. Pierre Lortie, chair of the committee, confirmed the intent of the proposed legislation when he smugly observed that "$1,000 doesn't buy a lot of TV."[10]

IGNORE THE FACTS

The Lortie Commission and others with restrictive views assumed that money spent on advertising sways helpless voters who cannot be trusted to parse through election time rhetoric, whether from a party or a citizens' group, and make up their own mind.

But there is little proof for a simplistic reflex. Even if one thought the 1988 election results were murky (i.e., not all who voted Liberal necessarily opposed free trade), and that advertising might sway *some* voters (a reasonable assumption), voters also demonstrated plenty of resistance to high-profile, high-pressure, lavishly funded pitches.

In 1992, after an earlier attempt to amend the Constitution failed, the Conservative government put a new package of amendments directly to the Canadian public. The Charlottetown Accord was perhaps the worst piece of constitutional committee work in the history of the country. It was a perfectly modern example of what happens when too many special interests and politicians are placed together in a room and deprived of fresh air. Moreover, much of it was vague and a mishmash of special-interest grievances writ large; it also possessed the predictable nanny-state solutions for Canada's ills.[b]

But the proposed amendments had the support of most of the country's talking heads, to say nothing of the federal and provincial governments. Also weighing in heavily on the "yes" side was the cheerleading state-owned radio and television network, the taxpayer-supported billion-dollar CBC. In addition to overwhelming elite support for the constitutional fix, the "yes" forces outspent the "no" side by a measure of *thirteen to one*. Given the theory about how easily political ads influenced Canadians and combined with the pundit advantage on the "yes" side, approval of the Charlottetown constitutional amendments should have been a slam-dunk.

Instead, despite the favourable odds for the "yes" side, Canadians could and did make up their own minds. They rejected the package with a 54.2 per cent win for the "no" side.[11] Insofar as the Liberal–Progressive Conservative–New Democrat–Lortie belief that Canadians were mindless sheep who needed protection from advertising, citizens were given the opportunity in 1992 to follow the money, politicians and much of the media. The majority marched in the other direction.

MPS, SHEEP AND *ANIMAL FARM*

There were Canadians who didn't think for themselves or take relevant facts, arguments and evidence into consideration; too many

b. They ranged from guaranteed special status for Quebec and 25 per cent of all seats in Parliament regardless of its population relative to the rest of the country, to a guarantee of all manner of social programs including "full employment," as if governments could wave a wand and make this magically come about. Among other proposals, regional economic development programs (read: business subsidies) were to be permanently entrenched in the Constitution.

of them were in Parliament. A majority of members of Parliament brought in yet another gag law in 1993, this time with the $1,000 limit as recommended by the Lortie Commission.

Members justified the restrictions in this manner: politicians were "particularly concerned about single-issue groups pushing a very emotional issue to the extent that it clouds the *real* issues of a campaign," said M.P. Harvie Andre.[12] Andre was the Progressive Conservative MP responsible for the 1993 law (even though he earlier opposed such restrictions): "I certainly recognize there are real benefits to me and everybody else in the system having limits.... The third parties can't come in."[13]

That was rich. In effect, Andre argued that Canadians (voters) should never be allowed to define the "real" issues (that was reserved for politicians) or become upset over an issue and make life difficult for a politician who didn't share the same passion. It was condescending, undemocratic and specious in its reasoning. Campaigns for the emancipation of slaves, suffrage for women and an end to discriminatory laws against Aboriginal, Chinese and Japanese Canadians were all based on at least some outrage about the indignity of their respective situations.

Passion is part of life and of politics. If a parolee murdered someone's child and the child's relatives wanted a change to Canada's lax parole system, their outrage would be entirely understandable—and justified. If citizens desire changed laws and policies, they should have the right to demand the same and without permission from the very people they pay to govern on their behalf. It is not for voters to crawl to politicians to beg for the right to express their opinion. If citizens channel their anger and frustration through democratic and non-violent channels, it is not the place of politicians to instruct voters as to when they may or not speak, as if such voters were children.

IF ADS ALWAYS PERSUADE PEOPLE, EXPLAIN $10 MILLION AND TWO TORY MPS

If politicians needed yet another demonstration that political ads do not always sway voters, shortly after the 1993 gag law was passed, the governing Progressive Conservatives served as a useful case study. The party spent $10.4 million in their 1993 re-election attempt (more than any other party) and elected just two members of Parliament.[14] If money and advertising always influenced voters in a straight cause-and-effect manner, to stay in power with a one-seat majority, the Tories would have required another $759 million.

Meanwhile, the National Citizens Coalition sued and the Alberta Court of Queen's Bench agreed that the revised federal *Elections Act* violated the Charter of Rights and Freedoms. The federal government appealed again, and lost, again. Mr. Justice Roger Kerans and two other justices almost laughed the government lawyers out of their courtroom.

The federal government lawyer, James Shaw, argued the restrictions merely attempted to create a "level playing field" during elections. The purpose, he said, was to prevent big spenders from twisting public debate with "excessive" advertising. The judges were having none of it. Judge Kerans noted the law could be seen as perhaps having another purpose: "to shut out people who disagree [with the political parties]. That's the other interpretation."[15] He labelled the $1,000 limit a joke, said it amounted to "absolute prohibition" and that it smacked of George Orwell's novel *Animal Farm*, where "everyone's equal as long as everyone's not able to speak."[16]

In striking down the law, the court made this argument:

> *Insofar as these impugned provisions severely limit the ability of third parties to participate in the very communicative process which allows a citizen's vote to be "informed," they undermine the rights of citizens to vote. Thus, this is the antithesis of an informed vote in a free and democratic country.*[17]

The court noted that the government presented no evidence that advertising by third parties has ever convinced any significant number of people to vote one way or another. And the judge noted:

In any event, I have great difficulty accepting that an opposite finding would justify suppression of expression ... there can be no pressing and substantial need to suppress that input merely because it might have an impact.[18]

Writing the judgement, Madame Justice Carole Conrad found that:

The spending restrictions ... force those who wish to participate by advertising in any meaningful way to do so through political parties and candidates. As such, the sections interfere with an individual's freedom of association to accomplish not only very legitimate, but essential objectives in a democratic country. [The result was] legislation which ironically purports to protect the democratic process, by means of infringing the very rights which are fundamental to democracy.[19]

The federal government did not appeal to the Supreme Court of Canada and so gave up, temporarily.

Pay Us and Keep Quiet:
The Thinking of Gag Law Proponents

Naturally, politicians who vote in favour of gag laws always have reasons. But for those who want to pipe up about the environment, labour issues, child care or taxes, the attitude from fans of restrictions is—sorry, during an election, the opinion bar is closed.

One politician, Ed Broadbent, made many of the arguments promulgated by those in favour of limits on citizens at election time. The former federal NDP leader delighted in such restrictions and argued they didn't extend as far as they ought: England, noted Broadbent, does not allow political advertising on television.

It meant that mindless and malicious political advertising, so typical in American elections and increasingly used in Canada (witness Reform's anti-Quebecois commercials), was absent from British television. Another benefit was that the policy saved all parties millions of pounds in election expenses.[20]

It was a fascinating justification. Canadians might think *Mr. Broadbent's* party, with its constant attack on free markets over the decades, was the mindless and malicious force in Canada. But Broadbent's desire to exclude citizens didn't pop out of an oxygen-deprived caucus meeting; he argued what many mistakenly assert. If there were fewer voices during elections, there would be more ideas.

Once the role of money is restricted, political parties are compelled to rely more on the voluntary efforts of their own members and other citizens. Parties—left, right or centre—that are most successful in winning individual citizens deserve to have greater impact. In a democracy, people and ideas, not money and power, should count. The same reasoning also holds for maintaining serious restrictions on "third-party" advertising during an election campaign.[21]

Note Mr. Broadbent's preoccupation with political parties as the vehicles of ideas, his *a priori* assumption that they deserved to have greater impact on elections, and that such a scenario would lead to deep policy debates. Depending on the year, about 1 to 2 per cent of Canadians belong to political parties. What Broadbent's errant assumptions ignored was that many people don't advance their ideas through political parties because they feel they cannot do so. Right or wrong in that belief, it ought to be up to voters to make such choices.

The gag law pushers see a decline in political party affiliation as unhealthy, but the opposite can just as easily be argued. Instead of contributing to a political party, Canadians may give to and work on behalf of advocacy groups as another avenue to express their convictions. This method also allows people to reconcile their desire to support diverse causes that may not be found within one political party.

For example, what if one takes a greener view of the environment than does the Conservative Party but is also more fiscally conservative than a federal Liberal or New Democrat? Maybe a Canadian cares to send his or her money to the World Wildlife Fund *and* the

Fraser Institute. Another person might support the Liberals on aerospace subsidies but not care for their foreign policy.

In any of the above examples, individuals can write a cheque to associations that represent both concerns in a manner a particular party might not or perhaps could not, given the tendency of parties to reduce platforms to the lowest and least controversial common denominator.[c]

What the Broadbents of the country fail to consider is that ideas may be advanced better—and primarily—through vigorous debates at election time by not only politicians but by every Canadian in every conceivable manner, including public debates sparked by a rainbow of various interests who fight it out on the airwaves and in the newspapers. Often, ideas are advanced and pondered that way more often than by those who run for political office; would-be politicians have an understandable desire to get elected but that often smothers a frank discussion of issues.

The assumption that Canadians must work primarily through political parties for the greater public good reveals much about those who hold such assumptions: a preoccupation with party politics as the preferred means to most ends—not a particularly deep or broad view of what contributes to a healthy debate, or a healthy civilization.

Political Parties = Substantive Debates? Where's the Beef?

When politicians ban free speech by those bothersome labour unions, environmental lobbies, citizens' groups, taxpayer associations and individuals—who work, vote, remit taxes and pay the salaries of MPs—there is no evidence that such restrictions have led to better, more informative and intellectually stimulating

---

c. This is desirable. The common complaint that "political parties don't represent me" is narcissistic. No single group or entity entirely represents one person's will or thinking or politics, nor should they. Political parties are useful in that compromise is hammered out in their platforms and in their governing if elected; such compromises are laudable and necessary in a democratic country. But the necessity of compromise in the art of governing or in seeking votes does not also require that political parties and politicians have a monopoly in the debate over ideas and policies at election time.

elections. It's a nice claim, but the evidence runs downhill in the other direction. Do most of our politicians discuss grave matters of state with the utmost of sobriety, without cheap political shots and without fluffy party advertising that insults the intelligence of voters? To pose the query is to answer it.

The argument that only political parties and their leaders can debate issues with the utmost of gravitas is laughable: political parties kill multiple trees to produce oft-meaningless motherhood-and-apple pie brochures that tell voters they are in favour of—what else—motherhood and apple pie. Ideas are mostly absent. Prospective MPs stick to script and dutifully mouth non-controversial statements. Governments pray to coast back into power while opposition parties hope the prime minister utters something questionable that might garner them extra votes. Understandably, that is the primary motivation: winning votes, but it comes at the expense of clarity for citizens who might well prefer would-be decision-makers be forced to explain their intentions *before* the ballots are cast.

This is not blind cynicism. One cannot be too critical of attempts by political parties to monopolize speech. When politicians talk about "third parties," it is a tip-off that they want the election-time sandbox to themselves. "Third party" means someone without a central interest in a dispute. So voters who will not play in the "political sandbox" according to the dictates set down by politicians—no messy divisive issues the politicians cannot spin away—are assumed to be merely "third parties." This pejorative term turns the core assumption of representative and accountable government on its head. From this view, no longer does power flow from citizens to their government, but the other way around; and those who disagree at election time can keep quiet or talk to the judge. Such a view, enforced by the power of government, is injurious to freedom and to a fairly fought battle of ideas.

Exhibit A on this one was the 2000 federal election, where taxpayers were forced to hand over $23.9 million to political parties and their candidates, entities that already benefited from generous tax credits that pump tens of millions of dollars into party coffers.

Substantive issues were not discussed, as demonstrated by the leaders' debate where Jean Chrétien, Stockwell Day, Alexa McDonough, Joe Clark and Gilles Duceppe all outdid each other to prove that original thinking about health care policy would never occur if *their* party were in charge.[d]

Advocacy group ads, which might have pried open the idea box by broadcasting fresh ideas on that and other issues, were effectively banned. The election was left safely in the hands of the play-it-safe professional political consultants whose philosophical, economic and historical horizons are either short-term or nonexistent. Both the 2000 and 2004 campaigns were notable for what wasn't discussed in serious terms: health care, terrorism, war, Quebec and multiple other issues. It was a contrast to the ideas debate that dominated the gag-free 1988 election and the substantial citizen discussion leading up to the referendum on the 1992 Charlottetown Accord.

It's Groundhog Day, *Again*

Similar to the movie *Groundhog Day*, in which a television weatherman wakes up only to relive the same day—over and over and over again—voters woke up to parliaments repeatedly trying to end critical citizen speech during elections. Unfortunately, in the last attempt, they were aided by a 1997 Supreme Court of Canada ruling (Libman) that struck down a Quebec law banning amounts higher than $600 spent to support or oppose separation in the 1995 Quebec referendum on separation. (The law allowed for amounts higher than $600 to be spent only by the official "yes" or "no" camps.)

While the Supreme Court struck down the $600 limit as too low, it was otherwise a good day for those who thought political debate in referendums and elections was for the politically privileged, not citizens. The court hinted that perhaps *$1,000*

---

d. The 2004 election wasn't much better, except that voters were forced to hand over $50.1 million to parties and candidates, and another $22.9 million in a now annual forced "allowance" to all parties from taxpayers. In the 2006 campaign, all federal parties have similarly avoided any substantive debate on health care—again.

might be an acceptable limit, coincidentally, the same amount suggested by the Lortie Commission. It also suggested that the federal government should have appealed the Alberta Court of Appeal ruling (in the earlier election law challenge initiated by the National Citizens Coalition). Apparently the difference between an unconstitutional law and one to be stamped "OK" by the court was $400.

Encouraged by the judicial tip-off, the federal government changed the *Elections Act* in 1997 to decree that no entity other than politicians and their party could spend more than $152,000 nationally, or about $500 per riding.[e] Spent all at once, the nationwide limit might buy one full-page ad in 10 major dailies across the country for a single day. If used in each riding, groups could, after they paid for the printing, paste flyers to telephone poles. The penalty for busting the third-party limit was a jail term of up to five years—this in a country where citizens are lucky if chronic drug dealers do time. An attempt to communicate with a majority of the country's voting age public is not inexpensive. In a riding with tens of thousands of voters and in a country with 30 million people, $500 per riding for everyone save political parties was a joke.

Political parties knew that, which is why politicians gave themselves generous limits. The largest political party in the country (the federal Liberals) could spend more than $12.7 million under the 1997 law; the Alliance, New Democrats and Tories were allowed similar amounts if they fielded a full slate of candidates. On average, political parties could spend $42,190 per riding, not including what candidates spent in addition. Thus, political parties could spend their millions on newspaper ads, mail-outs, radio and television commercials to inundate voters with their message.[f]

e. If advocacy groups (or anyone else) wanted to, they could spend up to $3,000 per riding, as long as the national limit of $152,000 was not breached. Thus, the average per riding was just over $500.

f. In total in 2000, all the registered political parties could collectively spend more than $74.1 million; (they spent $35 million). And the 49 "third parties" that registered with Elections Canada (given their individual limit of $152,000 each) could collectively spend $7.5 million; at the end, they spent just $666,000. In 2004, political parties spent more than $51 million; citizens, just $712,730 in total.

During the 2000 election, the National Citizens Coalition once again went to court in Alberta and had the law suspended, only to have the Court of Appeal restore the law for the duration of the election. Two years later, Alberta courts dumped the expense limits on third parties, but the Court of Appeal preserved sections of the law that required individuals and groups to register with Elections Canada and disclose their donors. Both the NCC and the federal government appealed sections of the ruling to the Supreme Court of Canada.

Meanwhile, other court battles continued. Elections Canada charged several people with violations of the law, including an elderly Nova Scotia man and B.C. libertarian Paul Bryan (both posted results on websites of election returns in eastern Canada before polls closed in western Canada). An anti-gun control lobby that posted signs decrying the federal gun registry was also targeted. By May 2001, Ottawa had spent more than $525,000 in taxpayer money to defend its restriction on the very taxpayers who were being muzzled by the law,[22] an amount almost equal to what all third parties collectively spent in the 2000 election.[g]

$83 v. $1: The Supreme Court's "Level-Playing Field"

Parliamentary persistence and come-hither hints from the justices in Libman resulted in a split, multi-layered verdict released in May 2004. The Supreme Court justices all agreed that a restriction on spending limits was a reasonable infringement on the constitutionally guaranteed right to freedom of expression. They differed, substantially, on most everything else, including whether it was fair to allow political parties to spend $83 for

g. There are other, bizarre measures in Canada's election law, which favour political parties at the expense of the private sector. During an election, radio stations must give preferred and cheaper rates to those advertising for election purposes. Obviously this makes advertising cheaper for such advertisers, primarily political parties and their candidates. And stations must even bump lucrative ads that may have been contracted long before the election to someone else and sold at a higher price. In effect, it would be as if the federal government passed a law that told hardware stores to price their products cheaper if a worker from a political campaign walks into the store to buy a product, and that the store must sell it to that worker even if they had already arranged to sell the same item to a regular buyer at a higher price. In essence, private industry is forced to subsidize political parties.

every $1 allowed to citizens during an election.[h] Six justices said yes; three said no.

The majority, led by Mr. Justice Michel Bastarache, criticized the original Alberta Court of Queen's Bench decision in 2001. Bastarache argued that the trial judge, Justice J. Cairns, erred because he placed little weight on the findings from the Lortie Commission. True, but the Alberta justice placed little emphasis on Lortie because the commission had relied heavily on a study written by Richard Johnston, a professor at the University of British Columbia. Johnston's work on third-party advertising in the 1988 federal election claimed that such ads affected voter intentions. But inconveniently for the gag-law proponents, Johnston later testified in a British Columbia trial on a similar, provincial gag law and retracted his conclusions. He made mathematical errors in his original study and disavowed his earlier conclusions as they were incorrect.

By extension, then, so too was the Lortie Commission and so were government lawyers and six Supreme Court justices and anyone else who argued from that report as a justification to restrict freedom of expression.[i] Johnston's new conclusion—that third-party advertising had no effect—was never challenged by other witnesses at the B.C. trial or by any other empirical study.[23] Even the Supreme Court admitted as much in its 2004 verdict: "There is no evidence before the Court that indicates that third-party advertising seeks to be manipulative," wrote Bastarache. "Nor is there any evidence that third parties wish to use their advertising dollars to smear candidates or engage in other forms of non-political discourse."[24]

Not that this lack of evidence of manipulation or meanness—which were anyway not illegal, even if committed or

h. The ratio in the 2006 election was even more lopsided: political parties could spend $106 for every $1 a citizen or citizens' group could spend on political advertising.

i. One reason advocacy groups and others may not have had a discernible effect on elections is due to the small amount of money spent by those groups. Even if they did spend large amounts of money and had an effect, the justification for restrictions would yet be odd. Voters *ought* to have an effect upon ideas and elections.

intended—would translate into a victory for free speech. The justices continued to tapdance on the basic civil rights they had now interred. "Nevertheless, the danger that political advertising may manipulate or oppress the voter means that some deference to the means chosen by Parliament is warranted."[25]

That "advertising" and "oppression" were used in the same sentence should be of much embarrassment to judges with any sense of history. Blacks in the American south were oppressed through slavery and through civil rights violations; natives in Canada were oppressed when they were denied the right to vote for decades; Japanese Canadians were oppressed when they were sent to internment camps during the Second World War; Jews can identify real oppression throughout history and in the present in selected countries. That six Canadian justices would use the word and do so as they carved up the right to full participation in the political affairs of the country was perhaps a sign of how separate the court had become from reality.

So they charged on to justify the restrictions and still quoted the Swiss-cheese-like Lortie Report to do it:

Johnston's preliminary findings regarding the effect of third-party spending on the 1988 federal election were not determinative of the position taken by the Lortie Commission on third-party spending generally. It is inconceivable that the findings of a Royal Commission would be based solely on one preliminary report in the presence of numerous other expert reports. Professor Aucoin, the Lortie Commission research director, confirmed that he would still recommend third-party spending limits to preserve the fairness of the electoral system.[26]

The Lortie Commission was biased from its creation. That led to its pre-determined claim that third-party advertising influenced the outcome of the 1988 election. But that conclusion has long since been disavowed by the professor who originally produced it. That was not in dispute and nor was the example of a defeat for the heavily funded "yes" side in the Charlottetown Accord. But none of that mattered to Canada's highest court.

Worse, unlike lower court justices, Supreme Court Justice Bastarache and his five colleagues who acceded to the gag law did not do their research. In 2000, Mr. Justice Brenner on the B.C. Supreme Court threw out a B.C. New Democrat government gag law and described just how central Professor Johnston's initial work was to Lortie. Johnston's work was *not*, as Justice Bastarache wrongly claimed, merely one voice with equal weight given to many others. According to Justice Brenner, it was pivotal:

Professor Peter Aucoin is a professor of political science at Dalhousie University. He was also qualified as an expert in the field of political science. He testified for the AGBC. Professor Aucoin was the research director for the Royal Commission on Electoral Reform and Party Financing (the "Lortie Commission"). He also gave expert evidence at the trial in Libman.

Professor Aucoin described the process by which Professor Johnston's conclusions in his 1990 paper were adopted by the Lortie Commission. He testified that Janet Agbert relied on Professor Johnston's paper when she produced a research paper for the commission. The commission's findings included findings on the impact of third-party spending in election campaigns. In every instance where there is a discussion of third-party spending in the Lortie Commission Report reference is also made to the 1988 federal election and the conclusion in Professor Johnston's 1990 paper ...

Professor Aucoin agreed that after the Libman trial, Professor Johnston published Letting the People Decide *in which he resiled from the position set out in his earlier paper.*

Professor Aucoin testified that the Lortie Commission's third-party spending recommendations were premised on the belief that third-party advertising had an effect on voter intentions and it relied on the Johnston 1990 memo for that conclusion.[27] (Emphasis added.)

Thus, the nation's highest court continued to rely on the Lortie Commission's faulty findings on the basis that the commission's *research director*—not the professor central to the original faulty findings he now disavowed—thought limits on citizen spending were a good idea.[28] On such flimsy foundations, the majority on the Supreme Court of Canada thought that warranted overriding an explicitly enunciated constitutional protection: freedom of expression.

BAIT AND SWITCH

The justices well knew that Lortie was a weak crutch when the issue of a constitutional right was in play. So in addition to the misplaced faith in the Lortie Commission, Justice Bastarache and Co. needed to at least pretend other reasons were weighty and mattered. The majority justices, he wrote, also relied on the idea of an "egalitarian" model of elections.

> *Under the egalitarian model of elections, Parliament must balance the rights and privileges of the participants in the electoral process: candidates, political parties, third parties and voters. Advertising expense limits may restrict free expression to ensure that participants are able to meaningfully participate in the electoral process. For candidates, political parties and third parties, meaningful participation means the ability to inform voters of their position.[29]*

Bastarache might have more credibility with this argument had he been more proficient at math. Citizens could spend $507 per riding and $152,550 nationally compared with limits granted to political parties of $42,226 per riding and $12,710,074 nationally. How were "third parties" supposed to "communicate their positions"? With carrier pigeons that collectively cost less than $152,550?

Then there was the justification that the courts must defer to Parliament.

> *Given the right of Parliament to choose Canada's electoral model and the nuances inherent in implementing this model, the Court must approach the justification analysis with deference ... In the end, the electoral system, which regulates many aspects of an*

election, including its duration and the control and reimbursement of expenses, reflects a political choice, the details of which are better left to Parliament.[30]

On balance, the contextual factors favour a deferential approach to Parliament in determining whether the third-party advertising expense limits are demonstrably justified in a free and democratic society. Given the difficulties in measuring this harm, a reasoned apprehension that the absence of third-party election advertising limits will lead to electoral unfairness is sufficient.[31]

But there was nothing reasonable about the apprehension, since voters had already proved—if such evidence were necessary to keep their rights—that they could ignore massive public relation attempts to sway their votes. They did so in the 1993 election and in the 1992 Charlottetown Accord referendum. The logic of reasonable apprehension should have been applied to an infringement on freedom of expression, not to voters.

In addition, curiously, deference to Parliament has not often been a virtue spotted at the Supreme Court. Regardless of what one thought of the debate over gay rights and marriage, for example, lower courts continually expanded equality rights provisions far beyond anything recognizable in the 1982 Constitution. In fact, the negotiations that led up to the Charter of Rights and Freedoms explicitly excluded sexual orientation as a protected Charter of Rights and Freedoms category. (As another example, the framers also excluded property rights.)

In order to override provincial and federal legislation as it concerned Canada's gay and lesbian community, lawyers and courts had to argue that the rather new Constitution was so flexible, so organic and growing, that categories of rights could be "read in" to the Charter despite explicit original avowals to the contrary.

The Supreme Court never once rejected a lower-court claim insofar as it concerned expanding rights on the basis of sexual orientation. (Nor did the highest court hesitate to override Parliament's law against self-created child pornography in a case involving John Sharpe three years earlier.) Incorrect or correct as such actions or non-actions were, the contrast to the court's approach in a case of a clearly enunciated constitutional right was stunning: *the Supreme Court now felt it necessary to "defer to Parliament" even though Parliament severely restricted freedom of expression—a clear constitutional right.* The court deferred despite a constitutional obligation to protect that freedom unless there was a compelling state interest and justification to injure it and even then to do so in a minimally intrusive manner. Instead, the majority of the court failed to protect freedom of expression and justified its failure on the grounds of mere possibilities and probabilities.

Justice Bastarache then delivered what he likely thought was his clincher argument: why would groups go to the trouble of fundraising and spending all that money if they didn't expect to influence the election debate in some fashion? "That political advertising influences voters accords with logic and reason. Surely, political parties, candidates, interest groups and corporations for that matter would not spend a significant amount of money on advertising if it was ineffective."[32]

But effective (or not)—a point that the justices already agreed had not been proven to anyone's satisfaction—and regardless of whether such groups *believed* their advertising was effective, that was not the issue before the court: the court was asked to uphold a law that banned widespread communication with other Canadians during elections. What groups thought about their own advertising was irrelevant.

In addition, there was the issue of the 83-1 advantage in spending limits given to political parties. Justice Bastarache and the majority on the court also attempted to defeat the argument given to him by the minority on the court: that the $500 per riding limit ($3,000, if citizens cared to skip some ridings and spend all $3,000 on leaflets in one electoral district) shut out citizens from mass communication with millions of other Canadians. Dissenting justices Major, McLachlin and Binnie argued this hardly met the test of minimal impairment, i.e., even if a restriction on speech is demonstrably justified, it should be as minimal as possible. Justice

153

Bastarache's answer? Citizens could communicate with each other with no restrictions *before* an election:

> *The Chief Justice and Major J. assert that short of spending well over $150,000 nationally and $3000 in a given electoral district, citizens cannot effectively communicate their views on election issues to their fellow citizens (para. 9). Respectfully, this ignores the fact that third-party advertising is not restricted prior to the commencement of the election period.*
>
> *Outside this time, the limits on third-party intervention in political life do not exist. Any group or individual may freely spend money or advertise to make its views known or to persuade others. In fact, many of these groups are not formed for the purpose of an election but are already organized and have a continued presence, mandate and political view which they promote. Many groups and individuals will reinforce their message during an electoral campaign.*[33]

The reference to pre-election communication was irrelevant; it was more smoke blown by Bastarache to divert attention from the rights now being peeled away by the very court that was supposed to uphold the same.

Bastarache continued and asserted that spending limits were practically irrelevant: "the vast majority of Canadian citizens simply cannot spend $150,000 nationally or $3,000 in a given electoral district."[34] Except that the justice's reasoning ignored—and not artfully—the reality that a lack of means was precisely why citizens banded together in unions, taxpayer groups, the National Citizens Coalition or environmental organizations. They wanted to spend more collectively and possibly have an impact in a way that they could not as individuals.

Still, the justice moved forward in his argument: "The proper focus is on protecting the right to meaningful participation of the entire electorate."[35] The justice explained how such "meaningful participation" would work:

Section 350 minimally impairs the right to free expression. The defi-
nition of "election advertising" in s. 319 only applies to advertising
that is associated with a candidate or party. Where an issue is not
associated with a candidate or political party, third parties may
partake in an unlimited advertising campaign.[36]

Bastarache's logic was on thin, translucent ice. A simple cold splash
of reason should have dissuaded him from even making this argument had he and the other majority justices cared to plunge below
the surface. It was and is impossible to imagine *any* issue not being associated with any or all parties. Conservatives, Liberals, New
Democrats and the Bloc all have a policy on the environment.
They all have opinions on taxes and spending, on the military and
war; they were then wrestling with gay marriage. In their pursuit
of votes, parties don't often take clear positions. But every party
produces a laundry list of policy positions that, while pulverized
to pablum in an attempt not to offend any possible voter, could
arguably be seen as an issue that citizens would then be banned
from speaking about during elections.

Thus, section 350, which so generously allowed citizens to
spend as much as they could on an issue—so long as it was not
associated with any party—was a velvet glove paragraph draped
over the iron fist of the *Elections Act*. It meant nothing in practical
terms. For an educated justice of the Supreme Court to pretend
that it did was transparent dishonesty of the highest order.

Nevertheless, the charade continued. Why was the $500 per
riding spending allowance so generous in the view of the six
justices?

[T]he limits are high enough to allow third parties to engage in a sig-
nificant amount of low cost forms of advertising such as computer
generated posters or leaflets or the creation of a 1-800 number. In ad-
dition, the definition of "election advertising" in s. 319 does not apply
to many forms of communication such as editorials, debates, speeches,
interviews, columns, letters, commentary, the news and the Internet
which constitute highly effective means of conveying information. [37]

How comforting. The gag law allowed for leaflets. Nor did it apply to newspaper editorials. But freedom of the press was not at issue in the trial. That citizens were supposed to be grateful that Parliament didn't also attack the press, or pre-election rights to advertising and debate, was an odd justification. It missed the salient fact that elections are normally an event and time when most politicians pay attention to citizens, and voters just might want to say something *then*. The reference to section 319 was another diversion and no more convincing than the argument that citizens had plenty of freedom during elections—so long as they never brought an issue that might also be touched on by a political party. It turned out some animals—the political kind—were indeed more equal. And they could speak.

Advertising and Free Speech Are Dangerous; "Self-Created" Child Pornography Is Not

Oddly, while a majority on Canada's highest court felt it necessary to protect innocent, easily led-astray voters on the justification that advertising may "oppress" citizens, the majority of the Supreme Court did not take a similar cautious just-in-case approach to "self-created" child pornography.

In its 2001 landmark decision involving child pornography (Canada *v.* Sharpe) the case of a Vancouver man charged under the Criminal Code with two counts of possession of child pornography was reviewed by the nation's highest court.[38] John Sharpe possessed child pornography that he intended to distribute and sell. Sharpe's defence was that his constitutionally guaranteed freedom of expression was infringed, and lower courts had mostly agreed. In response, the Crown admitted that freedom of expression was infringed upon, but argued it was justifiable under the section of the Charter that allowed just such an infringement where such an activity could be proved harmful to the public good—or more specifically in this case, to children.

The Supreme Court agreed that Sharpe's freedom of expression was infringed upon, but also that it was justified. *However*, the court then gutted the law by ruling that where child pornography is self-created (i.e., drawings or essays but not actual photographic images of a real child) and held by the person alone, and so long as it was for personal use and not distribution, the Criminal Code ban went too far. The same logic applied to adolescents who might engage in sex with each other and take "visual depictions," i.e., if they might videotape it. As long as the depictions were for personal use and not for distribution, the court argued banning such child pornography would constitute too great a danger to freedom of expression.

The court seemed not to consider several real possibilities. The first was that self-created child pornography might also be dangerous if it allowed the Sharpes of the world to fantasize about sex with children. The second overlooked reality was that some 15-year-olds are not at their empathic and maturity peak. It's entirely conceivable that a 15-year-old boy who videotaped consensual sex between himself and his 14-year-old girlfriend might post it to the Internet after they broke up—at which point it could be downloaded by the Sharpes of the world and be irretrievable. That the 15-year-old boy might then be charged with distribution of child pornography would be of little help to the girl.

But if self-created child pornography was permitted on the weak court claim that such individually created and used child erotica was not proved to be harmful to society and was an unjustified and too-great infringement on the constitutional freedom of expression, the Canadian court took the exact opposite view about freedom of expression during elections. Then, severe restrictions were necessary to protect Canadian adults from *advertising*.

A Masterful Dissent
The reasons of Justices McLachlin,
Major and Binnie in Harper *v.* Canada
There is much more that could be said about the illogic, straw man arguments, and Orwellian twisting of language evident in the majority Harper *v.* Canada decision by Iacobucci,

Arbour, Bastarache, LeBel, Deschamps and Fish. In contrast, here are some excerpts from the three dissenting justices, Chief Justice McLachlin and justices Major and Binnie. Note the clarity of language and the absence of any attempt to invert the commonly understood meaning of words. (*Emphasis added.*)

On the practical effect of the legislation:

The law at issue sets advertising spending limits for citizens—called third parties—at such low levels that they cannot effectively communicate with their fellow citizens on election issues during an election campaign. **The practical effect is that effective communication during the writ period is confined to registered political parties and their candidates. Both enjoy much higher spending limits. This denial of effective communication to citizens violates free expression where it warrants the greatest protection—the sphere of political discourse.** As in Libman *v.* Quebec (Attorney General), [1997] 3 S.C.R. 569, the incursion essentially denies effective free expression and far surpasses what is required to meet the perceived threat that citizen speech will drown out other political discourse. It follows that the law is inconsistent with the guarantees of the Charter and, hence, invalid.[39]

On the Chief Electoral Officer, Jean-Pierre Kingsley, who favours election-time restrictions despite his knowledge of how expensive it is to communicate with the public:

The limits do not permit citizens to effectively communicate through the national media. The Chief Electoral Officer testified that it costs approximately $425,000 for a one-time full-page advertisement in major Canadian newspapers. The Chief Electoral Officer knows from personal experience that this is the cost of such communication with Canadians,

because he used this very method to inform Canadians of
the changes to the Canada Elections Act prior to the last federal election. **It is telling that the Chief Electoral Officer
would have been unable to communicate this important
change in the law to Canadians were he subject—as are
other Canadians—to the national expenditure limit of
$150,000 imposed by the law.**[40]

*On the impossibility of even conducting a mail-out campaign dur-
ing an election:*

Nor do the limits permit citizens to communicate through
the mail. The Canada Post bulk mailing rate for some ridings amounts to more than $7,500, effectively prohibiting
citizens from launching a mail campaign in these ridings
without exceeding the $3,000 limit.[41]

On how the limits relegate electoral participation to minor expressions:

Under the limits, a citizen may place advertisements in a
local paper within her constituency. She may print some
flyers and distribute them by hand or post them in conspicuous places. She may write letters to the editor of
regional and national newspapers and hope they will be
published. In these and other ways, she may be able to
reach a limited number of people on the local level. But she
cannot effectively communicate her position to her fellow
citizens throughout the country in the ways those intent
on communicating such messages typically do—through
mail-outs and advertising in the regional and national media. The citizen's message is thus confined to minor local
dissemination with the result that effective local, regional
and national expression of ideas becomes the exclusive
right of registered political parties and their candidates.[42]

Comparative statistics underline the meagerness of the
limits. The national advertising spending limits for citizens

represent 1.3 percent of the national advertising limits for political parties.[43]

...

Political speech, the type of speech here at issue, is the single most important and protected type of expression. It lies at the core of the guarantee of free expression...[44]

...

On what the goals of Parliament and the courts should be:

Permitting an effective voice for unpopular and minority views—views political parties may not embrace—is essential to deliberative democracy. The goal should be to bring the views of all citizens into the political arena for consideration, be they accepted or rejected at the end of the day. Free speech in the public square may not be curtailed merely because one might find the message unappetizing or the messenger distasteful (Figueroa, supra, at para. 28).

Put simply, full political debate ensures that ours is an open society with the benefit of a broad range of ideas and opinions. This, in turn, ensures not only that policy makers are aware of a broad range of options, but also that the determination of social policy is sensitive to the needs and interests of a broad range of citizens.

Participation in political debate "is ... the primary means by which the average citizen participates in the open debate that animates the determination of social policy"; see Figueroa, supra, at para. 29.[45]

The right to participate in political discourse is a right to effective participation—for each citizen to play a "meaningful" role in the democratic process, to borrow again from the language of Figueroa, supra.[46]

"Effectiveness" means nothing if not the ability to persuade:

The ability to engage in effective speech in the public square means nothing if it does not include the ability to

attempt to persuade one's fellow citizens through debate
and discussion. This is the kernel from which reasoned
political discourse emerges. Freedom of expression must
allow a citizen to give voice to her vision for her community and nation, to advocate change through the art of
persuasion in the hope of improving her life and indeed
the larger social, political and economic landscape.[47]

...

How spending limits block debate:

The Canada Elections Act undercuts the right to listen by
withholding from voters an ingredient that is critical to
their individual and collective deliberation: substantive
analysis and commentary on political issues of the day.
The spending limits impede the ability of citizens to communicate with one another through public fora and media
during elections and curtail the diversity of perspectives
heard and assessed by the electorate. Because citizens cannot mount effective national television, radio and print
campaigns, the only sustained messages voters see and
hear during the course of an election campaign are from
political parties.[48]

...

*How we live in age of mass communication, not in the Athens of
Socrates and Plato:*

It is clear that the right here at issue is of vital importance to
Canadian democracy. In the democracy of ancient Athens,
all citizens were able to meet and discuss the issues of the
day in person. In our modern democracy, we cannot speak
personally with each of our co-citizens. We can convey our
message only through methods of mass communication.
Advertising through mail-outs and the media is one of the
most effective means of communication on a large scale.
We need only look at the reliance of political parties on advertising to realize how important it is to actually reaching

citizens—in a word, to effective participation. The ability to speak in one's own home or on a remote street corner does not fulfill the objective of the guarantee of freedom of expression, which is that each citizen be afforded the opportunity to present her views for public consumption and attempt to persuade her fellow citizens. Pell J.'s observation could not be more apt: "Speech without effective communication is not speech but an idle monologue in the wilderness"; see United States v. Dellinger, 472 F.2d 340 (7th Cir. 1972), at p. 415.[49]

...

The real question in this case is not whether there exists a rational connection between the government's stated objectives and the limits on citizens imposed by the Canada Elections Act. It is whether the limits go too far in their incursion on free political expression.[50]

On the need for minimal impairment of rights:

Here the concern of the Alberta courts that the Attorney General had not shown any real problem requiring rectification becomes relevant. The dangers posited are wholly hypothetical. The Attorney General presented no evidence that wealthier Canadians —alone or in concert—will dominate political debate during the electoral period absent limits. It offered only the hypothetical possibility that, without limits on citizen spending, problems could arise. **If, as urged by the Attorney General, wealthy Canadians are poised to hijack this country's election process, an expectation of some evidence to that effect is reasonable. Yet none was presented. This minimizes the Attorney General's assertions of necessity and lends credence to the argument that the legislation is an overreaction to a non-existent problem.**[51]

...

It is not an exaggeration to say that the limits imposed on citizens amount to a virtual ban on their participation in political debate during the election period. In actuality, the only space left in the marketplace of ideas is for political parties and their candidates. The right of each citizen to have her voice heard, so vaunted in Figueroa, supra, is effectively negated unless the citizen is able or willing to speak through a political party.[52]

On draconian limits:

There is no demonstration that limits this draconian are required to meet the perceived dangers of inequality, an uninformed electorate and the public perception that the system is unfair. On the contrary, the measures may themselves exacerbate these dangers. Citizens who cannot effectively communicate with others on electoral issues may feel they are being treated unequally compared to citizens who speak through political parties. The absence of their messages may result in the public being less well informed than it would otherwise be. And a process that bans citizens from effective participation in the electoral debate during an election campaign may well be perceived as unfair. These fears may be hypothetical, but no more so than the fears conjured by the Attorney General in support of the infringement.[53]

...

On the logical and intellectual errors of Justice Bastarache and the other majority justices:

Having had the advantage of reviewing the reasons of Bastarache J., we believe it is important to make three observations. First, whether or not citizens dispose of sufficient funds to meet or exceed the existing spending limits is irrelevant. What is important is that citizens have the capacity, should they so choose, to exercise their right to free political speech. The spending limits as they currently stand do not allow this. Instead, they have a chilling effect on political speech, forcing citizens into a Hobson's choice between not expressing themselves at all or having their voice reduced to a mere whisper. Faced with such options, citizens could not be faulted for choosing the former.[54]

Second, it is important to recognize that the spending limits do not constrain the right of only a few citizens to speak. They constrain the political speech of all Canadians, be they of superior or modest means. Whether it is a citizen incurring expenditures of $3001 for leafleting in her riding or a group of citizens pooling 1501 individual contributions of $100 to run a national advertising campaign, the Charter protects the right to free political speech.[55]

Spending restrictions in 2006 election: citizens v. political parties

	Allowed to a citizen or citizens' group under the *Elections Act*	Allowed to a *political party* with full candidate list
Allowed *per riding* (average)	$571	$59,172
Allowed *nationally*	$172,050	$18,225,260
RATIO	1	106
Amount spent annually* on advertising in general in Canada[56]	$5,110,000,000 (or $16,590,000 per riding)	

Sources: Elections Canada and Statistics Canada. Calculations by author. The allowable amounts are higher than the original 1997 legislation allowed as inflation adjustments occur with each election. *Latest year for which data is available from Statistics Canada.

Actual election spending in 2004 election

	ALL citizens/citizens' groups: TOTAL	ALL political parties: TOTAL
Average amount spent per riding	$2,314	$165,750
Total spent nationally	$712,730	$51,051,149

Sources: Elections Canada. Calculations by author. 2006 data not yet available.

Chapter 11

The Fumbling Fifth Estate:
Why some in the media drop the ball

Avoid labeling any specific bombing or other assault as a "terrorist act" unless it's attributed. For instance, we should refer to the deadly blast at that nightclub in Bali in October 2002 as an "attack," not as a "terrorist attack." The same applies to the Madrid train attacks in March 2004, the London bombings in July 2005 and the attacks against the United States in 2001, which the CBC prefers to call "the Sept. 11 attacks" or some similar expression.... The guiding principle should be that we don't judge specific acts as "terrorism" or people as "terrorists." Such labels must be attributed. [1]
    ~ A memorandum distributed to CBC staff, July 2005

An act of Jewish terrorism.[2]
    ~ Israeli Prime Minister Ariel Sharon, September 2005, after a West Bank settler killed four Palestinians in Shilo

Terrorism.[3]
    ~ Palestinian leader Mahmoud Abbas, December 2005, on a Palestinian suicide bomber who killed five Israelis in Netanya

What We Have Here Is a Failure to Analyze:
Example 1–the Sgro Scandal

"Judy Sgro lost her job as Canada's immigration minister because she resigned to defend herself against scurrilous allegations of misconduct,"[4] argued *Globe and Mail* columnist Jeffrey Simpson in a May 2005 essay entitled "Does politics mean never having to say you're sorry?"[5]

The Simpson column stemmed from a multiple-month opposition and media pounding against Sgro in late 2004 when it was revealed that Ihor Wons, Sgro's chief of staff, met with two stripclub owners in their establishments just before the previous election to discuss stripper immigration to Canada. That was what first landed Sgro in scalding political water. Odd as it was for a top bureaucrat to meet with concerned citizens in their place of work, the chief's bad judgment wasn't cause for Sgro's resignation and properly she refused to step down.

But what occurred next was an abuse of power and thus far more serious. After the "stripper story" broke, Sgro's political hires hinted to Ottawa media to back off the story or risk losing future inside scoops.[6] The same velvet-glove message was given to opposition members of Parliament as it concerned any special permits they might apply for one day on behalf of their constituents.[7]

Then there was the matter of a Pakistani businessman, Naseer Sadiq, who donated $5,000 to the minister's election campaign during the 2004 election but through one of Sgro's riding executives. It was an illegal campaign contribution under the rules written by the minister's own party. (The money was returned when the news became public, though the minister had earlier argued the money was not tainted.[8]) To cap off a bad run, allegations then floated to the surface from Harjit Singh, an immigrant pizza store owner about to be deported, who alleged the minister promised him he could stay in Canada if he provided pizza and campaign workers in exchange.

His allegation was false—he later admitted he never met Sgro, but coming after the other problems, they proved to be the tipping point for Sgro's resignation in early 2005. And there was one more difficulty: Sgro's office wouldn't break down the number of Temporary Resident Permits (TRP) on a per riding basis. The permits are discretionary and allow a minister to intervene in immigration cases for various reasons, humanitarian being the most obvious. But the hunch was that the immigration minister's riding or Liberal MPs might have been graced with a disproportionately large share.[a]

Several months after Sgro resigned, in May 2005, she then incorrectly claimed she had been exonerated, this based on a one-page letter from federal Ethics Commissioner Bernard Shapiro. That

a. These two allegations—that the minister's staff hinted that media and opposition MPs would pay a consequence, and that Sgro's staff could not break down the numbers—were not investigated by the ethics commissioner. As he noted in his June 2005 report, they were matters outside his jurisdiction. As for the allegation that "the Minister's agent accepted a $5,000 campaign donation from an individual named in her election return as Naseer Sadiq on behalf of Mr. Mohsin Sheikh," the commissioner noted this was true, though likely a violation of the *Elections Act*, not a violation of the Conflict of Interest Code, which empowered the commissioner.

provided the point of departure for Simpson, who then launched his politics-is-just-so-slimy missive in the *Globe*. Shapiro soon regretted the letter and for good reason: it was misinterpreted and it was bizarre of a commissioner to release a one-page excerpt of his thoughts one month in advance of the full report. In his letter to Sgro, the commissioner wrote that when the minister granted a TRP to immigrant Alina Balaican, the minister was unaware that Balaican also volunteered on Sgro's campaign; the minister's staff placed her in a conflict of interest. It cleared Sgro of intentional wrongdoing, but not the conflict of interest. That letter did not address any other complaint launched by the Opposition.[9]

On that basis, Simpson launched into rather un-*Globe*-like language—"scumbag" was his favourite term—while he simultaneously decried how politics was "now so venomous in Canada that the nastiest things can be said without anybody apologizing when the words are proven wrong."[10] Simpson then rhetorically queried why apologies were not forthcoming from Conservative leader Stephen Harper, newspaper editors who had "editorialized censoriously"[11] (in a manner Simpson would, of course, never do) or then prime minister Paul Martin.

Similarly, with reference to the one-page "exoneration," *Ottawa Citizen* columnist Susan Riley argued that "former immigration minister Judy Sgro is only one victim—an innocent one, as it turns out—of the debased and deteriorating atmosphere on Parliament Hill. It makes you wonder if yesterday's vindication is the first of many."[12]

In their rush to condemn their media colleagues and opposition parties, the *Globe* and *Citizen* pundits missed a few details. True, Sgro was falsely and maliciously accused by Singh. True, the ethics commissioner noted that it was Sgro's staff that placed her in a conflict of interest on the Balaican matter. But when ministerial responsibility once meant something, that would have been cause for a resignation. Sgro was owed a *mea culpa* on the Singh "pizza" lies—at least for anyone who based their criticism of the minister on that. But that was it. Yet outstanding were numerous and fair criticisms.

Contrary to the hasty exculpation by some, when the commissioner's gavel came down one month later there was no
exoneration. The ethics commissioner did find that during the
2004 federal election campaign, Sgro's ministry gave out 128
Temporary Residence Permits: 43 were handed out during the final week of the campaign. Seventy-four permits were granted for
requests from Liberal MPs, and two for Conservatives. Sgro was
"identified directly" with 24 permits, i.e., they were for people in
her riding.[13] The rush to hand out such permits occurred despite
early and laudable intentions to authorize as few as possible, precisely to avoid the charge of favouritism. Apparently that initial
preference collapsed as it upset a few of Sgro's parliamentary colleagues, which then led to the flurry of last-minute approvals.[14]

Sgro had a legal right and ministerial privilege to hand out 128
or 1,000 such permits. But the imbalance looked bad, especially
when a large chunk handed out were election-time dispensations
and coincidentally to Liberal MPs running for re-election. That
might explain why her staff balked at providing a per-riding breakdown. As the ethics commissioner noted, while only one worker
on Sgro's re-election campaign was given a special ministerial permit to stay in the country ...

*On the other hand, there appeared to be some indirect connec-
tion between working as a volunteer on the minister's campaign
and a benefit that might accrue to relatives, friends or specific
organization. In this context, there is, for example, the case of
Naseer Sadiq.*[15]

As it turned out, "$5,000" Sadiq sought and received TPRs for
six acquaintances.[16] Shapiro also found that Sgro's chief of staff,
Ihor Wons, who took a leave of absence from that position to
be involved in her re-election effort, "was active in managing
and promoting immigration cases when he should have been
limiting his own work to the re-election campaign and carefully
separating that responsibility from substantive ministerial and
departmental work."[17]

The commissioner also noted that "it was this very inability and/or unwillingness of Wons to separate himself from the department while he was working on the campaign that placed the Minister, with or without her knowledge, and however unintentionally, in the conflict of interest."[18]

THE SHAPIRO SHUFFLE: "NOT COMPLETELY NON-EXISTENT"

Shapiro argued it was "difficult to assess the extent to which the Minister was aware of Mr. Wons' inappropriate interventions and of the extent to which assistance in the campaign was used to make the case for Temporary Residence Permits for individuals usually related to someone working on Sgro's re-election campaign."[19] Nevertheless:

During Ms. Sgro's examination under oath when she was questioned, for example, regarding the issuance of TRPs for individuals wishing to attend the annual Ahmadiyya conference in July and, in particular, whether she was aware that anyone from that community was assisting on her campaign, she responded: "There was a representative who was assisting—I don't know how much, but that he was assisting on our campaign in one form or another, that was part of the organization of this conference but that was something that is done every year as far as assisting."

When Ms. Sgro was asked to confirm whether she knew if one or more of these individuals were working on her campaign, she replied: "I don't know if he was working on the campaign but he is someone we know very well. I can only assume that he would have given us some hours of volunteer time."

And finally, when questioned whether she knew these individuals were looking for assistance on the conference and at the same time working on the campaign, she replied: "I wasn't connecting the two," and "Probably ... I expect so."

With respect to specific cases, I have not been able to verify the circumstances in each instance. My judgement is that the Minister's knowledge of specific instances where those seeking permits or their sponsors were also working on her campaign seems limited, but is not completely non-existent.[20]

The commissioner noted that he was unable to determine "in each case whether there was a relationship between the person being given the permit and persons active in Ms Sgro's re-election campaign and, if that was the case, whether Minister Sgro was aware of this relationship."[21] Still, while "the main burden of responsibility for this conflict of interest environment appears to lie with the minister's staff, primarily Mr. Ihor Wons,"[22] this did "not absolve her of major responsibility; after all, it was on her direct authorization that the TRPs were issued."[23] Shapiro:

As is clearly outlined in Governing Responsibly: A Guide for Ministers and Ministers of State: "Ministers are individually responsible to Parliament and the Prime Minister for their own actions and those of their department including the actions of all officials under their management and direction, whether or not the ministers had prior knowledge."[24]

In particular, not only was Minister Sgro listed as the sponsoring MP in rather more cases than might have been expected, but also the permits themselves seemed available not to donors or individuals listed as volunteers directly but to the relatives and associates of those who were assisting the re-election campaign. This was in clear violation of Principle 7 of the Conflict of Interest Code for Public Office Holders.[25]

The veiled hints from Sgro's staff to media about access cut-offs and to the opposition about their requests for special ministerial permits, and the illegal $5,000 donation by a volunteer were all serious allegations—and which later turned out to be true. But as allegations, they were substantive and serious enough for Opposition members of Parliament and the editorial pages to call for Sgro to step down, quite apart from some later wacky accusation by a fellow about to be deported. All of that was known when Simpson and Riley wrote their columns. (Ethics Commissioner Bernard Shapiro had his ethical problems for which to answer, including why he hired a Liberal-connected law firm to investigate the Liberal member of Parliament.[26])

The Simpson–Riley condemnation was evidence of a failure to analyze legitimate concerns distinct from the spurious "pizza" allegation. In so doing, newspapers of record and their columnists gave the public the wrong impression that Sgro was the victim of a smear campaign and her resignation was unjustified. Far from it and far from being "scurrilous," the allegations were worthy of a cabinet minister's resignation.

But the failure of analysis prompted by impatience and likely a desire to save a decent person's political reputation was not the only recent example; other recent missteps have had a more damaging effect on public attitudes and policy.

A Failure To Analyze: Example 2–How the Media Fell for Rotten Numbers

If Simpson too hastily exonerated the minister of immigration, some in the media err when they quickly print numbers and paste them on the front pages of newspapers. It's another example of the failure of analysis in Canada's fifth estate.

One widespread example of this occurs whenever the Consumers' Association of Canada (CAC) publishes reports that purport to compare automobile insurance costs across Canada. "Drivers pay far more for private-sector vehicle insurance, consumer study says,"[27] headlined the *Halifax Daily News* in September 2003. "Ontario motorists saddled with skyrocketing insurance: Consumer study finds that Toronto drivers can pay 500 per cent more than other regions,"[28] claimed the *Charlottetown Guardian* based on the same study. "Insuring car can cost 6 times as much in TO"[29] repeated the *Montreal Gazette*, while the *Vancouver Province* blazed "Public auto insurance 'a big saver.'"[30] Even the *National Post* financial section, the *Financial Post*, put the CAC study front and centre: "Toronto drivers pay up to 500% more for auto insurance,"[31] said the prominent headline. One exception was Terence Corcoran in the *National Post*, who argued, sarcastically, about the CAC's numbers, "If it's in a [Canadian Press] news story, it must be true."[32] And about the only balanced headline came from the *Vancouver Sun*: "Private auto insurers accused of gouging."[33]

"Accused" was the right description. The CAC study had multiple errors that led to useless inter-provincial comparisons. It was a case of "junk in, junk out" and also of bought-and-paid-for advocacy but wrapped up in the pretension of neutral analysis.

Hilariously, unlike many reporters and front-page editors, even a director for the Consumers' Association didn't buy the data. While the CAC's national and B.C. office argued Ontario drivers paid almost $2,500 on average to insure their cars, trucks and SUVs, the president of the Ontario wing, Theresa Courneyea, said accurate research from her provincial wing showed an average Ontario insurance premium was $1,310.

The group's national study was faulty, noted Courneyea, because the Ottawa/B.C. office used Internet quotes. In contrast, Courneyea and Ontario Consumers' branch used government data and updated it; so CAC-Ontario's more accurate price was almost *half* the number the national office peddled in its statistically invalid studies.

Another problem with the CAC's national comparisons was that 50 per cent of their Ontario examples assumed a past claim or conviction. Not surprisingly, that boosted the average CAC estimate as past claims and convictions make for more expensive insurance quotes. That was a useful statistical assumption if one wanted to make it look like Ontarians were being gouged by insurance companies. But in the real-world population, only 11 per cent of Ontario drivers had a past claim or conviction.[34] With reference to the Consumers' Association national office and its exaggerated averages for drivers, Courneyea said her Ontario wing "doesn't use anything they've done."[35]

The inflated Ontario numbers were not the only flawed quotes from the Consumers' Association. In a comparison of the four western provinces, the group argued average consumers in private-sector Alberta paid twice as much as those who bought from government-run insurance companies in the other three jurisdictions. But that claim was based, again, on Internet quotes and also on the *median* number.[b] With a median quote, half the prices were above the one publicly published by the CAC price and half were below. In Alberta,

b. In 2003, I asked the CAC's national president for all the prices, i.e., the range of low to high prices used in his study. Bruce Cran refused to release them, or any other data, as he did again in 2005.

where the association obtained 10 different prices for various categories, it meant the CAC actually found four or five prices for each category that were lower than the median price it contrasted with other provinces, but they only published the mid-range quote.

The Consumers' Association wouldn't release the full range of prices to this author or anyone else. No mystery as to why: all else being equal, most drivers don't choose the fifth- or sixth-highest-priced policy from 10 quotes; most choose the lowest. If the lobby group revealed the range it would reveal that at least some insurance companies in the private sector beat rates in government-insured provinces. It would also pop the errant claim by the CAC that consumers were gouged in Ontario, Alberta and in Atlantic Canada.[c]

Because the group wouldn't make its data available and the media never bothered to query the Consumers' Association about its methods, the public was left to assume private insurance provinces were expensive. Extreme examples served as hyped assumptions about everyone's insurance, and averages from quotes were assumed to be representative of what people paid in the real world.

Not that it mattered; once the headlines appeared, the public was left with the intended impression advanced by the CAC: insurance was a great deal in provinces where the government sold all or basic automotive insurance.[d]

c. As an example, the CAC claimed that a 42-year-old female (with a 1996 Mazda Miata and one claim) had a median insurance quote of about $1,800 in Alberta compared to just over $1,500 in British Columbia. But because the Consumers' Association used the median quote it tacitly admitted *that it found at least four quotes that were below that "$1,800" Alberta "price,"* and possibly some that fell below the B.C. cost of insurance.

d. When the Consumers' Association refused to release their data, I asked Canadian Direct (which offers full insurance in Alberta and optional coverage in B.C.) to provide quotes for all 34 Consumers' Association-created categories for Alberta and to obtain the government rates for B.C. The results: out of five Alberta cities surveyed by the consumer group (and now by Canadian Direct) with 34 examples each (for a total of 170), *consumers could buy insurance cheaper in 137 cases in Alberta and only in 33 in Vancouver.* In a direct city comparison, consumers could pay less in 25 of the 34 categories if they were insured by Canadian Direct in Calgary as opposed to the government-run auto insurer in Vancouver. Those comparisons were made using the very categories created by Consumers' Association and from which it claimed prices were twice as high "on average" in Alberta as in other provinces. I compared B.C.'s rates with only *one* private insurance company though there were hundreds of other Alberta insurance companies. There was and is an excellent chance that Albertans might well be able to find a price that beats B.C. in most categories.

2005 INSURANCE FOLLIES: MORE APPLES, MORE ORANGES

In 2005, it was more CAC auto insurance studies, more misleading numbers and more hyped and inaccurate headlines.

"Ontario drivers pay through roof: Insurance $1,000 more than in B.C., study says,"[36] claimed the *North Bay Nugget* in July 2005. "Auto insurance cheaper in B.C. than Alberta,"[37] proclaimed the *Globe and Mail*. "Outrageous costs hammer Ontario drivers,"[38] noted the *National Post*. The *Calgary Herald* announced "Albertans pay more, consumer study finds."[39] Over in B.C., the papers gloated: "B.C. drivers pay less than Albertans for car insurance,"[40] said the *Victoria Times Colonist*. In a line paraphrased from a children's fairy tale—appropriate given the hollow claim—the *Vancouver Province* praised government auto insurance: "ICBC fairest in the land,"[41] and, added the tabloid in a sub-title, "Study gives public auto coverage top grade."[42]

Once again, newspaper headlines led the public to think the Consumers' Association studies were credible—why, the survey even "analysed 800,000 auto insurance quotes for 300 driver profiles in 219 communities in the two provinces,"[43] exclaimed the *Edmonton Journal*. A *National Post* reporter swallowed the bait and, based upon the cross-country comparison, wrote that the review of rates was "the largest such study done in Canada, [and] is based on nearly four million quotes across 300 different rating groups in Ontario, Alberta and British Columbia."[44]

The 2005 Consumers' Association auto insurance comparisons appeared comprehensive only until one drilled down into the data, which few reporters or editors did. The glaring statistical flaw in the "new and improved" CAC studies were the same as in the 2003 comparisons: the use of quotes to come up with averages instead of actual policy premiums paid by real drivers in the real world.

To understand why that's a problem, consider the following example. Suppose three drivers paid $1,000, $1,500 and $5,000 respectively. Divide the total ($7,500) by the number of insurance policies (three); the average premium is $2,500.

The CAC method to calculate averages was to obtain Internet quotes, say five: $1,000, $1,500, $3,000, $4,000 and $5,000. The result was an average price of $2,900. Even if one removes the lowest and highest prices (as did the CAC in their 2005 insurance studies), do the math and the average in this example is $2,833.[e]

But whether one uses three, five or the CAC's almost four million Internet quotes, the averages are always unreliable "ghost" comparisons because they're not based on what drivers actually pay in the real world. It wouldn't matter how many quotes were fed into a computer to spit out an average; the results mean nothing and represent nothing. It was as if, to find the average price of a "widget" sold on eBay, one had totaled all the bids and spit out an average based on that instead of calculating it from what buyers actually paid.

That's how the CAC claimed an average insurance premium was $2,383 in Ontario and $1,714 in Alberta in 2005 while the bullet-proof industry numbers were significantly lower at $1,279 and $1,127 respectively.[45]

In response to the criticism, CAC president Bruce Cran argued his methodology was "fully reviewed by a professor of actuarial science and confirmed as being valid."[46] All that meant was that four million Internet quotes were properly added up and then divided to arrive at an average. The CAC also claimed that its insurance studies measure what identical drivers would pay in each of the provinces. Except they didn't. To properly do that, the consumer group needed to use actual prices paid for by drivers in private- sector provinces. Instead, the CAC took wildly varying Internet quotes, which are the insurance equivalent of opening bids on eBay.

Most of the media overlooked the critical distinction and was suckered for the second time in three years. They also missed another obvious point: when government-run auto insurance companies such as British Columbia's calculate the average paid premium, they add up the total value of all premiums paid and then divide by the number of policyholders to arrive at a real-world average.[47] Likewise, when the CAC calculated averages for

e. One could play the opposite game with numbers. If one could find five quotes that were $2,000, $800, $700, $600 and $500, the average insurance quote would be dramatically low: $920. And it would be no more reflective of the real world because the average still starts with quotes, not actual premiums paid.

public-sector provinces, their numbers came from quotes that were exactly identical to what people would pay in the real world—*since in government-run systems, where basic insurance can only be bought from government, there is no other quote that matters.* That meant the CAC used wildly varying Internet quotes—"apples"—to arrive at averages in private-sector provinces, but used actual prices paid in public sector provinces—"oranges."

The CAC set out to prove private insurance was a bad deal and compared apples (bids) with oranges (actual prices) to do it; it's how the faux-consumers' organization claims that government auto insurance is a swell deal. It was never an accurate or statistically honest claim.[f]

PEEKING BEHIND THE WIZARD'S CURTAIN

The insurance industry's interests are obvious but they, unlike the CAC, provide requested information. The only time the Consumers' Association provided any comment to this author (but no data) was in 2003. The results were not flattering for Cran. Then Ontario director Theresa Courneyea said Cran's insurance comparisons "violate arithmetic" and "slant the picture."[48] That provincial branch even wrote the *Globe and Mail* to dispute a story published about the CAC national office's numbers in 2003. Courneyea noted the more accurate estimate was $1,310, not $2,504 as claimed by Cran, a figure that CAC-Ontario labeled "excessive."[49]

If the Ontario director for the Consumers' Association of Canada was frank and could point out the statistical flaws most media missed, there was another angle that most reporters forgot to explore: what is the CAC, who do they represent and where do they get their money? Some news outlets assumed the organization must be a straight-shooter because it claimed to represent consumers. Some newspapers troubled themselves to obtain

---

f. The CAC has long claimed that private-sector insurance is a rotten deal and often uses this example. As proof, the group gives the example of how Saskatchewan drivers on the Saskatchewan–Alberta border city of Lloydminster pay much less than those on the Alberta side. But here's what their studies do not point out: the average payout claim in Saskatchewan is $4,135 compared to $11,895 in Alberta. Differences in payouts affect premiums, though for reasons noted above, not to the extent of the CAC's exaggerated averages.

comment from more independent sources, the Insurance Bureau of Canada and the Fraser Institute, both of which disputed the Consumers' Association numbers, though that was never obvious from the headlines.

Some in the media played into stereotypes instead of asking rudimentary, sensible questions. In Sault Ste. Marie, the *Sault Star* looked at the Consumers' Association study and industry numbers and decided the proper way to parse through the forest of data for accuracy was to rely on the brand name:

What to make of these conflicting numbers? Consider the sources. The Consumers' Association of Canada represents, as the name implies, consumers. It has no stake in massaging or misrepresenting the results of its survey, which examined 2,973,980 auto insurance quotes in 357 Ontario communities and compared them with 803,017 quotes in 219 communities across Alberta and British Columbia. The Insurance Board of Canada, meanwhile, represents Canada's largest insurance agencies.[50]

Except that the industry was required to file its numbers and background data with government regulators and thus could be checked for accuracy and the Consumers' Association of Canada didn't represent many consumers, if any. In a 2003 interview, the then volunteer Alberta CAC director claimed the entire organization represented at most only 2,500 people, though he admitted even that was a ballpark figure.[51]

As for funding, the CAC has been in existence for five decades and mostly lives off taxpayer funds, though it now receives far less funding than it once did. Between 1989 and 1996, various CAC offices across Canada received over $5.5 million from Industry Canada. Between 2000 and 2003, its Ottawa office—the one that produced the faulty insurance studies—received almost $700,000 from taxpayers, courtesy of Industry Canada. In 2004, the CAC received at least $80,000 for its (then upcoming 2005) study on auto insurance rates (which cost $200,000 to create[52]); in 2005, two CAC offices received another $63,960 in government funds.[53]

In contrast to Greenpeace or the National Citizens Coalition or other advocacy groups that rely only on memberships and not government funds, groups such as the Consumers' Association can produce their flawed studies only because governments—and others—give them money to do so.

In an open letter published on its website, the CAC claimed its policy was to "not release its funding sources in order to conform with privacy legislation in Canada and to respect the confidentiality of its contributors."[54] This was diversionary smoke. Privacy legislation doesn't prevent any group from revealing how much they receive in general, i.e., $"x" amount from business, "this amount" from government and "that amount" from unions.

Coincidentally, in the same letter in which the Consumers' Association acknowledged government funds (a fact never printed in its studies, despite a requirement by Industry Canada), the CAC did proudly state: "We do not accept funding from industry."[55] Missing from the after-the-fact acknowledgment of government funds and an upfront note about no corporate money was any mention of union financial support—say, public-sector labour in British Columbia, Saskatchewan or other provinces where such unions have members who work for government-run auto insurance companies.

Contrary to the naïve belief of the *Sault Star*, if the CAC received funds from government unions—which might explain how it filled in the gap between what it received from government ($80,000) and what it spent on its 2005 studies ($200,000)—that would contradict the *Star*'s assertion that the Consumers' Association of Canada had "no stake in massaging or misrepresenting the results of its survey." When asked about just such funding, the response from CAC president Cran was blunt: "I won't give you anything; you can print that."[56]

Small membership numbers, government transfers and union cash from the public sector do not necessarily mean an organization produced error-prone research. Two plus two still equals four even if the whole world believes it adds up to five. But the CAC's data, methods, assumptions and auto insurance comparisons didn't withstand even a cursory examination.

POSTSCRIPT ON CHOICE AND COMPETITION

In their studies, the CAC was properly critical of insurance brokers in private sector provinces who sell policies from only one or two insurers. Ironically, the Consumers' Association solution is to kill competition and have just one insurer: government. The industry also has its bias. The Insurance Bureau of Canada favours the status quo in private sector provinces where, for example, banks cannot sell insurance directly to consumers, or tie insurance to discounts on other products. That's also an anti-competitive stance. Both the Insurance Bureau and the CAC ought to be pro-consumer, but that requires dropping self-interest and ideology and endorsing choice and wide-open competition.

As for the media, with apologies to Winston Churchill, never have so many done so little investigative work and asked so few questions—and produced such misleading headlines for a product bought by almost every Canadian.

A Failure to Analyze: Example 3—The CBC's Incurious Approach to George

In May 2005, two different media sources took distinctly different approaches to a controversial public figure, George Galloway, and his testimony before a U.S. Senate committee. The British member of Parliament appeared in Washington, D.C., to answer charges he took illicit money in the U.N. oil-for-food scandal. Television networks were there to record the anticipated fireworks; another observer, a Brit now based in Washington, also tracked the testimony. If there were any Canadians who yet wondered whether some of their more high-profile state television reporters have an obvious bias, the Senate hearings revealed that, yes, some wear it on their sleeve.

Up first for analysis is CBC-TV reporter Neil MacDonald. CBC anchor Peter Mansbridge framed the story this way: "We take you ringside now for a verbal dust-up over the Iraq Oil for Food scandal."[57] With the image of dueling boxers, Mansbridge described the combatants and, in Galloway's case, let the British M.P. off the hook in advance. "In one corner, a U.S. Senate sub-committee looking into who pilfered the missing billions," read Mansbridge. "In the other, George Galloway, anti-war politician from Britain accused of profiting from the program. His name is already cleared back home. As Neil MacDonald tells us, it hardly seemed like a fair fight."

The National then cut to MacDonald in the American capital. He noted the committee's charges and Galloway's responses, but then, as did Mansbridge in his introduction, never informed the viewer even in passing as to the existence of evidence (beyond the committee's) that might hint that Galloway was less than candid in his Senate testimony. In fact, CBC didn't even bother to air clips of any senator who might outline the case against Galloway, or someone who could provide balance and give context for how the committee obtained its information, reached its conclusions and what the strong and weak points of the Senate's case against Galloway might be.

Instead, the CBC piece became a cute game of MacDonald setting up Galloway as the charming, blustery, no-nonsense Scottish rogue against the Keystone Cop senators. After playing a clip of Galloway's you-lied-about-Iraqi-weapons-of-mass-destruction statement—which ignored the fact every intelligence service on the planet thought Saddam Hussein possessed them before the war, including the anti-Iraq-war French government—Neil MacDonald gave this brief rundown of the charges before he concentrated on the fluff of the appearance as opposed to the substance of the charges against Galloway:

NEIL MACDONALD: The Senate committee had accused Galloway, a British M.P., of accepting bribes from Saddam Hussein through the Oil for Food program. He denies it. In fact, he says, it's American payback for his anti-war activity.

GEORGE GALLOWAY: Now, you have nothing on me, Senator, except my name on lists of names from Iraq, many of which have been drawn up after the installation of your puppet government in Baghdad.

Chapter 11

MACDONALD: The committee says Galloway was an outspoken supporter of Saddam Hussein whom the committee says he visited many times.

GALLOWAY: As a matter of fact, I've met Saddam Hussein exactly the same number of times as Donald Rumsfeld met him. The difference is Donald Rumsfeld met him to sell him guns.

MACDONALD: The Senators, perhaps realizing what they had on their hands, tried to rein him in.

UNIDENTIFIED MAN: I'm looking for either a yes or no.

MACDONALD: Not likely.

GALLOWAY: Senator, this is the mother of all smoke screens. Have a look at the 14 months you were in charge of Baghdad, the first 14 months, when $8.8 billion of Iraq's wealth went missing on your watch.

MACDONALD: No response to that or to Galloway's challenge that they prove he took any money. Instead, after about an hour ...

UNIDENTIFIED MAN: You're excused, Mr. Galloway.

MACDONALD: And unlikely to be recalled. Neil MacDonald, CBC News, Washington.[58]

Television reporters cannot do *Atlantic Monthly*-type 10-page analyses of an issue in the manner available to authors, magazine scribes or even a newspaper reporter. But they can, if they choose, provide context and alternative voices on the likely veracity of someone like Galloway—if they bother. In CBC's case, there was no effort, though an opposing, informed viewpoint was easy to find. As it happened, there was another high-profile Brit in Washington the day Galloway testified. He had the requisite left-wing credentials that would appeal to CBC reporters and producers,[g] had lived in D.C. for some time, showed up to the Galloway testimony, and was every bit as entertaining on television as the Scottish M.P.

In contrast to the CBC puff job on Galloway, British author and columnist Christopher Hitchens, present at Galloway's May hearing, detailed the curious life of George later that month. Hitchens was hardly an apologist for conservatism, neo- or otherwise, or American Republicans. While Hitchens' support of the Iraq war was constant before and after the 2003 invasion, the writer had long been known for his independent mind. He once excoriated Mother Teresa in a book and was widely loved by the Left for his polemic on Richard Nixon's secretary of state, *The Trial of Henry Kissinger*. Hitchens still subscribed to some left-wing ideals, though he thought the same faction mostly daft at best or naïve, and culpable at worst, in its current approach to anti-liberal tyrants such as Saddam Hussein and radical anti-Western ideologies such as Islamism.

In his comments on Galloway, Hitchens threw cold water on the claim by some (and echoed by Mansbridge-MacDonald) that Galloway had been "exonerated":

He has, for example, temporarily won a libel case against the Daily Telegraph *in London, which printed similar documents about him that were found in the Oil Ministry just after the fall of Baghdad. The newspaper claimed a public-interest defense, and did not explicitly state that the documents were genuine. Galloway, for his part, carefully did not state that they were false, either. The case has now gone to appeal.*

g. An example of this bias can be found in Lydia Miljan and Barry Cooper's book, *Hidden Agenda: How Journalists Influence the News*. The political science professors had Compas pollsters ask Canada's media about their political affiliations. In 1997, fully three-quarters of the respondents at CBC radio cast their vote for the NDP compared to only 11 per cent of the general population that voted for New Democrats. In general among the media, the authors found that the only political party media respondents supported in greater proportion than the general public was the left-wing New Democrats. As for the CBC, they noted in a 2005 Fraser Institute study on anti-Americanism at CBC's *The National* that negative statements about the United States outnumbered positive statements by more than a two-to-one margin in 2002. In other words, the CBC has to try to be balanced when it reports on the U.S. Without it, the bias takes over.

Indeed, had Mansbridge or his script writer wanted to know the above fact, they could have and such knowledge would perhaps have tempered their enthusiastic Galloway-has-already-been-cleared-back-home preemptive public relations advocacy on his behalf. Normally, reporters are skeptical and couch their language if there is the slightest doubt about a person's veracity or about the propriety of using definitive language. Not Mansbridge and MacDonald on Galloway. In contrast, Hitchens detailed what was already known and beyond the in-court *Daily Telegraph* story:

> *Here then are these facts, as we know them without his help. In 1998, Galloway founded something, easily confused with a charity, known as the Mariam Appeal. The ostensible aim of the appeal was to provide treatment in Britain for a 4-year-old Iraqi girl named Mariam Hamza, who suffered from leukemia.... A letter exists, on House of Commons writing paper, signed by Galloway and appointing Fawaz Zureikat as his personal representative in Iraq, on any and all matters connected to the Mariam Appeal.*

Zureikat was well connected to Saddam Hussein's regime and was handed several lucrative oil-for-food contracts by the regime. In October 2005, the United Nations report on the oil-for-food scandal had this to say about Zureikat and Galloway:

> *A total of over 18 million barrels of oil were allocated either directly in the name of George Galloway, a member of the British Parliament, or in the name of one of his associates, Fawaz Abdullah Zureikat, to support Mr. Galloway's campaign against the sanctions. Mr. Zuerikat was a prominent Jordanian businessman. Mr. Zuerikat received commissions for handling the sale of approximately 11 million barrels of oil that were allocated in Mr. Galloway's name.*[59]

While *that* report was yet in the future when the CBC aired its Galloway report, Hitchens didn't have foreknowledge either, but was still able to detail Galloway in this manner promptly after his

Senate testimony earlier that year in May and far in advance of the U.N. report:

Although it was briefly claimed by one of its officers that the Appeal raised most of its money from ordinary citizens, Galloway has since testified that the bulk of the revenue came from the ruler of the United Arab Emirates and from a Saudi prince. He has also conceded that Zureikat was a very generous donor. The remainder of the funding is somewhat opaque, since the British Charity Commissioners, who monitor such things, began an investigation in 2003. This investigation was inconclusive. The commissioners were able to determine that the Mariam Appeal, which had used much of its revenue for political campaigning, had not but ought to have been legally registered as a charity. They were not able to determine much beyond this, because it was then announced that the account books of the Appeal had been removed, first to Amman, Jordan, and then to Baghdad. This is the first charity or proto-charity in history to have disposed of its records in that way.

... Galloway is not supposed by anyone to have been an oil trader. He is asked, simply, to say what he knows about his chief fundraiser, nominee, and crony. And when asked this, he flatly declines to answer.

We are therefore invited by [Galloway] to assume that, having earlier acquired a justified reputation for loose bookkeeping in respect of "charities," he switched sides in Iraq, attached himself to a regime known for giving and receiving bribes, appointed a notorious middleman as his envoy, kept company with the corrupt inner circle of the Baath party, helped organize a vigorous campaign to retain that party in power, and was not a penny piece the better off for it.

I think I believe this as readily as any other reasonable and objective person would. If you wish to pursue the matter with Galloway himself, you will have to find the unlisted number for his villa in Portugal.[60]

Television reporters don't have the luxury of long essays on such charges. But the CBC and MacDonald left viewers with the impression that Galloway was "cleared back home" as of the date of the Senate committee hearing.

Hardly. And it was worth at least a throwaway line that Galloway had very questionable friends, that they and he were under investigation by the U.N., and that Galloway had a history of being disingenuous. But that wouldn't have produced the "good cop" Galloway versus the "bad cop" White House neo-con story the CBC wanted that day.

The CBC and "Terrorism"

While the CBC could confidently pronounce, contrary to the facts, that George Galloway's name was "already cleared back home," Canada's state broadcaster becomes oh-so-cautious not to label acts of terrorism, well, terrorism, as evidenced by this July 2005 memorandum to CBC staff.

> *Avoid labeling any specific bombing or other assault as a "terrorist act" unless it's attributed. For instance, we should refer to the deadly blast at that nightclub in Bali in October 2002 as an "attack," not as a "terrorist attack." The same applies to the Madrid train attacks in March 2004, the London bombings in July 2005 and the attacks against the United States in 2001, which the CBC prefers to call "the Sept. 11 attacks" or some similar expression... The guiding principle should be that we don't judge specific acts as "terrorism" or people as "terrorists." Such labels must be attributed.*[61]

That memo was not the first time the CBC was reluctant to label suicide-bombers and others as terrorists. The state-funded broadcaster tussled with reporters and columnists in the past over the issue. CBC's problem is not unique; some private-sector news organizations have the same policy. But where it appears, it is less than helpful. At least one purpose of language is to communicate and do so clearly. When that doesn't happen, communication is hampered.

Many in the media properly object and "get this" when war departments use euphemisms to describe the brutal realities of combat: "collateral damage" instead of civilian casualties. To cloud a description of terror is no more proper when performed by the CBC. It offends the purpose of language and moral sensibilities at the same time. Morally descriptive neutrality on such a subject is probably the most deadly neglect of proper analysis in which a media outlet can engage.

Such diversions are an annoyance at a business meeting; it's deadening to the moral senses of the citizenry when the issue is terrorism. CBC's policy on terrorism is reflective of a deeper problem and it stems from moral confusion, ambivalence, nihilism, post-modern prattle about the inability to be objective or all of the preceding. There *are* issues and events that defy easy labels, but direct, purposed attacks on civilians—whether in Munich in 1972 or Madrid in 2004—are properly described as terror; to use any other label plays into the hands of those who use language to obscure rather than to illuminate.

Ten Reasons Why the Media Sometimes Miss the Story: Practical and "Postman"

My two-decade involvement with the media has placed me on both sides of the microphone. *For what it's worth*, here are my observations on why the media sometimes miss the real story:

1. There is no *one* "media bias," not in any monolithic sense, though the terms, solely or together—"media" and "media bias" is necessarily used in *general* fashion by everyone, including this author. However, every individual journalist has a bias, whether they're aware of it or not. Whether that's a problem depends on the individual journalist. (Columnists display their biases quite openly—as they should; that's why they're columnists.) Bias only injures the public interest when reporters and others make little or no attempt to understand the subject beyond their initial sympathies.

2. There is also no vast conspiracy, left or right, though some data indicates that many reporters and others lean further to the left

on economic matters than does the general public; on religious, social and cultural issues, many are simply tone-deaf.

3. On economics, the bias for government intervention exists partly because reporters need on-the-record comment and there is a tendency to seek out politicians or government spokespeople to find out "what government is doing about this problem." That's true even if a particular malady may be better dealt with by the non-profit or private sector. And because governments have spokespeople on almost every topic—and when they don't, the assumed question is "why is the ministry/this politician not dealing with 'X' ?"—reporters phone up the spokesperson most likely to give a quick comment. Beyond bias, on a two- or three-hour deadline, it's the nature of the beast.

4. There is the problem of "blind spots," both individual and corporate. When I began a five-year stint with the Canadian Taxpayers Federation, a prominent columnist told me to remember two facts: journalists are lazy and many don't understand what "the numbers" mean. I'll reserve comment on the first criticism, as it is an unfair generalization, but the second is accurate.

It's not always the fault of a particular scribe: whatever is taught in journalism schools, it's not the latest economic theories; even younger journalists may absorb warmed-over 1960s assumptions from their professors and they are generally anti-market in their orientation. The errant beliefs include (but are not limited to) the fallacy that if someone is poor it *must* be because someone else has gained at their expense—the zero-sum fallacy about wealth.[h]

If media outlets want more accurate reporting on an issue as it concerns dollars and cents, tax policy, fiscal and monetary policy or other issues, higher salaries are in order: a young person with a Master's degree in Economics, Science or History is not

---

h. It can be true on occasion; if a used car salesman sells a lemon, the customer will be poor and the salesman "rich," and at each other's expense. But general wealth creation does not conform to this model.

likely to seek a job with a newspaper, even in a major city, because they don't pay competitively. This is in contrast to some British broadsheets where reporters and editors are hired precisely for their advanced degrees in history, foreign policy and economics. Newspapers and owners that focus on simply putting words on a page as opposed to content do a disservice to their readers.

5. A related and particularly Canadian problem is that because ownership restrictions limit who can purchase our media publications, few people or companies can buy them outright without debt. That means money that could be invested in higher staffing levels and more in-depth reporting is instead spent on debt interest. Concentration of ownership is not the problem many assume, but a high level of debt associated with that ownership *is*.

6. On bias, observers should recall that like attracts like; journalists, editors and producers do "conspire" in the sense that if they think an angle or viewpoint needs to be trumpeted, they can and do make that happen. Sometimes that's unfair, sometimes it's a correction of a previous bias. So prejudice can and does exist, but it's not always the sole or most relevant explanation; sometimes a more banal reason explains coverage (or not) or a particular angle, as do cultural assumptions.

    This is most evident on socio-cultural-religious issues. If a reporter is a secular, upper middle-class urban male who has never lived off the North American continent, he may not care or understand deep national or religious currents that have carved out politics in Indonesia, China or Israel. Ignorance, in the non-accusatory sense of that word, often explains more than intention. When it's not that, it's a faulty approach to discourse based on either moral relativism or a loose post-modern view of the world that assumes there is no truth (thus CBC's problem with how to label obvious terrorist acts). Oddly, for journalists, who think of themselves as truth-seekers, it's not always clear they understand their own metaphysical assumptions and how such assumptions affect the stories they write and file.

So those who have never been to a church or a mosque will misunderstand religious folk; conversely, those deeply religious can mistake ignorance of their faith for hostility when some reporters may merely be bewildered because they have no context in which to place belief in the supernatural. The problem also exists in reverse. Many religious people cannot get beyond clichés or partisan religious affiliation to explain why a reporter should be concerned with their issue.

For example, one can oppose torture in Sudan or repressive Saudi Arabian policies because one believes men and women are made in the image of God and such suffering insults and destroys that unique, sacred creation. The basis of such opposition will reflect the religious beliefs of some people. But the explanation misses the key point—and one that all manner of people might embrace: torture and a repression of the right to choose one's own faith are wrong not just because they affect one's own religion or one's view of the universe. Christians, Muslims, Jews, other religious people, agnostics and atheists should oppose state restrictions on one's choice of faith (or not) and worse measures because such actions are a denial of human choice, a repression of the human spirit.

And *that* is how those with faith should express it: *"My" concern stems not only from a restriction on my human freedom but because this is deeply offensive to human rights for all.* In a pluralistic society, citizens of all beliefs should, quite properly, persuade others of the merits of their position *not based on sectarian appeals but on how it offends the values civilized people have in common, regardless of the origin of those norms*—the Enlightenment or a particular religion. Everyone except a tyrant has an interest in an end to torture, child slavery, the abuse of women, the smashing of the human spirit; not everyone has an interest in the success or failure of a particular religion or worldview.

7. Some journalists suffer from a lack of historical context. One example is in environmental reporting. That modern Western democracies are friendlier to and spend more on the environment than in any other age is an observable fact; but a 22-year-old

reporter without any historical context can be forgiven for hyping the latest alarmist study from an environmental group because he is unaware of the progress that has occurred. The reporter doesn't know that smog levels in Los Angeles today are dramatically below what they were 25 years ago or that cars pollute much less now than in the 1970s.[i] He is probably unaware of how London was soot-filled in the 19th century compared to today. Such historical facts are too often forgotten because they were never known in the first place, much less admitted by the chorus of Cassandras. That doesn't mean there are not legitimate current environmental concerns (there are), but they should be placed in context and that requires the perspective of and knowledge of history (and often economics) to parse through competing claims. This is a problem individually and corporately. Individually, there is a responsibility to gain more knowledge; corporately, media owners can help ameliorate this problem by hiring more staff; no one can know everything.

8. There is the "2 + 2 = 5" tendency in journalism. Confronted with a public policy problem and two contradictory claims on how to solve it, a reporter observes one group that argues 2 + 2 = 4 and another that claims 2 + 2 = 6[j] and assumes the truth must lie somewhere in the middle; he cuts the difference in "half." Thus, proclaims a columnist, the "answer" to the problem is in the "moderate centre" and 2 + 2 is proclaimed to equal "5." It is a common error; it assumes there are no quantifiable issues in public policy. While many aspects of a story are open to debate and the truth may lie somewhere in the middle of two competing assertions, some claims are simply in error. Sometimes, some figures are simply inaccurate in what they purport to represent; the insurance studies noted previously are an example.

i. For more details on our improved environment, see Stephen Moore and Julian L. Simon, *It's Getting Better All the Time*, The Cato Institute, 2000; Julian Simon, *The State of Humanity*, Blackwell, 1995; Julian Simon, *The Ultimate Resource*, Princeton University Press, 1996.

j. This should be obvious, but I don't mean this literally. This basic mathematical mistake is obviously recognizable, but not everything is, including basic statistical assumptions.

Chapter 11

9. Reporters, columnists, radio talk-show hosts and anchors are human beings. That means mistakes will occur (this author has made his own). The best media outlets can do to limit such errors is to construct a firewall of fact-checkers who double-check assumptions, claimed facts and the final product. That happens less than the public may guess or realize.

10. There is a deeper malady at work. Jerry Mander and Neil Postman identified the problem in several books in the 1970s and 1980s: television. The idiot box has dumbed-down public discourse.[k] But the existence of television is a reality and, contrary to Mander's fear, the diversification and fragmentation of television networks at least improved *some* aspects of television viewing; the Arts and Entertainment channel is an improvement on mainstream television from the 1970s; the History Channel is superior to daytime soap operas and cheap-to-produce voyeuristic television that peeks into the most banal and tragic aspects of others' lives. The multiplication of channels has allowed for better TV, if viewers seek it out, but also an explosion of banality, crudeness and hype.[l]

The solution to the latter is not more state control or funding for government networks; that brings its own bias and an

k. See Jerry Mander, *Four Arguments for the Elimination of Television*, 1977, 1978, and Neil Postman *Amusing Ourselves to Death* (1985) and *The Disappearance of Childhood* (1982, 1994). I don't agree with some of the authors' conclusions or selected anti-market positions, which I think are anachronistic. But Mander and Postman are persuasive on the anti-rational, anti-literate aspect of television and its effect on public discourse.

l. For any critic of television, it is best not to throw stones from glass houses. Unlike Mander, I do not argue television should be eliminated or that it should never be watched; also, it has arguably not had wholly negative results. But more discrimination is in order. And full confession: I unapologetically use television. I am a realist. If the majority of the public receives its news and information from television, those who want to persuade the public must deal with that reality. So, arguments are encapsulated for television (*because they have to be*) in an attempt to enlighten, cajole and persuade for those who might never encounter my views elsewhere. The luxury of columns, longer pieces and books, obviously, is that one can go into detail unavailable in a visual medium. There is no point in railing against the existence of a technology that will not be un-invented. Television should be critiqued, used sparingly and hopefully more wisely.

unaccountable Leviathan with its own set of problems. Also, no matter how well a particular network or program attempts to elevate public discourse, television as a medium will never match the printed word for its ability to provoke thought and analysis. As Postman noted in *The Disappearance of Childhood,* our minds don't argue with images. The eyes receive, the brain records and the mind accepts images as "real." An image is neither correct nor incorrect, it just *is,* and images primarily evoke emotion, not rational, sequential, logical thought. It is a retreat to pre-literacy and a world without much intellectual rigor—to the cave, to images, and all that implies. In contrast, the written word demands a response. We read from left to right and can spot logical flaws in an argument.

This is why those who dumb down newspapers and magazines to compete with television are in error; people who are primarily interested in visual stimulation will seek out the choice medium, television. Owners, publishers and editors who try to compete by fluffing up their own product will inevitably fail; they will disappoint readers who look for rational content, depth and excellent writing. The attempt will bring about the very decline in readership already in progress and so feared when media conglomerates look into their crystal-ball future. Why pick up a newspaper if it offers nothing above the level of newscasts—which by their visual nature cannot themselves compete with a well-crafted article or editorial? Or offers insights no better than weblogs? The attempt to paint visual mascara on the printed word is a distraction and contains within it the seeds of its own demise.

But if media owners, publishers and editors have a responsibility, so too do citizens. Individuals have their own duty to pick up a newspaper, a well-written magazine and a book. If adults rarely read and instead reach for the remote and click on visual vapidity, and if their children by example choose the same fate, the blame for the poor state of politics, the media and public discourse properly starts with individuals, with parents. The failure of analysis—as with most problems—begins at home.

Chapter 12

Survivalists and the State:
How the garrison culture reinforces
inept government

Privations such as they had never known were now their daily lot, and the long snowbound winter nights, which they were forced to spend in rough log huts or army tents, gave ample opportunity for bitter thought in reference to the authors of their misfortunes. The fierce anger with which they had resented the indignities of war gave place to a deep and acrid hatred, which pervaded every aspect of their lives and constituted one of the strongest influences in molding the outlook of their children.[1]
~ Historian Hugh Keenleyside, in 1929, on the early Loyalist experience.

Abominable pests of society.[2]
~ George Washington, on the Loyalists

The Dominant Canadian Narrative: Survival

Canada, her politics and the tendency of voters to place too much faith in government cannot be understood apart from the historical river that carved our national discourse. The shape of that discussion has been greatly affected by the power south of the border. This is obvious in regions such as southern Ontario and in the Maritimes, but it also means that cultural-political assumptions—insofar as they emanate from those regions, especially population-rich Ontario—will dominate the national discourse. Margaret Atwood called it survivalist; Northrop Frye labeled the phenomenon the "garrison mentality." Whatever the tag, the effect upon many Canadian attitudes has been lasting.

This particular regional identity and self-understanding is not the sum total of Canadians' self-understanding; other regions have their own narratives. Quebec, British Columbia and the prairies have theirs. Very different immigration patterns and reasons for arrival in Calgary or Vancouver led to a cultural and national self-understanding distinct from the Loyalist version; a Ukrainian who flees Josef Stalin's USSR in the 1930s and settles in Edmonton will have a very different view of the world than families with 18th-century roots in southern Ontario. Over time, immigration waves dilute the potency of the survivalist-garrison narrative and its power over political discourse. But it is still the dominant one in part because of Ontario's population, wealth and cultural clout; it partly explains the modern-day attitudes of many toward government.

British North America before the War of Independence

In a 1945 survey of the historical interplay of Canada, the United States and Great Britain, historian John Brebner queried how it was that in a North America peopled by men and women of the same stock, closely intermingled by marriage and migration, resulted in two separate, self-conscious nations. He surmised that there were at least three reasons: "the natural dividing line of the St. Lawrence and Great Lakes with the Canadian Shield to the north of them, the slight but perceptible height of land between the Missouri Valley, and the valleys of the Assiniboine and the Saskatchewan."[3] And, perhaps, more importantly, although he does not suggest this factor is the most decisive one: "men's inclinations to find comfort in the fact that they and their regional groups are not as other men are."[4]

That regional division of early European settlements and the time-worn exacerbation of the same was noted earlier than Brebner, in 1929, by Hugh Keenleyside, who detailed the early freedom that North American colonies enjoyed and how that provided the impetus for later upheavals. "Between 1660 and 1763 American colonies had enjoyed an economic freedom unknown in any other colonial system of the period. Legally, the Regulatory Laws of 1660[a] were operative during this period, but in fact were consistently ignored."[5]

The colonies were accustomed to a measure of self-government already advanced beyond that available in England itself. English colonies in the Americas also enjoyed economic and legislative freedom unavailable in French and Spanish colonies. A century's

a. The regulatory laws governed trade and commerce between the colonies and England, and were mercantilist in nature.

worth of isolation, independence and new social conditions reinforced by habit all combined to produce a hatred of restraint. And
no matter how legally sound the decision was (or seemed) in the
eyes of London when it began to enforce long-established laws,
the existing conditions meant that English rulers and their North
American colonies were in for a systemic shock when King George
III strictly enforced the Regulatory Laws.[6]

Brebner notes that while for many North American colonists
British regulations were ignored by two generations when they interfered with profitable pursuits, there was a significant difference
between the colonies:

> In these matters there were important differences between the colo-
> nies south of the mouth of the Bay of Fundy and those north of
> it, that is, between the regions which were to become the United
> States and Canada. Nova Scotia, although remarkably like New
> England and peopled largely by New Englanders, was a marginal
> or debatable land where New England and Old competed for eco-
> nomic mastery and between them retarded the maturing of the
> region to economic independence. Newfoundland, dependent on a
> single staple export, was just beginning to shake herself free from
> English West Country control and, for lack of capital and capital
> equipment, was as yet unable to pursue a self-directed course.
>
> Quebec, cut off from France and no longer able to trade with
> the French West Indies through contacts around the Gulf of St.
> Lawrence, found that she needed the British connection in order
> to secure attention to her interests in the stern competition of the
> Gulf fisheries and of the fur trade in the interior. The Hudson's Bay
> Company was a living extension of the British industrial and com-
> mercial organism, and severance from it was unthinkable to the
> directors and shareholders. In fact, the District of Maine (then part
> of Massachusetts) might well have been taken as a sort of bound-
> ary between British colonies which were able and inclined to resent
> British mercantile control and those who looked to it for nourish-
> ment and aid.[7]

The difference between the two sections of colonies and their dependence on—*or competition with*—British mercantilist controls, helps explain why in early colonial history the separate identities existed and might one day become more apparent.[b]

THE ROAD TO SERFDOM RUNS THROUGH HALIFAX

Over in Halifax, notes Brebner, "the usual colonial oligarchy of officialdom, finance, and business had fallen under the sway of a London mercantile group which had the advantage of enjoying the confidence of the colonial authorities in England."[8] Also, the mercantilists had a strong colonial grip over the rest of the colony regardless of sympathies because the representative system was heavily weighted to favour the propertied classes in Halifax (i.e., those most sympathetic to English rule).[9] The distance and expense made it difficult for elected representatives from the poorer, distant settlements of the colony to attend legislature sessions. There were numerous outbursts around Nova Scotia that agitated for the independence movement in New England. But the geographical disadvantage *within* Nova Scotia for latent New Englanders worked against a more solid link to revolutionary politics. Brebner:

> *As the revolutionary tensions heightened, the Nova Scotians found that the sea cut off most of them from direct contact with their former homelands in New England and that roadless Nova Scotian wildernesses separated their settlements from each other.... It was impossible for them to get together, to maintain close relations with New England, to bend the provincial administration to their will, or to break down the private and public controls which were exercised from London. Loyalism not only had a natural appeal in pensionary Halifax, but it also promised to confer many material benefits,*

b. Nova Scotia provides an example of geography and its influence on a colony's destiny. New England's grasp on Nova Scotia was weaker after 1749 despite the migration from there, which occurred after that year, and despite the colony's population, which by 1775 contained an estimated 17,000 to 18,000 settlers, of whom three-quarters were New Englanders and thus had sympathy with delegates at Philadelphia then agitating for independence. (Brebner, 1945, p. 51)

and Halifax was determined to keep the lid on the out-settlements in order to reap them.[10]

While the impetus for rebellion against British rule originated in New England colonies such as Massachusetts and Virginia, sympathy did exist in British colonies farther north, and the first Continental Congress that met in Philadelphia in September 1774 openly discussed the inclusion of Canada in the independence movement. And reports of royal oppression in Boston provoked sympathy among merchants in Montreal and Quebec who organized a shipment of grain and money to send to the New England port.

In February 1775, American leaders in the independence movement drew up a letter to the merchants of Montreal in which they stated their grievances against the Crown and denounced the *Quebec Act* (which among other items had re-imposed compulsory tithes—something appreciated by the Catholic Church in Quebec, though perhaps not necessarily by its parishioners) as despotic. Canadians were invited to revolt and to send delegates to the second session of Congress, soon to meet in Philadelphia. The Montreal reply, sympathetic though it was, was that the local British administration was simply too strong to be effectively opposed.[11]

In early autumn 1775, American forces crossed the St. Lawrence River near Montreal and Quebec, and while initially successful in their advance, the campaigns faltered over the winter months and were defeated in the spring of 1776, a development crucial to the maintenance of British rule. Keenleyside:

The American defeat at Quebec was indeed the crucial event in the struggle for possession of Canada. Larger bodies of troops were placed in the field in 1776, but never again did the danger of Quebec appear imminent. Never again did the habitants, disillusioned by this defeat, risk their lives and property, in comparable numbers, on behalf of a losing cause. British authority here was established, to remain unquestioned for more than three decades.[12]

The War of Independence

The American invasion of British territory, with hopes that other English colonists would join New Englanders in their independence movement, had the *opposite* effect of solidifying British control. The American Revolution and the migration that followed (voluntary and forced) for those loyal to the Crown reinforced the growing separateness of the two peoples.

Keenleyside argues a plurality of New Englanders at first opposed a separation and retained such sentiments even after July 4, 1776. Perhaps, but the treatment the United Empire Loyalists received from the victors reinforced their acrimony.

Loyalists were barred from all civil rights; they could not collect debts, nor claim legal protection from slander, assault or blackmail. They could not hold land or present a gift. The professions were closed to them and military service in the Whig ranks was frequently demanded. Freedom of speech, press, and travel were rigidly curtailed, and, on the charge of treason, Loyalists were hanged, exiled, or imprisoned. On the same charge property was confiscated. Heavy fines and forced donations were levied, and in many districts those suspected of Tory sympathies were herded together in concentration camps—camps which in some cases compared unfavourably with the worst of British prison ships.[13]

Loyalists were not innocent of such crimes either, but after the Treaty of Paris in 1873, which ended hostilities and provided for a more orderly return of Loyalists to their properties, if for no other reason than to dispose of it before a final move, some faced persecution worse than that which occurred *before* the end of hostilities. Keenleyside quotes John Adams—who previous to the war's end had recommended hanging all who were disloyal to the Revolution. Keenleyside, on the excesses of the Whig mobs:

Profaneness, intemperance, thefts, robberies, murders and treason; cursing, swearing, gluttony, drunkenness, lewdness, trespassing ... they render the populace, the rabble, the scum of the earth, insolent and disorderly, impudent and abusive. They give rise to lying, hypocrisy, chicanery, and even perjuring among the people....[14]

For example, George Washington declared Loyalists to be "abominable pests," and only urged against executing them on tactical grounds: he feared revenge might be exacted against patriots. He advised Loyalists to commit suicide instead.[15]

Keenleyside asserts that the departure of Loyalists, many of whom had been among the wealthier elements of pre-revolutionary society, led to an American polity that was less law-abiding, a charge thrown at the U.S. throughout its history. When 100,000 Loyalists departed, America also lost the most conservative, stable and arguably law-abiding segment of its population.[c] It also added a feeling of moral and cultural superiority to the north-south divide. [16]

The migration of so many Loyalists solidified the Canadian–American divide and the conditions that greeted the new settlers reinforced an understandable bitterness:

Privations such as they had never known were now their daily lot, and the long snowbound winter nights, which they were forced to spend in rough log huts or army tents gave ample opportunity for bitter thought in reference to the authors of their misfortunes. The fierce anger with which they had resented the indignities of war gave place to a deep and acrid hatred, which pervaded every aspect of their lives and constituted one of the strongest influences in molding the outlook of their children.[17]

The separateness grew with the failed attempt by some Americans in the War of 1812 to, as they saw it, "liberate" Canada from the British. There were divisions within American states as to the

---

c. The effect of this migration on Canadian colonies was dramatic: Nova Scotia and Prince Edward Island together had a population of 13,000 before the Loyalist emigration, but 35,000 by 1790. New Brunswick saw 10,000 American exiles arrive, which greatly swamped the 700 people then living there. The western settlements (later known as Upper Canada), which then had few white settlers, added 12,000 Loyalists to the population. (Keenleyside, 1929, p. 47)

wisdom of the 1812 effort, but when hostilities officially ended with the Treaty of Ghent in 1815, the fact was that British North American colonies emerged intact and the effect was that governing classes found their distaste for the Yankees reinforced. [18]

The Survivalist Complex

Canada's existence is a conscious result of and response to resisting America's founding. The loyalist migration north during, before and after the War of Independence, the War of 1812 and later events such as the St. Albans raids and the Alaskan boundary dispute all contributed to Canadian attitudes towards the United States.

In addition, the early isolation among communities that were not naturally sympathetic to the status quo, as in the example of Nova Scotia save Halifax, is a recurring theme in Canadian literature and our politics: the outpost forced to make do and thus reliant on the authorities because distance and isolation prevent other options; thus, loyalty to the group becomes paramount for survival.

Those historical events, combined with the physical nature of Canada, produced what Northrop Frye noted was a "garrison mentality" where the moral and social values of the group are not questioned. In reviewing Canadian poetry, he noted the prevalence of the "tone of deep terror in regard to nature" and its effect on one's psychological state:

The human mind has nothing but human and moral values to cling to if it is to preserve its integrity or even its sanity, yet the vast unconsciousness of nature in front of it seems an unanswerable denial of those values.... Small and isolated communities surrounded with a physical or psychological "frontier," separated from one another and their American and British cultural sources: communities that provide all that their members have in the way of distinctively human values, and are compelled to feel a great respect for the law and order that holds them together, yet confronted with a huge, unthinking menacing and formidable physical setting—such communities are bound to develop into what we may provisionally call the garrison mentality.[19]

203

Similarly, in another widely recognized motif pointed to by Margaret Atwood, she wrote that if "The Frontier" is what symbolizes America and "The Island" represents England, "the central symbol of Canada ... is undoubtedly survival." And Atwood notes this is so whether one looks at early explorers or settlers, the French vis-à-vis the English, and now English Canada in relation to the United States.[20]

It is an understandable psychological reaction, but by now should also be a curious relic. On a physical level, no region in Canada is less like the small and isolated communities described by Frye; the current reality—Ontario's large population, crisscrossed transportation networks and wealth—defies the psychological constructs that yet exist. (Other regions are actually more recognizable as the garrison both in relation to the United States and in relation to southern Ontario. The prairie West, British Columbia, the Atlantic, and even northern Ontario are more likely to feel like garrisoned communities, which attempt to survive in contradistinction to the power and force of Toronto, Montreal and Ottawa.)

But to expand on Atwood's theme, despite separate regional myths from other parts of the country (which do not share the loyalist narrative), there is at least one common bond of Canadians in not only traditional loyalist regions but in others: *survival* in contradistinction to the American nation.

Frye beautifully describes and asks rhetorically about the differences between regional identities in relation to geographic setting. He begins with a description of Newfoundland, "an environment turned outward to the sea,"[21] moves to the Maritimes—"turned toward inland seas"—and then to eastern and central Canada: "Anyone brought up on the urban plan of southern Ontario or the gentle *pays* farmland along the south shore of the St. Lawrence may become fascinated by the great sprawling wilderness of northern Ontario or Ungava..."[22] As Frye moved west, he poses this question:

And what can there be in common between an imagination nurtured on the prairies, where it is a centre of consciousness diffusing

*itself over a vast flat expanse stretching to the remote horizon, and
one nurtured in British Columbia, where it is in the midst of gi-
gantic trees and mountains leaping into the sky all around it, and
obliterating the horizon everywhere?*[23]

What there *can* be in common is a joint political project, the goal
of which is unity and the means of which are expressed though
the mechanism of politics, occasionally using the "glue" of fear of
American absorption if the project should fail.

Thus, whether in the original act of Confederation or in successive additions to the country, Charles Doran and James Sewell
note that the Canadian federation:

*… was a deliberate effort to create a political society distinct from
the United States while accommodating both European founding
nations. The saga of extending the Dominion from sea to sea similarly bespoke an aim of protecting the Canadian project from its
neighbour and its neighbour's way of life…."*[24]

Thus, proper or not, survival is used to justify not only a link-up of
lightly populated British Columbia with central Canada by means
of a railway in the late 19th century; it can (and was) as easily used
by magazine publishers in the mid-20th or early 21st centuries to
protect themselves against substantially larger American publishers. ("Survival" is in fact the very word attached to the Canadian
culture and the magazine industry in the context of such discussions.) It is used to justify policies as diverse as a billion-dollar
budget for a state television network or a foreign policy that on occasion appears more about an assertion of difference vis-à-vis the
Americans rather than derived from a clear idea about Canada's
national interest.

The garrison mentality, strongest in Ontario, explains some
attitudes including those towards the United States but also do-
mestically to build up government; the project of national unity—a
political one—was a survivalist one, the theme of which could
be and is adapted for use across the country, by various actors

and with multiple means and ends. Faced with a rich, powerful neighbour with overwhelming military might, government, most obviously on the military level, was the only force to give any hope of protection against the American colossus. *An unquestioned preference for authority, for government in a variety of forms, but especially for security, made sense.*

The Survivalist Theme in Other Areas:
Quebec, Academia and Business

Some of the preference for strong Canadian government resulted from the historical reality of garrison and survivalist mentalities. In the 20th century, a more recent factor was the rise of Quebec separatism and the belief in parts of English Canada (as well as English Quebec) that only a powerful central government could combat regional distinctiveness, which might otherwise tear at the country's unity. In addition, there was a significant change in mainstream economic perspectives from the late 19th century to the mid-20th century, the latter of which produced the interventionist Keynesian state.

Each of those developments fed each other. Quebec nationalism dispensed with the paternalistic Catholic Church only to retain paternalism (post-Quiet Revolution) in the form of a strong interventionist provincial government. That tilted the country even more in the direction of economic intervention given Quebec's population, national leaders and electoral clout. Threats of separation reinforced English Canadian beliefs in the role of the state. And all sailed on the assumptions of John Maynard Keynes.

While Canada has shifted away from Keynes over the last two decades, that development has arguably not diminished the more basic orientation and economic assumptions. It's also a shift that has been strongly opposed by many in academia, who still possess significant influence on Canadian culture, our self-understanding and even what constitutes a "good" Canadian. In a 1989 survey, a Hungarian émigré to the United States, Paul Hollander, surveyed Canadian academics on their views of the U.S. He concluded that

attitudes towards America among intellectuals depended on their
political orientation.

*Insofar as they are of leftist persuasion they object to the exploit-
ativeness they associate with the most powerful representative of
capitalism and the commercialization of cultural values; if they are
conservative, they see themselves as custodians of national culture
and identity and most sensitive to threats to these values.*[25]

Thus, the Loyalist-survivalist-garrison fears are yet nourished by
the existence of the superpower next door, especially when one
takes a very skeptical view of American capitalism as does the political left and much of academia. Conservatives, in the operational
rather than ideological sense, also have their fears reinforced given
the dominance of American cultural exports.

Even arguments over morality play out and dance with
the survivalist self-understanding. Odd as it is to present-day
Canadians when Canada is the more liberal country, past criticism once included accusations that America was too socially
liberal. It was an accusation that could also be combined with
economic arguments and could also be used to advance domestic
business interests.

Thus in 1926, when 50 million copies of American magazines
were bought in Canada, domestic publishers could appeal both to
the swamping of the Canadian cultural boat but also the need to
protect Canadians from depraved Americans and their "smut-filled
literature."[26] As a result, the Canadian publishers soon obtained a
substantial rebate on tariffs on selected imports of paper (in 1928)
and three years later Parliament began to heavily tax imported pe-
riodicals, of no small help to Canadian publishers, who saw their
circulations soar while American ones declined.[27]

Similarly, in 1999, when then-Heritage minister Sheila Copps
argued for a legislative bill to continue to prevent "split-run"
American magazines into Canada, protectionism could be defend-
ed on cultural and economic grounds: "Canada is not looking for
a trade war, of course not. What Canada is doing is standing up

for Canada's interests," said the minister in 1999.[28] In short, and beyond whether the particular policy prescription was the proper one, the underlying justification was a familiar one: pace Atwood and Frye, Canada was a garrison outpost that needed government protection to *survive*.

Economics and Nationalism Infuse New Life into Survivalism

Two hundred and thirty years after the American war of independence and almost two centuries since Americans crossed our border on war-footing, the survivalist impulse should have much less resonance. Even deep cultural patterns can be diluted over time by massive immigration waves and subsequent political developments. But in the mid-20th century, an ascendant economic doctrine from Keynes nicely fits with Canadian nationalism to reinvigorate the garrison fear in Canadians: fear of foreign control of our economy.

Writing in 1989, diplomat and York University International Relations professor John Holmes argued that because Canadians write about U.S.–Canada relationships far more often than Americans, that when discussions surrounding the two countries take place, "Canadians get away with more nonsense."[29] Unfortunately for Holmes, an example occurred in his own essay.

Holmes claimed (contra U.S. claims about Canada in the 1980s) that Canada was "the least ideologically nationalist state in the Western world."[30] As proof and with a look back before 1984, the diplomat-professor argued that former prime minister Pierre Trudeau was "ideologically *anti*-nationalistic." That Trudeau was more cosmopolitan than a nationalist was true, though it remains an open question as to whether a country can be so anti-nationalist that it one day lacks a core set of principles and distinctive features that allow successive immigrant waves to mold together in a cohesive unit. It's another version of post-modern confusion, which assumes all values are relative, and that has nothing to draw people into a community other than pulverized, atomized self-interest. But that problem aside, Holmes then described a belief he says Canadians often hold: that we're not ideological in *any* sense. Trudeau again served as the example. His coming to power merely coincided with a "maturing of the Canadian economy and a consequent insistence on a greater share of native control,"[31] wrote Holmes.

Holmes' essay appeared just as the presumption that state intervention is benign—long since expired among most mainstream economists—was about to crumble politically beneath the Berlin Wall. But Holmes was a useful example of how a leftist preference for state intervention was able to keep alive centuries-old survivalist fears and also produce a new modern Canadian myth: Canadian governments are non-ideological.

Ours has always been a functional approach. We did not for practical reasons seek independence from Britain because we needed Britain for our markets, our defence, and as a deterrent to "manifest destiny" from the outside. There was no cutting off our noses in the name of some fashionable ideology like anti-colonialism. We worked out with the British a peaceful evolution of self-government with mutual respect. That experiment set the pattern for the transformation of the world's greatest empire into a Commonwealth and it saved the world oceans of blood in the process. If the French had followed our example, America would have been saved from Vietnam. Ours was a triumph of functionalism over ideology. We are the least ideologically nationalist state in the Western world.... Our governments have been more interventionist because they had to be.[32]

Holmes theorized that because some federal and provincial governments bought up the commanding heights of the economy between the 1950s and 1970s, that this was all a "very Canadian, functionalist view, and it is totally un-ideological ... our economy has reached a higher level of maturity; and we are going to do whatever is practical to raise the level of national control and ownership."[33] Holmes seemed not to notice that his non-ideological approach—nationalization of industry—was coincidentally wrapped in *very* ideological hard-left economic assumptions about the role of the state.

The claim that such actions were not ideological is unpersuasive and amounts to a badly disguised rhetorical ploy; because left-wing economic preferences were implemented in Canada's history on the justification of functional necessity, those who initiated such moves were not ideological because such actions were argued to be necessary and functional. It was a circular argument and one that barred experience and skeptical counter-claims from disrupting the loop.

The myth that Canadians are not ideological is yet widely believed but no less mistaken for that. With some perspective since the Holmes essay was published (if not before, for those who care to dissect economic assumptions), one can argue on any number of grounds that state ownership of gas and oil companies, airlines and coal mines is ideological, given the practical failure of the same and the tremendous cost. But myths endure long after the original events that gave rise to them have faded, be it the loyalist-survivalist-garrison narrative or the belief that interventionist government of the sort practised by governments in the 1970s was non-ideological. The Holmes' thesis was evidence that the survivalist narrative was alive and well—*Canada needed state ownership to protect us against foreign control; it was necessary for our survival.*

Such a preference might be described as akin to serfdom; in historical Canadian terms it might be described as an updated version of survivalism. Labels aside, the result is that many citizens yet retain an attachment to government as their protector and beyond just a sensible utilitarian end. But many of our past leaders—far closer in temperament and time to the events that produced such an orientation—never felt the need to give government quite such latitude and space as it now occupies.

Chapter 13

In the Beginning … Early Dominion
attitudes towards taxes and government

All taxation is a loss per se. It is the sacred duty of the government to take only from the people what is necessary to the proper discharge of the public service; and that taxation in any other mode, is simply in one shape or another, legalized robbery.[1]

~ Honourable Sir Richard Cartwright, Dominion Minister of Finance, Budget Speech, 1878.

Where Taxes Began

To find the origins of tax, travel back in time to the ancient world and to a fertile plain between the Tigris and Euphrates rivers, now modern Iraq. History's first recorded tax was brought to mankind in Sumer, 6,000 years ago. It is there, inscribed on clay stones excavated at Lagash, that we learn of the first taxes, instituted to fight a ferocious war. But as has often been the case throughout history, when the battles ceased, the taxes stayed—a cause of no small discontent on the part of the locals, who complained that taxes filled up the land from one end to the other.[2]

Six millennia later, taxes have appeared, risen and fallen and are intertwined with the history of peoples and states. When limited and coupled with specific aims, taxes have helped some countries keep and build empires. The case of the English income tax, first instituted in 1798 under Prime Minister William Pitt, is often cited as a key factor in England's success in her war with France. (Napoleon refused to institute a similar levy to prosecute his war.) The new tax provided a third of the additional revenue needed to win the war with France.

Unsurprisingly, though, Pitt's income tax was hardly popular. A naval officer spoke for many in 1799 when he ventured: "It is a vile, Jacobin, jumped up Jack-in-Office piece of impertinence—is a true Briton to have no privacy? Are the fruits of his labour and toil to be picked over, farthing by farthing, by the pimply minions of bureaucracy?"[3] Pitt's tax was repealed in 1802, and the modified version introduced by his successor was cancelled at the end of hostilities in 1815, and gave exception to the general rule that wars come and go but taxes stay.[a]

But if some taxes were helpful to nations and peoples, others have been injurious and fatal to freedom. In pre-Bolshevik Russia, serfdom evolved as overtaxed peasants could not fulfill their obligations to the state and accepted bondage to landowners in preference to taxation. In theory, peasants could work off the debt they owed to wealthy landowners (incurred after the landowner paid taxes on their behalf); in practice, it rarely occurred. It was not the first time in history that the interests of a government in pursuit of tax and a special interest (i.e., landowners) coincided to penalize the very poor.[4]

CANADA'S FIRST TAX–ON NATURAL RESOURCES
In Canada, the first known instance of taxation was, with the view of history, rich with symbolism: an export duty on beaver pelts (at 50 per cent) and moose pelts (at 10 per cent) in what was then New France, in 1650.

And while the tax on beaver furs was soon reduced to 25 per cent three years hence, by 1662, every import into the country was subject to a 10 per cent tax for six years, necessary to help pay off colonial debt. (That levy stayed for *eight* years and was then replaced by equivalent duties on imported tobacco, wine and brandy.)

From there, the taxes of the colonial outpost multiplied. Excise taxes on both imports and exports sprouted as the European settlers grew in number and in geographic reach. The beaver pelt tax was abolished in 1707, but duties had already increased on tobacco and alcoholic imports. A new tax, on property, was instituted in Montreal in 1716, where it paid for a stone wall built around the settlement.

Duties and Excise Taxes
Much of Canada's early and pre-Confederation governments relied heavily on duties and excise taxes applied to imports and exports

a. The exception was itself temporary; another income tax introduced in 1842 in Britain remains to this day.

as their main source of revenue. While other taxes existed, such as a land tax in Nova Scotia, most colonial governments used customs duties for their revenues, applied in various ways. Ships that left Halifax, for example, were charged according to tonnage.

And the nationality of the colonial master mattered little; after the 1763 Treaty of Paris that gave the English formal control over French colonies, the existing tariff system was preserved and expanded. Over in Nova Scotia, import duties were applied to sugar, bricks, lumber and billiard tables in 1764. One year later, excise taxes were levied on coffee and playing cards. Those were followed later that century by duties on chocolate and rum, and also a 10 per cent tariff on American imports (with the exception of lumber, grain and cattle).

From the end of the 18th century to Confederation, the average tariff rate rose from 3 per cent to 12-15 per cent,[5] which was increasingly joined by poll taxes[b] and property taxes as the main revenue providers for governments. Some were levied by cities, other by the provinces of Upper Canada, Lower Canada or the Atlantic colonies.[c] Provincial licences were necessary for peddlers in 1807 in Upper Canada. By 1882, New Brunswick required municipalities to levy poll and property taxes. In 1827, Upper Canada levied the first stumpage fees (the tax paid for cutting down trees on Crown land).[6]

PRE-CONFEDERATION INCOME TAXES: FEW, AND LEVIED BY MUNICIPALITIES

While many Canadians might think the first income tax arrived in 1917 to help finance the First World War, tax historian J. Harvey Perry speculates that the country's first income tax, at least in rudimentary form, may well have been in 1775. In that year, Nova Scotia instituted a temporary poll tax (for one year), which was graduated according to income.

b. "Poll taxes" are uniform fees assessed on each person, usually as a prerequisite to voting.

c. Prince Edward Island became a separate province apart from Nova Scotia in 1769; New Brunswick followed by splitting off from Nova Scotia in 1784.

Another type of income tax, more recognizable to the modern citizen, was instituted in 1831 in the few New Brunswick municipalities then in existence. Perry notes that over in Nova Scotia, Halifax levied an income tax from its incorporation in 1849 and that tax continued for more than three decades.[7]

With new governments came more taxes, and the establishment of a municipal system in Upper Canada in 1849 led to new levies exacted by elected municipal councils (as opposed to justices of the peace). After the 1850 *Assessment Act*, local taxes also included incomes, as long as the value of that income along with one's land and some other personal property exceeded £50.[8] Power to tax income was expanded again three years later. Meanwhile, over on the lightly populated West Coast colony of Vancouver Island, a "salaries tax" was imposed in the mid-1860s.[9]

Thus, while Upper and Lower Canada and the Atlantic colonies relied more on tariffs and duties for revenues, local governments relied on taxes applied to real estate and personal property, and lightly on tax from incomes where it was included in the overall assessment of one's property.

The marginal nature of income tax in particular is evidenced by one of the earliest comprehensive records of municipal revenues. Total tax revenues to municipalities in Ontario in 1867 amounted to $3.2 million (based on a total assessed value of $244.7 million). Only *3 per cent* of that revenue came from the tax levied on incomes; the rest came from real estate taxes (87 per cent) and taxes levied on personal property (10 per cent).[10]

The Dominion of Canada in 1867

By 1867 and the founding of Canada, the colonies of Upper and Lower Canada had been the largest tax collectors, a position then abandoned as they relinquished most taxing power (of the type that was important at the time—duties and excise taxes) to the new Dominion government.

To gain an understanding of the makeup of federal revenues at Confederation, it is helpful to examine the revenues that flowed into the public treasury. In 1867, total revenues to the Dominion government totalled $13.7 million. Almost two-thirds (62 per cent) of the revenue came from customs[d] while excise[e] taxes accounted for 22 per cent. Miscellaneous revenues and post-office money accounted for the other 14 per cent.[11] At this point there were few of the taxes most modern Canadians are most familiar with, such as sales and income taxes.

In terms of the Dominion government's priorities, in 1867 debt payments accounted for the largest share of federal expenses at $4.1 million (30 per cent) of a $13.7-million budget. Transfers to provinces and municipalities accounted for $2.6 million (19 per cent); resources and development spending (on agriculture and surveying, for example) accounted for $1.5 million (11 per cent).

General government outlays (policing, other law and order, justice and general administrative costs) accounted for $1.5 million (11 per cent). Defence expenditures totalled $800,000 (6 per cent) while $300,000 (2 per cent) was spent on other transfers, including treaty payments. Another $1.1 million (8 per cent) in spending is not listed under any particular category. Transportation and communication (for outlays mainly for public infrastructure, such as railways, for example) amounted to $1.7 million (12 per cent).[12]

With the addition of own-source revenues and expenditures from the provinces and municipalities, it is estimated that Dominion, provincial and local government revenues and expenditures would not have amounted to much more than $25 million in the Dominion's first year.[13]

d. *Webster's Dictionary* defines "customs" as "duties imposed by law on imported, or, less commonly, exported goods."

e. *Webster's* defines "excise" as "an inland tax or duty on certain commodities, as spirits, tobacco, etc., levied on their manufacture, sale or consumption within the country."

Dominion Government Revenues and Expenditures in 1867

Revenues ($ million)		Expenditures ($ million)	
Excise Duties	3.0	Defence	0.8
Customs Import Duties	8.6	Other	0.3
Post Office	0.5	Transportation and Communication	1.8
Other	0.2	Resources and Development	1.5
Miscellaneous*	1.4	Public debt charges	4.1
Total budgetary revenue	**13.7**	General government	1.5
		Payments to Provinces & Municipalities	2.6
		Unclassified	1.1
		Total budgetary expenditure	**13.7**

*Miscellaneous revenues includes revenue from bullion and coinage, licenses and permits, sales, and receipts for services.
Sources: Urquhart and Buckley, Historical Statistics of Canada.

KEEP US AWAY FROM THOSE HIGH-TAX YANKEES

In Canada today, it is often assumed that our identity rests upon a higher tax burden vis-à-vis the United States. For some, high taxation takes on an almost mystical meaning and justification. For those who equate compassion with the exclusive or primary domain of government intervention in the economy with its requisite high levels of taxation, such involvement is often equated with Canada's very identity as a country.

There are problems with such an assumption, not least of which is the existence of other countries with higher standards of living—including longer life expectancies and an educated populace equal to our own—but lower levels of taxation relative to the economy. While *some* government is necessary for the rule of law, the security of property, defence of the nation and other foundational elements to a civilized society, a government that expands for its own sake is subject to the law of diminishing returns and *diminished* returns once it grows so large that it inhibits prosperity.

The curious attachment to high taxes on the part of some Canadians is questionable in its means to prosperity and in its moral assumption about what makes a country compassionate, i.e., that it is *government* spending and not personal charity or voluntary cooperation or non-government activities and attitudes that nurture and define compassion. But debates over the proper size of government aside, the historical record is that Canada's identity was originally found in its attachment to limited government, lower taxes and more robust desire for liberty in *contrast* to the United States in the 19th century. At Canada's founding, and for at least 50 years after Confederation, Canada's leaders argued that such policies were necessary for the country's well-being.

Welcome to Low-Tax Canada:
Love It So You Won't Leave It

For our earliest founders and finance ministers, attracting immigrants and investment to Canada through the promotion of a low-tax regime was the stated goal for at least the first 50 years of our country's existence. The Dominion's leading politicians trumpeted Canada's lower taxes compared to the tax-happy Americans, an advantage they argued was needed to ensure citizens and would-be immigrants were not lost to the Yanks.

The idea that citizens existed as vassals for the state, to be emptied of money at the whim of a government that wanted revenue for higher purposes, was largely absent from Canada's founders. Theirs was a classic liberal world, in which the role of the state was to protect the citizen *from* government and to provide basic services, the latter of which was defined quite narrowly at the time.

This view was true as it concerned taxes in general, but was also held by the Liberal Party of the day as it concerned the main revenue of the day: tariffs. That tax, unlike most, had political appeal as it could be used to stoke protectionist sentiment where a politician thought he would win votes. The Liberals, who in that age understood themselves as disciples of Adam Smith and thus stood in the tradition of English free-traders and economic liberals, thought higher tariffs were not only uneconomical but also morally questionable.

At the time, while the Conservatives were generally more sympathetic to higher tariffs (the protectionist element was more politically tempting to them), both parties attempted to renew a reciprocity treaty even after the Americans opted out of the previous pact in 1866. The implicit foundation of such a treaty was, of course, fewer and lower tariffs. Even after the abrogation, the Canadian governments continued to allow many American products cross the border for free or imposed a low tariff while it attempted to sign another agreement on the issue.[14]

In 1876, the first post-Confederation finance minister for the Liberals, Sir Richard Cartwright,[f] responded critically to the call for higher tariffs. He pointed out that such a hike would be injurious to most Canadians, as it transferred wealth from the many (in rural Canada) who bought a good, to the few (in the cities) who might manufacture or import the product:

> *To enrich a very few and seriously impoverish the great mass of the people ... is not to add to any great extent to the population of the country, but to promote an artificial transference from the rural districts to the towns and cities at the expense of the agricultural interests ...*[15]

Cartwright's attitude to tariff hikes was buttressed by his philosophy towards taxes in general, which was in line with the classic liberal thought of the late 19th century, which by default favoured free markets. It was notably distinct from liberalism one century later in Canada and the U.S., where "liberal" and "socialist" were at times nearly interchangeable. That was not the liberalism of Cartwright's time, as his 1878 budget speech makes clear:

> *All taxation is a loss per se. It is the sacred duty of the government to take only from the people what is necessary to the proper discharge of the public service; and that taxation in any other mode, is simply in one shape or another, legalized robbery.*[16]

Another Liberal expressed much the same sentiment in the closing decade of the 19th century. In his 1894 campaign swing through Winnipeg in 1894, Liberal Opposition leader Sir Wilfrid Laurier

---

f. Cartwright was the Liberals' first finance minister (1874-1878), but the new country's fourth. The other three, Conservative all, were the Hon. John Rose (1867-1869), Sir Francis Hincks (1870-1872), and the Hon. S.L. Tilley (1873).

(soon-to-be prime minister in 1896) attacked the protectionist pol-icies of the Conservative government and emphasized freedom in a manner that today might be equated with modern American political rhetoric.

> *The good Saxon word, freedom; freedom in every sense of the term, freedom of speech, freedom of action, freedom in religious life and civil life and last but not least, freedom in commercial life.*[17]

For the 50 years between Confederation and the introduction of the wartime income tax in 1917, Canada's budget speeches had two central themes: attract people to Canada and build the country. As another tax historian, Irwin Gillespie, has written, our Confederation-era politicians assumed a policy of taxes lower than the U.S. as crucial to filling the country with immigrants and with investment, as both were the natural conditions necessary for prosperity:

> *Dominion governments feared losing potential immigrants, as well as those immigrants who were newly settled in Canada, to the United States. Thus the principle applied to numerous tax rate changes was that they should not exceed the tax levels in the United States. Competition for those mobile human resources, not to men-tion the capital with which these immigrants (be they farmers or businessmen) arrived, was fierce. Consequently, all Dominion gov-ernments were determined to keep tax rates low.*[18]

And the preference went beyond just lower taxes in general; in the specific case of an income tax, Canadian politicians between 1867 and 1917 routinely dismissed any call for such a tax as a political death wish. George Foster, the Conservative finance minister be-tween 1889 and 1896, remarked in 1893 that he "would like to see the man who could be elected in any constituency on a policy of direct taxation."[19]

Also, many politicians noted that such a tax would constitute interference with the taxing jurisdiction of the provinces and urban areas that already levied such a tax. As late as 1915, the federal finance minister, also a Tory, noted the fact of income taxation in many municipalities and two provinces as one more reason why the Dominion government should not impose an additional income tax.[20]

Canada's Past Health Taxes

Canada's politicians have always used health care as a reason to raise old taxes or impose new ones. Over time, some taxes introduced specifically for health care were gradually diverted for other uses. Alternately, the reason for the tax was forgotten or made irrelevant as the money flowed into general revenues where a large portion of expenditures were already devoted to health care. But the combination of forgetfulness and a refusal to divert existing spending invariably leads governments to what some think is a "new" idea: a health care tax.

Here are selected past examples of taxes or tax increases justified by references to health care:[21]

1916: Prince Edward Island's *War and Health Tax Act* raises all taxes by one-third except for the road tax. Saskatchewan's *Union of Hospitals Act* authorizes local municipalities to set up hospitals to serve common needs and to finance the same through land tax levies.

1939: Saskatchewan passes the *Municipal and Medical Hospital Services Act*, and extends the municipal taxing right to include personal taxes, though not to exceed a $50 charge per family.

1944: Ontario's *Municipal Health Services Act* permits municipalities to levy property taxes or a poll tax for health plans.

1947: Saskatchewan introduces a new tax—compulsory monthly premiums—for health insurance.

1948: Ontario enacts a 20 per cent amusement tax in the *Hospital Tax Act*. British Columbia introduces a 3 per cent retail sales tax under the *Social Security and Municipal Aid Tax* partly to fund medical services. The same year, B.C. passes the *Hospital Insurance Services Act*, which, like Saskatchewan's, mandates personal and family premiums.

1950: Saskatchewan increases and renames its 2 per cent retail sales tax to 3 per cent for health funding under the *Education and Hospitalization Tax Act*.

1951: British Columbia raises its health care premium rates.

1953: Newfoundland introduces an entertainment tax of five cents per theatre ticket for cancer control.

1954: Saskatchewan health care insurance premiums are raised. Newfoundland broadens the entertainment tax. British Columbia increases the retail sales tax from 3 per cent to 5 per cent, now known as the "social services tax."

1959: Nova Scotia imposes a 3 per cent retail sales tax known as the "hospital tax."

1965: British Columbia reintroduces health care premiums.

With the introduction of Medicare in 1969, the provinces once again moved to raise or initiate new taxes over the following several years. Nova Scotia raised its retail sales tax from 3 per cent to 7 per cent in 1969 and directed the money for health programs. Quebec increased the corporate tax by 2 per cent and in 1972 introduced a payroll tax on employees, employers and the self-employed.

In Manitoba, a 5 per cent addition to personal income taxes was labelled the Hospital Services Tax, though proceeds from it were not specifically earmarked. Monthly premiums were introduced in 1969, and eliminated in 1973, but a payroll tax was introduced in 1982 for health care and education costs. Saskatchewan levied a 5 per cent retail sales tax and earmarked half the proceeds for health services. Alberta introduced health care premiums in 1969.

In 1984, British Columbia introduced a 4 per cent surtax on personal income tax as a "health care maintenance" tax and increased the surtax to 8 per cent in 1985.

Health care tax increases continued into the last decade when, in the early 1990s, Ontario New Democrats introduced a new high-income surtax which the Ontario Conservatives later kept and re-labeled as the "fair share" health care levy. And in 2002, two governments that are supposed to be fiscally conservative—British Columbia's Liberals and Alberta's Conservatives—raised their health care premiums to pay for wage settlements in government health care.

In the fall of 2002, then Prime Minister Jean Chrétien echoed the remark of Oliver Wendell Holmes: "It has been said before and we on this side of the House agree that, like it or not, taxes are the price one pays to live in a civilized society."[22] Thus, in an age where governments do not account for a mere 10 per cent of national income (as was the case one century ago) but 41.7 per cent, the default impulse is yet to try and squeeze a bit more out of the public. Chrétien didn't follow through on his threat, but another Liberal did: Dalton McGuinty in early 2004.

Pre-election, in September 2003, the Ontario Opposition leader signed a pledge with the Canadian Taxpayers Federation and with media cameras clicking—not to raise taxes without a public referendum.[23] Nine months later, McGuinty (now Premier), introduced a "new" Ontario tax that would cost each Ontarian from $300 to $900 annually. The justification was the deficit. The name of the new impost: a *health* premium.[24]

Changing expectations

Canada's leaders have had distinctly different views on taxes and the role of government over the course of Canada's political history. They range from conservative (sometimes referred to in the 19th century as classic liberalism or just liberal) to socialism and everything in between. Some excerpts from Canada's past:

The good Saxon word, freedom; freedom in every sense of the term, freedom of speech, freedom of action, freedom in religious life and civil life and last but not least, freedom in commercial life.[25]

> ~ *Liberal Opposition leader, Sir Wilfrid Laurier, in 1894*

During the war there has been considerable criticism to the effect that the Business Profits Tax was not sufficiently heavy. In my view this criticism is not sound and fails to take into consideration many vital aspects of the subject. A Business Profits Tax is justifiable during a prolonged war, because money is urgently needed and it is a ready method of obtaining it in large amounts. There is also a justification in the fact that public opinion is offended at the sight of abnormal profits in a period of great suffering and privation. On principle, however, the tax is not sound and tends to produce much economic evil in the State. It is really a tax upon business success, and consequently tends to discourage business enterprise and administrative efficiency....[26]

> ~ *Sir Thomas White, Conservative Finance minister, in a 1916 budget speech*

I have placed no time limit upon this measure, but merely placed upon Hansard the suggestion that a year or two after the war is over, the measure should be definitely reviewed by the Minister of Finance and the Government of the day, with a view of judging whether it is suitable to the conditions which then prevail.[27]

> ~ *Sir Thomas White, Conservative Finance minister, in a 1917 speech in which he introduced the federal income tax*

The old order is gone. It will not return. I nail the flag of progress to the masthead. I summon the power of the State to its support.[28]
~ *Prime Minister R.B. Bennett, in a 1935 radio broadcast*

Socialists are Liberals in a hurry.[29]
~ *Prime Minister Louis St. Laurent, in a 1949 speech*

Poverty is a passport to prison.[30]
~ *Prime Minister John G. Diefenbaker*

We can't rely on the free market system any more. We need rules even if that means you and I end up being called Communists or Socialists.[31]
~ *Prime Minister Pierre Trudeau, to Liberals in Toronto, 1975*

The goal of economic progress is the extension of human liberty, not, as the critics allege, the open-ended servicing of human greed.
~ *Opposition leader Joe Clark, giving a 1976 address in London, England*[32]

All we've been saying is that the country is broke. We've been trying to tell you for some time this country is bankrupt.[33]
~ *Prime Minister Brian Mulroney, in a 1985 comment to media*

It has been said before and we on this side of the House agree that, like it or not, taxes are the price one pays to live in a civilized society.[34]
~ *Prime Minister Jean Chrétien, in 2002, in Parliament*

We have brought forth a plan to reduce taxes for Canadians—some $30 billion in tax cuts that will contribute to our collective prosperity.[35]
~ *Prime Minister Paul Martin, in 2005, in his opening statement after calling an election for early 2006*

And forgive me jesting again, but the NDP is kind of proof that the Devil lives and interferes in the affairs of men. This party believes not just in large government and in massive redistributive programs, it's explicitly socialist.[36]

~ *Stephen Harper (Prime Minister in 2006), in a June 1997 address to the Council for National Policy in Montreal*

Chapter 14

Thank the USA: How America invented Canada's taxes

Henry Ford and his Model T, in Buffalo, New York, 1921. From the Collections of Henry Ford Historical Museum. Ford's invention of the assembly line was a boon to provincial governments in Canada. By the end of the 1920s, the revenues from automobile licences and gasoline taxes accounted for one-quarter of all provincial revenues.

The Siamese Twins of North America who cannot separate and live.[1]
~ Historian John Barlett Brebner, in 1945, on the interplay of
Canada and the United States

Canada's Modern Taxes:
As American as Yankee Doodle

So how did the Dominion change from a nation where politicians
looked down south and saw a republic a little too cozy with higher taxes and perhaps too willing to intervene in the economy?
A combination of events and American policy, actually. The First
World War and the introduction of federal income tax are the
most obvious examples of how an event propelled the introduction of that previously forbidden levy. But while events provided
the context, new American policy often provided the justification.
When Canadian politicians imposed additional and higher taxes
in the late 19th and early 20th centuries, they invariably did so only
after the Americans. As well, there were direct legislative influences on Canadian tax laws both federally and provincially. Think of
almost any modern Canadian tax: on federal income tax, gasoline,
property or on corporations; almost all have American origins.

For example, the first provincial corporate tax, in Quebec in
1884, came from an American precedent. The taxation of personal property, common in many Canadian municipalities at
Confederation, was also American in origin, not British, as that
country abandoned such taxes centuries before.[2] When Ontario
and the other provinces introduced succession duty levies (known
also as estate taxes or more bluntly as "death taxes"), the influence
of American legislation in the Canadian versions was clear. As tax
historian J. Harvey Perry writes:

> *The Canadian provincial legislation was inspired by and modelled*
> *after legislation of the American states. Clear testimony to this*
> *fact is given in the work of R.A. Bayly (1902). Bayly said this*
> *about the original Ontario Succession Duty Act, on which many*

of the other provincial acts were based: "That the New York and Pennsylvania Acts in force at the time were copied in principle and detail must be at once apparent to anyone who compares them with the Ontario Act of 1892."[3]

At another point he notes:

The first Canadian Act was drafted in the office of the Attorney General for Ontario and was modelled upon the Acts of New York passed in 1887 ... The Ontario Act of 1892 was purely American in its origin.[4]

The pattern established in the last 20 years of the 19th century— where Canadian governments copied the taxing habits and also the legislation of American governments—continued unabated into the new century.

WAS THE FEDERAL INCOME TAX INTENDED TO BE PERMANENT?

American influence aside, it is assumed that the federal income tax introduced in 1917 was meant to be temporary. Certainly it seems that way from a reading of budget speeches of the period, and the federal government made every effort to avoid levying an income tax. Sir Thomas White, the Conservative Finance minister who eventually brought in the income tax, first attempted to finance the war effort with increases in existing duties and tariffs.

In the 1914 budget, tariffs were increased on coffee, sugar, spirits and tobacco and excise duties were also upped. In 1915, additional tariff increases were applied once again to most consumable goods. "The chief source and mainstay of our revenue is the tariff and it is to this we look principally for relief of our present financial condition,"[5] noted White, who was also forced to borrow heavily to finance the war effort. (It is estimated that in the second year of the war effort, $166 million would be required for that purpose; the tax increases were to bring in between $28 million and $35 million.)

In 1915, White still resisted an imposition of an income tax. His chief objection was that the provinces had very few taxes that they could levy under the Constitution, and thus, because several provinces already did so, it was his view that "the Dominion should not enter upon the domain to which they [the provinces] are confined to a greater degree than is necessary in the national interest."[6]

By 1916, however, the war had lasted longer than anyone had foreseen in 1914 and the reality of wartime needs forced a change in policy. Public opinion, prompted by sacrifices brought about by war, also led to criticism of firms that made large profits during wartime. Thus, in the budget, the Finance minister introduced a tax upon business war profits. Some thought he did not go far enough, but White cautioned such critics in this manner:

During the war there has been considerable criticism to the effect that the Business Profits Tax was not sufficiently heavy. In my view this criticism is not sound and fails to take into consideration many vital aspects of the subject. A Business Profits Tax is justifiable during a prolonged war, because money is urgently needed and it is a ready method of obtaining it in large amounts. There is also a justification in the fact that public opinion is offended at the sight of abnormal profits in a period of great suffering and privation. On principle, however, the tax is not sound and tends to produce much economic evil in the State. It is really a tax upon business success, and consequently tends to discourage business enterprise and administrative efficiency....[7]

White also took exception to the view that a tax on business was in some way neutral to the average citizen. He noted that taxation costs, like any other, are built into the price of products and thus transferred to the public:

There is no doubt in my mind that the taxation of business profits in England, United States and Canada has had much to do with the increased price of commodities. Taxation always tends to transfer

*itself to the consuming public, no matter what its immediate inci-
dence may be.... It is not difficult to see the national disadvantage
of such a tax beyond the abnormal war period.*[8]

Canada's Federal Income Tax: Following an American Lead

As late as April 1917, and despite increases in the Business Profits
Tax, the Finance minister still resisted introducing a personal
income tax. But three months later, another 100,000 men were
called up. This was to be an extra cost to the nation not only in
dollars but of more obvious importance—potentially in blood.
Thus, White introduced the Dominion's first national tax on
July 25, 1917, in the *Income Tax War Act*. He noted that this
was a reluctant action given that several provinces already imposed such a tax (Prince Edward Island and British Columbia).
Also, some municipalities levied taxes on income similar to the
amount the Dominion government was then poised to bring
into force.

Canada's federal income tax, introduced three years after the
American federal income tax, also bore the mark of U.S. legislative
influence. Canada's first federal income tax,[a] brought into being
by the *Dominion Income War Tax Act* of 1917, "bore an unmistak-
able resemblance to the similar 1913 American legislation," wrote
one historian.[9]

Was income tax meant to be permanent? White's prior reluctance to see a permanent business tax imposed was matched by his
distaste for a levy on personal income, but he seemed to realize that
the final decision about its permanence was not likely to be his:

*I have placed no time limit upon this measure, but merely placed
upon Hansard the suggestion that a year or two after the war is over,
the measure should be definitely reviewed by the Minister of Finance*

a. The Americans brought in a federal income tax briefly in the 19th century, during the Civil War, abandoned it afterward, but after a skirmish in the country's
Supreme Court in the 1890s and then a constitutional amendment, introduced
it again in 1913.

and the Government of the day, with a view of judging whether it is
suitable to the conditions which then prevail.[10]

Thus was Canada's first federal income tax born. The rate began
at 4 per cent for any income above $1,500 (then the basic exemp-
tion), or just above $20,300 in today's dollars.[b]

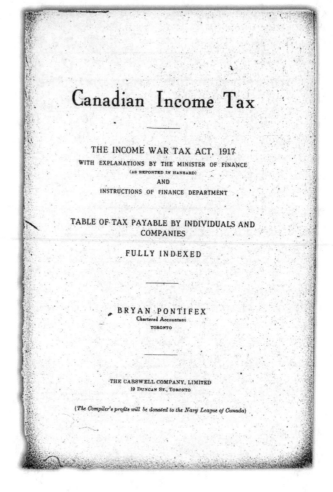

b. Given inflation, that $1,500 basic personal exemption would now be worth
$20,384. How does that compare to today's exemption? As of 2005, the federal
exemption was $8,148, while provincial basic exemptions in 2005 ranged from
$14,523 in Alberta to $7,231 in Nova Scotia.

THE PATTERN CONTINUES: ALBERTA (!) FOLLOWS U.S. LEAD ON GASOLINE AND SALES TAXES

The combination of events and American influence can be seen in the incidence of Canada's first gasoline taxes. With the provinces responsible for road construction during this period, the burgeoning growth in vehicle ownership in Canada necessitated new taxes to pay for the additional roads. In 1905, the number of registered passenger cars in all of Canada had totalled just 553. That jumped to more than 60,000 10 years later and to more than one million by 1930.[11]

The first gasoline tax in Canada was levied by Alberta in 1922 at a rate of two cents per gallon. But Alberta was hardly the first North American jurisdiction; the Americans already taxed fuel in Oregon, Colorado and North Dakota by 1919; in Kentucky in 1920 and in 15 other U.S. states in 1921. In all, 19 states placed a tax on gasoline before Alberta. But once the "wild rose province" taxed gasoline, other Canadian provinces soon followed. Only Saskatchewan held out until 1928—and took pride in having waited that long.[12]

In terms of revenues, the automobile was an ever-increasing component of provincial revenues. Minimal in 1920 when revenues for vehicles came solely from registration, gasoline taxes and vehicle licensing accounted for 26 per cent of all provincial revenues by 1930.[13]

The American precedent was also evident in other taxes. When Canadian provinces introduced sales taxes over the course of several decades, beginning with Alberta in 1936 under the *Ultimate Purchasers Act*[c] (though the province yanked the tax just one year later), American states had already ventured into that territory.

After the Americans: The Great Depression and World War Two

While World War One and new and easily taxed inventions such as the automobile boosted government taxation—and spending—in

---

c. While Alberta was the first province to introduce a retail sales tax, Montreal had already begun to levy a civic version in 1935 and was followed by Quebec City in 1940. Both city sales taxes were eventually taken over by the province.

the first several decades of the 20th century, the Great Depression (and later World War Two) propelled government to new heights. The Depression sent Canadian governments in search of more revenues and resulted in taxes and intervention previously thought unlikely by citizens of that period. The burden was small compared to today, nonetheless, judged by expectations of the day, it seemed as if every tax lever was pumped for higher revenues. Moore and Perry:

> In the scramble for tax revenues, corporate and personal incomes were particularly the subject of attack. Only the Dominion, British Columbia and Prince Edward Island taxed corporate profits in 1930; a decade later all provinces were in the field. Similarly, the number of provinces levying personal income taxes increased from three to seven. While these new provincial taxes were being imposed the federal income tax rates approximately doubled. The federal sales tax was increased from a rate of 1 per cent to 8 per cent and many new excise taxes were introduced. Provincial gasoline taxes were raised 50 per cent on average; retail sales taxes were introduced in the provinces of Saskatchewan and Quebec and in the cities of Montreal and Quebec, succession duty rates were raised, exemptions lowered and enforcement stiffened. New flat-rate taxes were introduced and old ones increased. In terms of increased rates and new levies, the onslaught on the taxpayer was comparable to that of World War II, but in addition the hidden burden in the form of double or triple taxation, overlapping administration, multiple accounting and multifarious forms was also onerous.[14]

One clear measure of the increased tax burden is in the ratio of taxes relative to the economy. In 1929, taxes amounted to just over 15 per cent of Gross Domestic Product (GDP). As the Depression deepened, the combination of a shrunken economy and new and higher taxes meant that by 1932, taxes as a percentage of the economy had climbed to more than 25 per cent. That ratio declined slightly during the ensuing years but was broached again by 1941.

And that height was soon surpassed again. The necessity of revenues for the war effort resulted in taxes equal to 48 per cent of all economic output in 1944.

One measure of the tax burden for individuals is shown in the decreased personal exemption and higher rates; mid-war, in 1942, the basic exemption was lowered to just $660, significantly less than the original $1,500 allowed when income tax was introduced in 1917. Thus, 25 years later and despite inflation, more personal income than ever was subject to taxation. And marginal federal tax rates, which ranged from 4 per cent to 29 per cent in 1917, hit a 1944 wartime peak of between 33 and 98 per cent.

Post-war taxes (as well as spending) were consistently reduced both in actual rates and also relative to the growing economy; by 1950 taxes amounted to just 21 per cent of the economy. The trade-off was slower debt reduction, but as Liberal Finance minister D.C. Abbott remarked at mid-century, "the present level of personal income taxes is regarded as excessive by a large proportion of the public."[15] Indeed.

The Canadian cliché for higher taxes: American Justice Oliver Wendell Holmes Jr.

"There is no art which one government sooner learns of another than that of draining money from the pockets of people," said Adam Smith in *The Wealth of Nations* in 1776. "Taxes are the price we pay for civilization," replied U.S. Supreme Court justice Oliver Wendell Holmes Jr. in Compañia de Tabacos *v.* Collector in 1904. And ever since, in an act of supreme cross-border irony, the U.S. justice who assuaged the concerns of Americans about imposts in a low-tax age has become the poster child for Canadians who like to argue—in a high-tax age—for present tax levels or even higher takings from government.

However, similar to any statement with a nugget of truth, once a saying becomes a cliché, the reasonableness of the original point is lost in present justifications. What may be appropriate to live by in one age may hardly be prudent in another; the applicability of a statement depends on context. About the time Justice Holmes uttered his now-famous dictum, federal taxes in the United States amounted to 1.3 per cent of the U.S. economy.[16] One century later in America, federal taxes alone amount to nearly 20 times that.

In Canada, and to go beyond just federal taxes to a more comprehensive measurement of government near to the time of Justice Holmes' remark, total government expenditures amounted to 9.5 per cent of Gross National Expenditures (GNE) in 1900 and 11.4 per cent in 1910.[17] If taxes, which presently constitute 33.9 per cent of the economy in Canada, make for a superior civilization (with actual government expenditures higher yet at 41.1 per cent and total revenues at 41.7 per cent), the logical corollary is that 38 per cent or 39 per cent or 75 per cent would equal even *more* civilization. The riposte is that a glance around the world at lighter-levied countries—Switzerland and Japan, to name just two—who are arguably as pleasant, or more so, than Canada in terms of prosperity, health, life expectancy and culture, shreds the simplistic link. Taxes may be a "good" at moderate levels, but it's a mistake to extrapolate the taxes = civilization concept to an extreme.[d]

Adam Smith was correct about the tendency of governments to tax as a default option. The belief that enough smart people plus more tax dollars equal a solution to any public problem is a perennial temptation for intellectuals and politicians. But Canada long ago passed the point necessary for taxes as a foundation for civilization. The debate now should be how to achieve moderate levels and how to properly divvy up the resulting tax revenues. Instead, increased taxation is too often presumed a cure-all for any public or private ill. Justice Holmes was right about taxes and civilization—but only to a point.

---

d. The high taxes = higher civilization link is now more ironic given that, as I've noted elsewhere, many of Canada's crime rates—with the exception of murder—are higher than those of the United States.

Live long and prosper, even if your government is smaller than Canada's

Does the size of government need to be as large as Canada's in order for a society to be healthy, experience less crime and live as long? While there are countries with larger size of government relative to the economy when compared with Canada, there are also some notable exceptions. And while many Canadians would count out the United States and argue it is less civilized than Canada, that argument is more difficult (and incorrect) when it concerns Australia, Ireland, Japan and Switzerland, all of whom have smaller governments but enjoy similar if not better social indicators.

There are many variables that influence life expectancy and other social indicators and there are many diverse ways to measure a civilized country. But that is just the point: many countries prosper, their citizens live longer, they have more doctors and more beds to stay in when they are sick—with a smaller size of government relative to the economy.

	CANADA	Australia	Ireland	Japan	Switzerland	United States
Total general government revenue % of GDP	41.7	**36.6**	**35.6**	**30.3**	**35.6**	**31.9**
Total general government expenditure % of GDP	41.1	**36.2**	**34.2**	**38.2**	**35.5**	**36.5**
GDP per capita (PPP) in $US	31,500	30,200	**35,800**	29,600	**33,600**	**39,700**
Infant mortality per 1,000 live births	5.4	**4.8**	**5.1**	**3.0**	**4.3**	7.0
Life expectancy at birth years Women	82.1	**82.8**	80.3	**85.3**	**83.0**	79.9
Men	77.2	**77.8**	75.2	**78.4**	**77.8**	74.5
Practising physicians per 1,000 population	2.1	**2.5**	**2.6**	2.0	**3.6**	**2.3**
Acute care beds per 1,000 population (in patient care)	3.2	**3.6**	3.0	**8.5**	**3.9**	2.8
CO2 emissions per capita	17.49	**17.35**	**10.28**	**9.41**	**5.96**	19.68

Source: OECD in Figures. Statistics on the Member Countries, OECD Observer 2005 / Supplement 1
Social indicator advantages for other countries vis-à-vis Canada in **bold**.

Chapter 15

The Perfect Storm: How discontent in Ontario, Alberta, B.C. and Quebec will change Canada

It should be glaringly obvious that national unity historically based on taxpayers in two jurisdictions writing large cheques to others is not a responsible concept.[1]

~ Ontario Chamber of Commerce, November 2005

If Ontario Is Unhappy ...

A business organization—centred in the largest, most populous, powerful province and which dates from 1911—is not normally the organization to press for radical change. Whether a government is Conservative, Liberal or New Democrat, chambers of commerce usually issue bland press releases with Dilbert-like jargon.

So when the Ontario Chamber of Commerce issued a broadside blast at the federal Liberal government and have-not provinces—not once but twice in 2005—it was a sign that the discontent formerly spotted in British Columbia, Alberta (and eternally in Quebec) was now entrenched in the Ontario firmament.

"Ontario has never failed to help other regions and provinces. But the current level of transfers out of Ontario are not sustainable,"[2] warned Chamber president Len Crispino in a news release. "There is evidence that excessive inter-regional transfers, both the transfer payments programs, have almost certainly contributed to excessive spending in receiving jurisdictions,"[3] noted the report. It then breached another protocol normally respected in the formerly polite central Canadian province: it named names. "Atlantic Canada is home to approximately 100 hospitals, at least 15 public universities, four complete provincial governments (and civil services) to serve a population of about two million."[4]

It was the adjective and the extra colour that gave away the sentiments Chamber members must have expressed behind closed doors. It wasn't just that the Atlantic provinces were—read between the lines—duplicates of each other. It was that they possessed "complete" governments and civil services in addition. And they and the other have-not jurisdictions cost Ontario money—$23 billion annually was the dollar figure pinned on the discontent.

Then the Chamber argued a line that 20 years ago might have appeared at a western protest rally:

> *It is amazing that Ontario has acquiesced to the federal government
> and the other provinces for so long with no serious effort to discern the
> impact on Ontario or the results achieved elsewhere. It is even more
> amazing that the other provinces and the federal government do not
> recognize the heavy burden Ontario and Alberta taxpayers carry on
> behalf of the receiving provinces.[5]*

The reason other provinces did not recognize Alberta's and
Ontario's contributions was obvious: because it's never been
in the interest of their political leadership to go there. But the
Chamber continued:

> *As of this date, other provincial governments are proposing further
> transfers seemingly without regard to Ontario's or Alberta's abilities
> to contribute.... There is doubt however that the federal govern-
> ment or other provinces will get engaged in the problem at all unless
> Ontario is very forceful. It should be glaringly obvious that national
> unity historically based on taxpayers in two jurisdictions writing
> large cheques to others is not a responsible concept.[6]*

The Chamber's $23-billion gap between what the federal govern-
ment collects in taxes and spends in Ontario was labeled a "fiscal
imbalance," as in: the federal government takes too much while
Queen's Park needs money.

The "fiscal imbalance" claim is a myth, at least applied to the
federal government. That claim assumes the national government
doesn't have areas of responsibility and bills to pay that might
have first call on the cash, such as shoring up the armed forces or
repaying a half-trillion-dollar federal debt. The Ontario Chamber's
assertion also contained several unjustifiable assumptions: that a
federal government should spend money primarily in the same
province where it is collected, that Ontario cannot hike taxes even
though Premier Dalton McGuinty is quite adept at that art, and

that the Ontario government cannot solve its own fiscal problems with more careful spending.[a]

The "fiscal imbalance" exists all right, but *between* provinces; the federal government is only the middleman, the supplier of the equalization and transfer drugs that originate in the more economically robust regions.

But the Chamber was properly irritated about the $23 billion[b] transferred *when such transfers are unjustified*, i.e., when they do not actually solve the problem. That Ontario was long polite about such inter-provincial cash calls resulted from eternally assumed prosperity and a noble impulse that believed that such transfers could keep Canada together and could bring prosperity to have-not provinces.

But it was one thing to hand over billions every year when Ontario ran surpluses and cut taxes; as well, under Mike Harris, any complaint about equalization and transfer programs would have been met with claims that another Conservative was being greedy, regardless of the strength of the underlying economic argument. But it's another matter, including on the perceptions front, when deficits are in play, the government can't guarantee the lights will come on, taxpayers have a swollen Hydro debt, and Ontario loses physicians to Alberta. Then, the insanity of the federal equalization and transfer programs—which encourage counterproductive economic behaviour—become clear, even in downtown Toronto and to Queen's Park Liberals.

CASCADING DISCONTENTMENT: MCGUINTY, THE *STAR* AND TAXPAYERS

The Chamber's irritation was not the first sign of discontent. Ontario premier Dalton McGuinty brought up the $23-billion-elephant-in-the-room at a meeting of provincial premiers in

a. Ontario's per capita spending average for the first two years under McGuinty was $6,431—higher than the New Democrat average in the first half of the 1990s at $6,380. (All figures adjusted for inflation. *Source*: Canadian Taxpayers Federation.)

b. This was one figure; a more comprehensive estimate from the Institute for Sustainable Energy, Environment, and Economy in Calgary noted that Ontario's annual net loss was $28.7 billion for the 2002 fiscal year. See Chapter 2 for more explanation on equalization, transfers and the much-discussed "fiscal imbalance."

September 2004. "We're all for supporting equalization *per se*,"[7] said McGuinty. "We're real partners in this. We're committed to this. We're putting our money where our mouth is." He then added the fine print: "It's very important that the provinces understand that they've got to protect the golden goose here."

Even the *Toronto Star* chimed in, perhaps inadvertently, when in March 2005 it editorialized that "McGuinty is on solid ground in arguing that a fiscal imbalance between Ottawa and Ontario is hurting the province,"[8] and that "If McGuinty is unable to persuade Ottawa that fairness demands more federal money for Ontario, the province, in all likelihood, will just keep limping along. For all our sakes, it is imperative that McGuinty succeeds in winning Ontario's fair share of federal support."[9]

McGuinty's professed support for equalization and the *Star*'s demand for more "federal" money was a call for more tax dollars. It's just that the *Star* and the Liberal leader wanted the cash for the Ontario and not the federal government. But the message from both corners meant the same thing: a dramatic cut in equalization and transfer payments to poorer provinces so Ontario, B.C. and Alberta could keep more at home.

It's possible the *Star* and McGuinty didn't understand the implication of their own rhetoric. But there was only one way to cut through that Gordian knot of less money for Manitoba, Nova Scotia and the other have-nots but more for Ontario, B.C. and Alberta. That's if Ottawa shifted enough of its tax power over to provincial governments. Anything else, such as increasing equalization and transfers, would only recycle money in greater quantities from the very jurisdictions (Ontario, B.C. and Alberta) that complain about the imbalance in the first place. And larger federal-provincial transfers would only increase—not decrease—that Grand Canyon gap.[c]

c. Even then, wealthy provinces will always pay more to Ottawa than they receive
  in return because of other federal programs not likely to be run by individual
  provinces any time soon, Employment Insurance, for example. Employees in
  booming provinces such as Alberta collectively pay much more into EI than they
  "take out" because of low unemployment rates; others receive more from the EI
  program than they collectively pay into it. But a provincial EI program would
  likely be undesirable for that very reason (fewer benefits and much higher rates
  because of the smaller pool of contributors), though it might have a salutary effect on perverse incentives built into the current federal program.

UNINTENDED CONSEQUENCES

Many taxpayers might welcome a shift in the tax burden away from Ottawa to the provincial capitals, but it will open up options and force choices that some proponents may not welcome. Ontario may use all the extra tax room vacated by Ottawa to pay for programs formerly funded by federal transfers; B.C. and Alberta might do some of that but cut business and personal taxes in addition, as might the Atlantic provinces.

McGuinty and the *Star* properly wanted less money forwarded to inefficient ends. But the result would be an end to a national one-size-fits-all approach to social policy so beloved by most Liberal governments (federal and provincial) and the *Toronto Star.*

For some, that would be a pleasant development. The failed record of regional development programs, corporate welfare, and the perverse effect of transfer and equalization programs was noted for years by market-loving think tanks such as the CD Howe Institute, the Fraser Institute and, somewhat bravely given the region, the Atlantic Institute for Market Studies (AIMS) in Halifax.

Economist Fred McMahon, a one-time policy analyst at AIMS, has long detailed why many transfers hurt Atlantic Canada (and other have-not areas) instead of help; he recommended a policy approach based on incentives to put the four provinces on the road to the wealth in Ireland and the northeastern American states: trade wasteful make-work programs for reduced business tax levels, among other options.[d] It was a better strategy than a perpetuation of Ottawa's approach, the latter of which was designed to buy votes, not prosperity, and failed in the same way and for the same reasons the federal government's strategy to bring prosperity to remote native reserves has been a disaster.

It was odd that an Ontario Liberal premier and the *Star* editorial board agreed with libertarian and conservative think tanks and economists. But it was proof that even politicians and

---

d. See Fred McMahon, *Looking the Gift Horse in the Mouth: The Impact of Federal Transfers on Atlantic Canada,* and *Road to Growth: How Lagging Economies Become Prosperous,* and *Retreat from Growth: Atlantic Canada and the Negative Sum Economy.*

interventionist-friendly newspapers are not beyond the redemptive power of common sense.

THE OTHER ONTARIO TEMPEST: TAXPAYERS

If free-market think tanks and the Ontario Chamber of Commerce on one side of the dinner table, and McGuinty and the *Star* on the other, make up an odd *ménage a quatre*, Ontario's taxpayers were the background kitchen help whose behaviour should not be ignored.

Before the 2003 election, McGuinty promised never to hike taxes without giving taxpayers a chance to first vote on the idea; he even affixed his *Dalton McGuinty* to a pledge in a prime-time news conference with the Canadian Taxpayers Federation (CTF). It was meant to dispel any lingering doubts that Ontario Liberals would reverse the 1990s tax relief and act more like New Democrats than federal tax-cutting Liberals. McGuinty succeeded. And then post-election, in the premier's chair, he chose instead to imitate the Ontario Reds; he broke his pledge and signalled his intent to ignore and then revoke Ontario's *Taxpayer Protection Act,* which mandated a referendum on tax hikes. He also managed to rouse 209,045 Ontarians to sign a CTF petition that called on him to respect his original vote-getting promise and also the voters who believed him.[10] But the side benefit of the deception was that, while Ontario is not normally a protest culture, McGuinty ensured a segment of Ontarians are no longer as docile as they might have been 10 or 20 years ago. Lying can do that.

And Now for the Fireworks

If taxpayers in Ontario are primed because of the McGuinty backflip; if the province's Chamber of Commerce, Liberal government and leading left-wing daily are unhappy with Ottawa and the current state of inter-provincial arrangements, there are two interpretations. First, they are part of a potentially explosive cocktail that results from grievances already brewing in B.C. and Alberta, the other powerful provinces that in most decades also are net contributors to the country's finances. Second, and more positively, the discontent has created the possibility for national reform on a number of issues ignored in polite Ontario until now.

Add Quebec to the mix and, despite its status as a chronic have-not recipient, the pressure it can add to the national debate may yet break the status quo on the role of the federal and provincial governments and how social programs are delivered.

Thus, four provinces now have motive, pressure and vehicles for reform: provincial financial pressure in two cases (Ontario and Quebec) and desire in the other two (Alberta and B.C.); popular pressure as is most noticeable in the Ontario $23-billion claim and the Chamber report; and vehicles: governments and politicians with their own agendas.

Each province also has "sparks" that won't be doused easily. If Ontarians now realize how much money is transferred away from their province and to questionable projects with failed outcomes, British Columbians and Albertans have been unenthused for some time. In B.C., the annual per capita loss between 1961 and 2002 was $428, while Alberta lost $2,510 per person annually compared to $758 in Ontario.[e]

And it's getting worse: the 2000-02 average was a net loss per person of $1,396 in B.C., $2,725 in Ontario, and $3,401 in Alberta—every year. The recipient provinces may not like a reduction in those numbers, but with 62 per cent of the population, Alberta, B.C. and Ontario have clout if they use it and take a hard line on federal transfer payments.

In addition to the have provinces, which each have at least one significant issue it wants addressed, there is Quebec, where health care reform will go further than most, thanks in part to the 2005 Supreme Court Chaoulli ruling. Ontario's Liberal government might object to more private health care, delivered or insured, but on this issue it won't matter: if Quebec combines with B.C. and Alberta to press for reform, those three provinces represent 51 per cent of the population of country. Also, Quebec is volatile for

---

e. In total, between 1961 and 2002, British Columbia was subject to a net loss of $54.2 billion, Alberta lost $243.6 billion, while Ontario gave up $314.5 billion. (*Source*: Institute for Sustainable Energy, Environment, and Economy.)

federal politicians; none dare trample on provincial powers lest separatists be given a club with which to beat Canada.

British Columbia was out of the loop on major national issues for 10 years because of a government that hobbled its economy, but its government is again friendly to wealth creation, the economy is booming and living there has become *expensive*. The first two factors contribute to rapid population growth and all the influence that implies: more wealth, additional cash transfers out of the province to Ottawa and more seats in Parliament. The last factor contributes to irritation with current federal-provincial arrangements especially because it's so costly to live in many parts of that province. Massive transfers of tax dollars with mortgages two, three and four times higher than those in have-not provinces will increasingly be ill-received by homeowners who spend well over half a million dollars for a Vancouver bungalow.

Add to that economic aggravation B.C.'s historic sense of grievance. Ottawa is viewed as a distant colonial capital that wastes money (and for which B.C. voters harshly punish provincial governments), is corrupt and caters overmuch to Quebec. Any national reform that could give the West Coast more control, allow it to keep more money and provide clout will be attractive to British Columbians.

As for the smaller provinces, it would be a mistake to assume they will necessarily oppose reforms. It will depend on the issue and some might well join in the occasional "coalition of the willing" on a particular issue because it is in their interest.

Thus, Newfoundland and Saskatchewan governments may not care for a discussion on reduced transfer payments; they may go along if the reward is federal tax points and solid control over how they deliver their social programs including health care. Likewise, Prince Edward Island, Nova Scotia, New Brunswick and Manitoba may see any talk of equalization reform, an end to business subsidies and cancelled regional-development schemes as anathema. But should the federal transfer of tax room be large enough to allow such provinces to dramatically reduce personal and business taxes to re-engineer government and stimulate investment, there may be enough incentive combined with a "major power" press to push it through.

Most significantly, Alberta is the winner in any equation. If all other provinces block a reform high on Alberta's priority list, its natural resource revenues allow it to conduct its own policy experiments.[f] But Alberta would have a national effect even then, by example, but also through competitive pressure and especially on Ontario.

If there is no reform of programs, and federal spending and taxing powers, Alberta can and likely will cut business and personal taxes further; it has the room. That action makes it much more difficult for Ontario to rebound economically. The giant sucking sound will be head offices, small businesses and entrepreneurs who move to Alberta. (And, as population follows jobs, the clout of that province will also increase in Parliament.)

Another side effect is on government services, the attraction for physicians, for example, of Alberta: higher pay and significantly lower personal and business tax rates. Given Alberta's leverage and room to maneuver, Ontario will press the federal government to vacate tax room for three reasons: first, on the justification that only then can Ontario balance its budget more than occasionally; second, to pay more for increased health care; and third, to reduce provincial taxes to compete with Alberta.

But Alberta yet holds the trump card in all of this. If the federal government refunds tax points to the provinces as per Ontario's request, a sensible Alberta government will call "checkmate," cut rates, and increase the distance between its taxes and those paid at similar incomes in Ontario. That deepens the competitive advantage and forces other provinces to lower *their* rates, especially the major competitors. Those who dislike what they see as Alberta's current oversized influence will not care for Canada's economic

f. I should note that I am opposed to the so-called Alberta Agenda published by a group of prominent Albertans who called for the province to collect its own provincial tax and run its own police service (instead of the RCMP), among other suggestions. Such measures would only add to costs incurred by provincial taxpayers, and insofar as provincial tax collection is concerned, would be inefficient. Such measures would do absolutely nothing to increase Alberta's power within the country; they would be expensive and useless distractions.

future: it has Alberta Advantage spray-painted all over it. It is an influence that will only increase with the presence of an Alberta-friendly Tory government in power in Ottawa.

The Perfect Storm and Survivalist's Worst Fears

As much as the "fiscal imbalance" claim is incorrect when applied to federal-provincial relations, the combination of provincial interests, Alberta's unique clout and a resurgent threat of Quebec separation will likely lead to a two-pronged federal strategy: a permanent transfer of tax room and, in an attempt to prevent future requests for more, a loosening of or a complete end to requirements on how provinces spend their revenues, something now tightly bound up by Ottawa when it transfers cash and existing tax points. It will be a retreat to provincial and federal jurisdictions as originally envisioned by Canada's founders—on balance, a positive development. That will also unleash experimentation in the provincial capitals; it will happen in areas from health care to child care and in a manner similar to diverse approaches to welfare reform in the 1990s.

In a four-province alliance that consists of Ontario, Quebec, B.C. and Alberta, 86 per cent of Canada's population is included. On any one issue, that coalition can suffer a defection of one and still represent over half the country's people in battles with the federal government.[g] Experimentation will be quickly noticed and, where successful, copied.

For some in Canada, the "survivalists" who fear change and retain a garrison psyche and look to government (most often the federal one) for security, such changes will be unwelcome. For others, possibly a majority and certainly those guided by a different historical narrative about Canada, some delegation of authority, responsibility and taxing power from Ottawa will be welcome. From the perspective of federal politicians who desire

g. I wouldn't assume that everyone in a province will or does follow a provincial government approach. But those in power in the provincial governments can still pursue their agenda and the fact of their large populations allows them bargaining power with Ottawa just in case a plurality of the population happens to agree.

to channel dissent that now simmers (and in Ontario of all un-expected places), it will also be an attractive option. It will also open up the possibility for other regional narratives and self-understanding to more greatly affect the national discourse on these issues than has occurred to date.

The other alternative, from those attached to current gov-ernment models, is to block reform on major federal-provincial issues. But that would frustrate Ontarians' newly found sense of grievance, aggravate the historical irritation present in British Columbia and Alberta, and risk fomenting separatism again in Quebec—even, admittedly, but especially—because the separatists are better at propaganda than math.

Those opposed to reform of the Canadian polity may not have a choice but to consider devolution of money and power to the provincial capitals. The discontent exists in the four major provinces, as do the political and psychological elements that will sustain and continually provoke it: grievances (real or not), deficits in some provinces, desire for more control in others, impatience with slowed reforms and antagonism should they be hindered. Such "rebellion" may finally fracture the fear of change innate in the survivalist-garrison psyche, the dominant Canadian narrative for more than two centuries; it may fatally weaken what amounts to a serf-like, garrisoned timidity and open up the country to a newer and more positive vision of its future.

Provincial discontent, from some of the unlikeliest sources, has brewed the perfect storm.

Endnotes

Chapter 1

1. C.S. Lewis. *The Abolition of Man.* Oxford: Fount, 1981, p. 20.
2. Andrew Mills. "Politics of Quebec, then and now; Critics question the company that Jean once kept; old separatist controversy still dogs new GG," *Toronto Star,* 20 August 2005, p. A18.
3. Jack Aubry. "Article unearths more about Lafond's separatist ties," *National Post,* 13 August 2005, p. A1.
4. Ibid.
5. Andrew Coyne. "Does Jean believe in Canada?" *National Post,* 13 August 2005, p. A18.
6. Ibid.
7. Jack Aubry. "Jean 'committed' to Canada: G-G's statement doesn't address 'independence' toast," *National Post,* 18 August 2005, p. A1.
8. Ibid.
9. Andrew Coyne. "This new adventure. Jean's siren song of freedom: Jaw-dropping boldness of speech seductive," *National Post,* 28 September 2005, p. A1.
10. Chantal Hébert. "Michaëlle Jean will turn out to be hard to dislike or to dismiss," *The Hill Times,* 3 October 2005, Issue 807, p. 11.
11. Jack Aubry. "Jean 'committed' to Canada."
12. Ibid.
13. Rhéal Seguin. Untitled, *Globe and Mail,* web edition, 27 October 2005.
14. Philip Preville. "Michaëlle Jean, Installed," *Saturday Night,* Winter 2005, p. 34.
15. Ibid.
16. Quoted in Rhéal Seguin, Untitled, *Globe and Mail.*
17. OECD. "Society at a Glance"/International Crime Victims Survey, March 2002, data Chart CO3.1, http://www.oecd.org/dataoecd/39/44/2492201.xls.
18. Vancouver Board of Trade, Report on Property Crime in Vancouver, 24 October 2003, available at http://www.boardoftrade.com/policy/PROPERTYCRIME-FINAL-OCT24-03-web.pdf, p. 2.

19. Tracy Huffman. "'We have got to get the guns'; New squad to gather intelligence on gangs and firearms. 'There are a lot of youngsters who are at risk,' says officer," *Toronto Star*, 25 November 2005, p. AO1.

20. Statistics Canada. "General Social Survey: Criminal victimization, 2004." Reported in *The Daily*, released 24 November 2005, pp. 5-7.

21. Statistics Canada. "Crime Statistics, 2004." Reported in *The Daily*, released 21 July 2005, pp. 2-6.

22. Keith Gerein. "Mandel wants share of income tax for cities: Idea will be presented at mayors' conference," *Edmonton Journal*, 25 November 2005, p. B9.

23. Trevor Lautens. "The outrage is: There was no outrage," *North Shore News* (North Vancouver), 30 January 2004, p. 6.

24. Daryl Slade. "Prison time cut due to lack of vegetarian meals," *Calgary Herald*, 23 August 2005, p. B5.

25. Chris Purdy. "In vegetative state after beating, man attends hearing on attacker's status: Attacker was on probation at time of incident and had a history of violent crime," *Vancouver Sun*, 28 October 2004.

26. Chris Purdy. "'We won,' victim's wife says," *Edmonton Journal*, 1 March 2005, p. A3.

27. Joey Thompson. "Is 14 old enough for age of sexual consent? Most other countries have raised age to 16." *The Province* (Vancouver), 16 November 2005, p. A6.

28. Canadian Press. "Top court won't review case of man spared jail," *Daily News* (Halifax), 21 October 2005, p. 8.

29. Alberta Justice statistics on James Roszko. Williamson Kerry and Renata D'Aliesio. "Families of slain RCMP fume over report: Roszko escaped dangerous offender status," *Calgary Herald*, 7 October 2005, p. A1.

30. Editorial. "Evidence shows Harper's justice policies would exacerbate drug problem," *Vancouver Sun*, 6 December 2005, p. A10. *The Sun* argued that "a 2001 study commissioned by Justice Canada found absolutely no correlation between the crime rate and the severity of sentences." The editorial missed the salient point that if someone convicted of three violent offenses was placed in jail for, say, 20 or 30 years, that convict would no longer have a chance to affect the crime rate.

31. Linda Diebel. "We know the numbers. Forty-eight shooting deaths this year. Forty of those victims were under the age of 30, the last an 18-year-old gunned down at his best friend's funeral. Isn't it time we did something more?" *Toronto Star*, 20 November 2005, p. AO8.

32. Matt Ramsey. "Cops say no to drugs: Downtown eastside: Crackdown on open drug use as streets littered with needles." *The Province* (Vancouver), 27 November 2005, p. A23.

33. Rondi Adamson. "Thugs know they won't be severely punished," *Toronto Star*, 1 January 2006, p. A16.

34. Linda Diebel. "We all have to act to push for change," *Toronto Star*, 31 December 2005, p. A18.

35. Ibid.

36. Siri Agrell and Kelly Patrick. "Boxing day shootings suspect fresh out of jail: gun violence: Many charges dropped," *National Post*, 31 December 2005, p. A10.

37. Patrick Evans et al. "Girl's slaying has 'touched each one of us'; Hundreds gather to mourn Yonge St. victim. Many undeterred from New Year's revelry," *Toronto Star*, 31 December 2005, p. A21.

38. Les Whittingon. "Ex-chief of ad firm faces MPs; Groupe Everest founder testifies; Denies doing anything wrong," *Toronto Star*, 20 April 2004, p. A06.

39. *Globe and Mail*, 19 April 2004, web edition.

40. William Marsden. "Memory lapses plague testimony of Montreal businessman," *National Post*, 2 March 2005, p. A7.

41. William Marsden. "Ad firm made $31M from sponsorships: President earned $9M." *National Post*, 1 March 2005, p. A6.

42. Herbert Bauch. "Lafleur's son admits billings seemed excessively high," *National Post*, 10 March 2005, p. A6.

43. Ibid.

Chapter 2

1. Sir Wilfrid Laurier as quoted in *Canadian Quotations and Phrases: Literary and Historical*, Robert H. Hamilton and Bruce Hutchinson, eds., Toronto: McClelland & Stewart, 1965, p. 219.

2. Quoted in Kevin Dougherty, "Ante up, Charest tells feds as Quebec Liberals meet," *Montreal Gazette*, 17 May 2004, p. A11.

3. Ibid.

4. James Baxter and Jason Markusoff. "Show us the money, premiers say: Goodale rebuffs demand to reinstate $2.2B for education," *Edmonton Journal*, 13 August 2005, p. A1.

5. Ibid.

6. Ron Ryder. "Respect provinces' jurisdictions: Charest's message to Ottawa," *Guardian* (Charlottetown), 9 November 2004, p. A1.

7. A. Milton Moore and J. Harvey Perry. *Financing Canadian Federation*, Canadian Tax Foundation, Canadian Tax Papers, No. 6, Toronto, 1953, p. 5.

8. Ibid.

9. J. Harvey Perry. *Taxes, Tariffs, and Subsidies*, Toronto: University of Toronto Press, 1955, p. 619.

10. Ibid.

11. Moore and Perry, p. 6.

12. Ibid.

13. Perry, *Taxes, Tariffs, and Subsidies*, p. 621.
14. Moore and Perry, p. 16.
15. "Federal Transfers to Provinces and Territories." Department of Finance, Ottawa, 7 November 2005, http://www.fin.gc.ca/FEDPROV/mtpe.html.
16. "Federal Support for Health Care: The Facts." Department of Finance, Ottawa, 7 November 2005, http://www.fin.gc.ca/facts/fshc7_e.html.
17. Robert Mansell, Ron Schlenker and John Anderson. "Energy, Fiscal Balances and National Sharing." *Backgrounder*, Institute for Sustainable Energy, Environment and Economy, University of Calgary, 18 November 2005, p. 11.

Chapter 3

1. John Robert Colombo. *New Canadian Quotations*. Edmonton: Hurtig Publishers, 1987, p. 370.
2. Reid Scott. Quoted on CBC *News Sunday*, 11 December 2005.
3. Reginald W. Bibby. Section 5, "Parenting and Parents," *The Future Families Project: A Survey of Canadian Hopes and Dreams*. Ottawa: Vanier Institute of the Family, 2004, p. 55.
4. Government of Quebec. Rapport Annuel 1998-1999. La Ministère de la Famille et de l'Enfance. Saint Foy, QC: Les Publications du Quebec, 1999. http://www.mfacf.gouv.qc.ca/ministere/rapports_annuels_en.asp. See chapter 2. Government of Quebec. Public Accounts 2003-2004, Volume 2. http://www.finances.gouv.qc.ca/en/documents/publications/pdf/vol2-2003-2004.
5. Stephen Harper. "A new $1,200 choice in child-care allowance for pre-school kids." Announcement in Ottawa, 5 December 2005. Available at www.conservative.ca/1004/33758/.
6. Statistics Canada. "Longitudinal Survey of Immigrants to Canada." 13 October 2005. http://www.statcan.ca/Daily/English/051013/td051013.htm.
7. Hon. Patricia J. Mella, Provincial Treasurer, Prince Edward Island. "Presentation to the Senate committee on national finance concerning the equalization program," 24 October 2001.
8. For more on this, see Angus Maddison, *The World Economy: A Millennial Perspective*. Paris: Development Centre Studies, Organisation for Economic Co-operation and Development, 2001.
9. Thorvaldur Gylfason. "Natural resources and economic growth: what is the connection," CESifo Working Paper No. 530. Munich: Center for Economic Studies and Ifo Institute for Economic Research, Munich, www.CESifo.com, August 2001.
10. Organisation for Economic Co-operation and Development. *OECD in Figures*. Paris: OECD, 2005, p. 38.

11. Ibid., p. 36.
12. Ibid., p. 36.
13. Department of Finance. Fiscal Update 2005. Ottawa: 14 November 2005. http://www.fin.gc.ca/news05/05-077e.html.
14. Calculations by author using Department of Finance data. Note that federal revenues including CPP revenues on the assumption that pocketbooks feel higher CPP taxes in the same manner they feel lower employment insurance taxes. In 2005, revenues were forecast at $228 billion. By my calculations, personal tax relief in 2005, after accounting for 2000 and 2005 announcements and offsetting tax increases, would round out close to $12.4 billion, or about 5.4 per cent of total revenues that year.
15. M.C. Urquhart and K.A.H. Buckley, eds. *Historical Statistics of Canada*, series G26-44. Toronto: MacMillan Canada, 1965, p. 96 of series 219; p. 99 of series 287.
16. J.H. Perry. *Canadian Fiscal Facts: Principal Statistics of Canadian Public Finance.* Toronto: Canadian Tax Foundation, 1965, pp. 102-104.
17. Derek Hum and Barry Ferguson. "Aspects of the Chinese head tax." Winnipeg: Department of Economics, St. John's College, University of Manitoba. http://home.cc.umanitoba.ca/~dhum/re_aspects.html. Also R.L. Hayley, "The Chinese head tax class action: No legal basis." Vancouver: Lawson Lundell, Barristers and Solicitors, 2002. www.lawsonlundell.com. Information on provincial revenue amounts from J.H. Perry, *Taxes, tariffs, and subsidies, Volumes 1 & 2* (1955).

Chapter 4

1. Jacqueline Thorpe. "Bay Street to Harper: Let's hear more on tax plan: Tough on subsidies," *National Post*, 3 June 2004, p. FP1.
2. Rod Ziegler. "Computer chip plant won't get aid—Klein," *Edmonton Journal*, 28 May 1999, p. B1.
3. "Canada's top business associations unite in call for tax cuts," The Canadian Chamber of Commerce, the Alliance of Canadian Exporters Canada, and the Business Council on National Issues, joint media release, 28 September 1999.
4. Michael Bliss. "The company that built a country," *Report on Business Magazine*, September 2001, pp. 46-52.
5. Source: Alberta Public Accounts, compiled by the Canadian Taxpayers Federation.
6. Report of the Auditor General of Canada. Ottawa: September 1999, pp. 19-27.
7. Ibid., pp. 19-28.
8. Audit of Technology Partnerships Canada, Audit and Evaluation Branch, Industry Canada.Ottawa: October 2003, p. 6.

9. Ibid.
10. "Government of Canada Announces New Program to Promote Innovation, Technology Adoption." Montreal: Technology Partnerships Canada, Industry Canada, news release, 20 September 2005. http://tpc-ptc.ic.gc.ca/epic/internet/intpc-ptc.nsf/en/hb00476e.html.
11. Jack Aubry. "Federal fund recoups only 20 per cent of $2 billion," *Ottawa Citizen*, 31 January 2005, p. A6.
12. Ibid.
13. Author interview with Industry Canada, 22 September 2005.
14. Jack Aubry. "Technology firms broke rules on commissions: audit," *National Post*, 23 September 2005, p. FP23.
15. Anne Dawson. "Liberal MPs slam payout for Dingwall: Caucus backlash: Martin urged to quash severance for ex-Mint boss," *National Post*, 6 October 2005, p. A4.
16. Kevin Restivo. "Ottawa replaces much-maligned loan program for tech firms: To focus on sharing 'risks,' rather than 'cost recovery,'" *National Post*, 21 September 2005, p. FP4.
17. Business Credit to Small, Medium and Large Customers, Canadian Bankers Association, July 2001. http://www.cba.ca/eng/statistics/stats/loan_loss.htm.
18. See Stephen Moore and Dean Stansel, "Ending Corporate Welfare as We Know It," Policy Analysis No. 225, Washington D.C.: Cato Institute, 1995; Stephen Moore, "Welfare for the Well-Off: How Business Subsidies Fleece Taxpayers," *Essays in Public Policy*, Stanford, CA: Hoover Institution, May 1999; Fazil Mihlar, "The Government of British Columbia, 1991-1998: An Assessment of Performance and a Blueprint for Economic Recovery," *Critical Issues Bulletin*, Vancouver, B.C.: Fraser Institute, 1998; and Fred McMahon, "Looking the Gift Horse in the Mouth: The Impact of Federal Transfers on Atlantic Canada," Halifax, Atlantic Institute for Market Studies, 1996.
19. See Lynn Bachelor, "Business Participation in Economic Development Programs: Lessons from Six Ohio Cities," *Urban Affairs Review*, Vol. 32 (5), 1997, pp. 704-23; Timothy J. Bartik, "Better Evaluation Is Needed for Economic Development Programs to Thrive," *Economic Development Quarterly*, Vol. 8 (2), 1994 pp. 99-107; Margaret E. Dewar, "Why State and Local Economic Development Programs Cause So Little Economic Development," *Economic Development Quarterly*, Vol. 12 (2), 1998, pp. 134-46; Il Grant and Don Sherman, "Measuring State-Level Economic Development Programs," *Economic Development Quarterly*, Vol. 9 (2), 1995, pp. 134-36.
20. Terry F. Buss. "The Case Against Targeted Industry Strategies," *Economic Development Quarterly*, Vol. 13 (4), 1999, pp. 339-57.

Chapter 5

1. Elizabeth Nickson. "Feeling betrayed in B.C. for battle: Campbell's election promises ring false, labour head says," *National Post*, 23 February 2002, p. B1.
2. Morley Gunderson, Douglas Hyatt and Craig Riddell. "Pay differences between the government and private sectors: labour force survey and census estimates," Ottawa: Canadian Policy Research Networks, February 2000, p. 4.
3. Derek Picard. "Wage Watch," Canadian Federation of Independent Business, October 2003, p. 1.
4. Patrick Brethour and Peter Kennedy. "Public pay settlements double private sector," *Globe and Mail* online, www.globeandmail.com., 21 February 2004.
5. Maurice Bridge. "Hospital workers' strike cost $6.4 million, high court told," *Vancouver Sun*, 18 May 2004, p. B5.
6. Irwin Block. "Clash at Ste. Justine Hospital: Charest cancels event after demonstrators show there's muscle behind union backlash," *Montreal Gazette*, 2 December 2003, p. A1.
7. Jeremy Hainsworth. "Labour leaders discuss supporting B.C. teachers," *Winnipeg Free Press*, 16 October 2005, p. A6.
8. Judith Lavoie. "Budget cuts draw terror comparison: Unions lambaste B.C. government's bid to 'dismantle' civilized society," *Times Colonist* (Victoria), 24 October 2001, p. A1.
9. Ibid.
10. Seth Klein. Interviewed on the "Rafe Mair Show," CKNW Radio, Vancouver, 11 December 2001.
11. Justine Hunter. "Traditional NDP votes in limbo: Labour allies being lured away with promises of tax cuts," *National Post*, 16 November 2000, p. A11.

Chapter 6

1. F.L. Morton and Rainier Knopf. *The Charter Revolution and the Court Party*. Peterborough, ON: Broadview Press, 2000, p. 97.
2. Public Accounts of the Province of British Columbia, Ministry of Finance, 1992-2001.
3. Results from Access to Information request from the Canadian Taxpayers Federation to the federal department of Canadian Heritage, Multiculturalism Program, Ottawa. Fulfilled January 11, 2002.
4. Results from Access to Information request from the Canadian Taxpayers Federation to the federal department of Canadian Heritage, Multiculturalism Program, and Environment Canada, Ottawa, 2002.
5. Results from Access to Information request from the Canadian Taxpayers Federation to Environment Canada, Ottawa, 2002.

6. Ibid.
7. News release from the Pembina Institute, 18 September 2002, www.pembina.org.
8. Data on grants and contributions and other suppliers of money from the public accounts of British Columbia, 1992-2002. Details from Access to Information requests filed by the Canadian Taxpayers Federation, 2002.
9. *Winnipeg Free Press*, "In brief," 29 November 2002, p. A10.
10. Status of Women Canada, Estimates 2002-2003, Part III, tabled in Parliament, 31 March 2003.
11. Data provided by REAL Women, interview by author, 27 September 2002.
12. Morton and Knopf, *The Charter Revolution and the Court Party*, p. 99.
13. Ibid., p. 97.
14. Ibid., p. 99.
15. "The left's secret slush fund," *The Report*, 14 April 2001.
16. Walter Robinson. *Atlantic Canada Opportunities Agency: The Lost Decade, A 10-year Quantitative Analysis*. Ottawa: Canadian Taxpayers Federation, 9 May 2000.
17. Walter Robinson. *WED: Wasted Effort and Tax Dollars? A 13-year Quantitative Analysis of Western Economic Diversification*. Ottawa: Canadian Taxpayers Federation, 2 November 2000.

Chapter 7

1. Mark Vaile. "A Missed Chance to Trade Up from Poverty," 8 April 2003. http://online.wsj.com/article/0,,SB104976504270926700,00.html.
2. National Farmers Union. "Solving the Farm Crisis: A Sixteen-Point Plan for Canadian Farm and Food Security," Submission to Hon. Wayne Easter, Parliamentary Secretary to the Minister of Agriculture and Agri-Food, 20 January 2005, p. 2.
3. Salil Tripathi. "India leaves anti-globalizers in the dust," *Wall Street Journal*, 21 January 2004, web edition.
4. Nicholas Kristof. "Inviting all Democrats," *New York Times*, 14 January 2004, p. A19.
5. Ibid.
6. Ken Georgetti. "Time for a new debate on Canada-U.S. trade," *National Post*, 1 December 2005, p. A19.
7. Editorial. "The Rigged Trade Game," *New York Times*, 20 July 2003, p. A10.
8. "Running into the Sand: Why failure at the Cancun trade talks threatens the world's poorest people," September 2003, Oxfam. http://www.oxfam.org.uk/what_we_do/issues/trade/bp53_cancun.htm.

9. Ibid.

10. Cato Institute. March 2002. http://www.cato.org/dailys/03-06-02.html

11. "U.S., EU farm subsidies 'devastating' to Africa: Goodale in group looking for solutions," *Ottawa Citizen*, 6 May 2004, p. A12.

12. National Farmers Union. "Solving the Farm Crisis: A Sixteen-Point Plan for Canadian Farm and Food Security," pp. 1-14.

13. Ibid., p. 2.

14. Organisation for Economic Co-operation and Development. OECD in Figures 2005, *OECD Observer*, Supplement 1, pp. 26-27.

15. OECD. Agricultural Policies in OECD Countries: Monitoring and Evaluation 2005, Highlights, http://www.oecd.org/dataoecd/33/27/35016763.pdf, p. 12. Currency conversion based on Bank of Canada rate, 31 December 2004.

16. OECD. Agricultural Policies in OECD Countries: Monitoring and Evaluation 2005, Executive Summary, p. 1.

17. Oxfam Press Release. "Sugar company, Lords and Dukes top farm handout list," 22 March 2005, www.oxfam.org.uk/press/releases/subsidies220305.htm

18. Cato Institute. *Cato Handbook on Policy*, 6th edition (2005), p. 315. http://www.cato.org/pubs/handbook/hb108/hb108-30.pdf.

19. Industry Canada. Trade and Investment Monitor 2004, p. 12. http://strategis.ic.gc.ca/epic/internet/ineas-aes.nsf/vwapj/tim2004e.pdf/$FILE/tim2004e.pdf

20. Statistics Canada. "Corporations Returns Act: Foreign Control in the Canadian Economy, 2003," (61-220-XIE), *The Daily*, 20 June 2005, pp. 3-4.

21. Statistics Canada. "Foreign direct investment 2004," *The Daily*, 17 May 2005, pp. 2-4.

22. Statistics Canada. "Impact of foreign ownership on head office employment in manufacturing, 1973-1999," *Foreign Multinationals and Head Office Employment in Canadian Manufacturing Firms*, no. 34, (11F0027MIE2005034), reported in *The Daily*, 8 June 2005, p. 5.

23. Statistics Canada. "Impact of foreign ownership on growth in productivity, 1980-1999," *The Daily*, 5 December 2005, pp. 2-3.

24. Ibid.

Chapter 8

1. Edmund Burke. *Reflections on the Revolution in France*. Harmondsworth, England: Penguin, 1987, p. 356. First published 1790.

2. Daniel Yergin and Joseph Stanislaw. *The Commanding Heights: The Battle for the World Economy*. New York: Touchstone/Simon & Schuster, 1998/2002, p. 189. Original quote in David Goodman. *Deng Xiaoping and the Chinese Revolution*. London: Routledge, 1994.

3. Charles Gordon. "The myth of Canada's 'tax hell,'" *Maclean's*, 26 April 1999, p.13.
4. Jonathan Gatehouse. Quoted in "Submit joyfully to taxes," *National Post*, 20 April 1999, p. A3.
5. See Hugh Segal, *Beyond Greed*. Toronto: Stoddart, 1997.
6. Jock Finlayson. "A look at income in British Columbia," Vancouver: Policy Perspectives, Business Council of British Columbia, June 2000. From Statistics Canada data.
7. Angus Maddison. *The World Economy: A Millennial Perspective*. Paris: Development Centre Studies, Organization for Economic Co-operation and Development, 2001. All figures adjusted for inflation to 1990 Geary-Khamis dollars.
8. See Niels Veldhuis, Joel Emes and Michael Walker, *Tax Facts* 13. Vancouver: Fraser Institute, 2003, p. 62.

Chapter 9

1. Jack Layton. "Status quo no solution," *Victoria Times Colonist*, 1 August 2002, p. A11.
2. John H. Gomery. *Commission of Inquiry into the Sponsorship Program & Advertising Activities: Who Is Responsible? Fact-Finding Report*. 1 November 2005. Ottawa: Public Works and Government Services Canada, p. 223.
3. Layton, "Status quo no solution."
4. Canadian Press. "Corporate scandals will benefit labour, says CLC chief; Union movement is on the rise, says Georgetti; Criticizes right-wing but Liberal Paul Martin as well," *Toronto Star*, 20 September 2003, p. D24.
5. Susan Delacourt. "Pendulum swings to activist government," *Ottawa Citizen*, 1 August 2002, p. A14.
6. Peter Foster. *Self-Serve: How Canadians Pumped Canada Dry*. Toronto: Macfarlane, Walter and Ross, 1992, p. 2.
7. Ibid. Additional calculations on privatization revenues by Milke and inflation adjustments courtesy of the Bank of Canada on-line inflation calculator.
8. "WorldCom will emerge intact, CEO promises," *Financial Post*, 23 July 2002, p. FP1.
9. Roger Altman. "The Market Punishes Its Own," *Wall Street Journal*, 23 July 2002.
10. Leon Lazaroff. "White collars, black hearts: Sentences are getting tougher for corporate crooks," *Calgary Herald*, 25 September 2005, p. C2.
11. Theresa Tedesco. "Radler chastened, Black remains defiant: Former partner refuses to bargain, sources say," *National Post*, 21 September 2005, p. FP3.

12. Charles Frank. "Canadian justice lacks bite," *Calgary Herald*, 21 September 2005, p. D1.

13. "White-collar crimes U.S. scandals," *Toronto Star*, 15 July 2005, p. DO4.

14. "The Gomery Affair: Who's who," *Montreal Gazette*, 1 November 2005, p. A4.

15. Anonymous. "What the judge found," *National Post*, 2 November 2005, p. A8.

16. Mark Milke. *Barbarians in the Garden City—The BC NDP in Power*. Victoria: Thomas & Black, 2001, pp. 174-90.

17. Ibid., pp. 64-72, 191-95.

18. Vaughn Palmer. "Liberals opt for a high-profile professional," *Vancouver Sun*, 13 February 2001, p. A18.

19. Gomery, *Commission of Inquiry*, p. 76.

20. Maurice Bridge. "For sale: the ring that tempted Svend Robinson," *Vancouver Sun*, 27 October 2004, p. A1.

21. Anonymous. "Martin refers report to RCMP; PM moves to mop up after scandal, bans Gagliano from Liberal party for life," *The Record* (Kitchener), 2 November 2005, p. A3.

22. "A review of the estimates process," Office of the Auditor General, Province of British Columbia, February 1999, pp. 139, 151.

23. All details from Report of the Auditor General to the Legislative Assembly, Charlottetown: Auditor General of Prince Edward Island, 2002.

24. Ibid., p. 25.

25. Ibid., pp. 25-26.

26. Ibid., p. 26.

27. Ibid., p. 27.

28. "Lessons learned from our audit investigations," Winnipeg, MB: Office of the Provincial Auditor, March 2001, p. 4.

29. Annual report. Toronto: Office of the Provincial Auditor, 2001, p. 2.

30. Editorial. "Look south, Eric," *Saskatoon Star Phoenix*, 15 July 2002.

31. Report of the Auditor General of Canada to the House of Commons, Matters of Special Importance. Ottawa: Office of the Auditor General, 2001, p. 1.

32. Ibid., p. 6.

33. Report of the Auditor General of Canada to the House of Commons, Matters of Special Importance (2001), p. 12.

34. Report of the Auditor General of Canada to the House of Commons. Ottawa: Office of the Auditor General, November 2003, Chapter 3, pp. 10-12.

35. Gomery, *Commission of Inquiry*, p. 225.

36. Ibid.

37. VIA Rail Annual Reports, 1998-2004.

38. Report of the Auditor General of Canada (November 2003), Chapter 3, p. 12.
39. Ibid.
40. Ibid.
41. Gomery, *Commission of Inquiry*, p. 233.
42. Report of the Auditor General of Canada (November 2003), Chapter 3, p. 11.
43. Ibid.
44. Ibid.
45. Tim Naumetz. "Canada Post sees red ink ahead: Must adjust to market: Pension fund insolvency required $267-million infusion," *National Post*, 26 October 2005, p. A12.

Chapter 10

1. Alexander Solzhenitsyn. Letter to the Writers' Union, Moscow, originally quoted in the *New York Times*, 15 November 1969. Reprinted in the *Quotable Conservative*, Holbrook, MA: Adams Publishing, 1995, p. 216.
2. W.T. Stanbury. "Reforming the Regulation of the Financing of Federal Parties and Candidates," Faculty of Commerce and Business Administration, University of British Columbia. Prepared for the 2nd Annual B.C. Taxpayers Conference, 3 June 1995, p. 2.
3. Notes from "NCC battles gag laws," National Citizens Coalition, www.morefreedom.org.
4. Stanbury, p. 13.
5. Lorne Gunter. "End campaign spending limits," *Policy Options*, September 1999.
6. Ibid.
7. "The political establishment digs in," *Alberta Report*, 22 February 1993.
8. Ibid.
9. "Royal Commission Proposes New 'Voter-Friendly' Election Law for Canada," Ottawa: Main Communiqué from the Royal Commission on Electoral Reform and Party Financing, 13 February 1992.
10. Notes from "NCC battles gag laws," National Citizens Coalition, www.morefreedom.org.
11. Patrick Boyer. *Direct Democracy in Canada*. Toronto: Dundurn Press, 1992, p. 76.
12. "Why does Harvie Andre really want to stifle your freedom of speech during elections?" National Citizens Coalition campaign ad, 1991.
13. Ibid.
14. "Ads don't buy votes," *Globe and Mail*, 30 April 1994.
15. Alanna Mitchell. "Election-ad gag law has difficulty in court," *Globe and Mail*, 9 May 1995.

16. Ibid.
17. "Ottawa's gag law struck down," *Globe and Mail*, 7 June 1996.
18. Ibid.
19. "Elections are not for parties alone," *Globe and Mail*, 9 October 1996.
20. Ed Broadbent. "Let's deodorize political influence," *Globe and Mail*, 22 June 2000.
21. Ibid.
22. National Citizens Coalition news release, 10 May 2001, based on Access to Information requests.
23. Pacific Press & Garry B. Nixon *v.* Attorney General of British Columbia (2000). Supreme Court of British Columbia, par. 167.
24. Harper *v.* Canada (2004). Supreme Court of Canada, par. 85.
25. Ibid.
26. Ibid., par. 96.
27. Pacific Press & Garry B. Nixon *v.* Attorney General of British Columbia, Reasons for Judgment, Honourable Mr. Justice Brenner, 9 February 2000, par. 32-34.
28. Harper *v.* Canada, par. 95.
29. Ibid., par. 87.
30. Ibid., par. 87.
31. Ibid., par. 88.
32. Ibid., par. 106.
33. Ibid., par. 112.
34. Ibid., par. 113.
35. Ibid., par. 113.
36. Ibid., par. 114.
37. Ibid., par. 115.
38. Canada *v.* Sharpe (2001). Supreme Court of Canada.
39. Harper *v.* Canada (2004). Supreme Court of Canada, par. 2.
40. Ibid., par. 4.
41. Ibid., par. 5.
42. Ibid., par. 7.
43. Ibid., par. 8.
44. Ibid., par. 11.
45. Ibid., par. 14.
46. Ibid., par. 15.
47. Ibid., par. 16.
48. Ibid., par. 19.
49. Ibid., par. 20.
50. Ibid., par. 31.
51. Ibid., par. 34.
52. Ibid., par. 35.
53. Ibid., par. 38.

54. Ibid., par. 42.
55. Ibid., par. 43.
56. Statistics Canada. Annual Survey of Advertising and Related Services, *The Daily*, 15 April 2005, p. 7.

Chapter 11

1. Obtained by and reprinted in the *National Post,* 19 July 2005, p. A16.
2. Conal Urquhart. "West Bank settler kills 4 Palestinians," *Toronto Star,* 18 August 2005, p. A06.
3. Tim Butcher. "Five Israelis killed in mall suicide bombing," *Daily Telegraph,* Wed. edition, 6 December 2005, http://www.telegraph. co.uk/news/main.jhtml?xml=/news/2005/12/06/wmid06. xml&DCMP=EMC-new_06122005.
4. Jeffrey Simpson. "Does politics mean never having to say you're sorry?" *Globe and Mail*, 13 May 2005, p. A17.
5. Ibid.
6. Don Martin. "At Immigration, dead Minister walking," *National Post*, 9 December 2004, p. A20.
7. Robert Fife. "Sgro aide tried to silence critics by withholding permits, MPs allege," *Ottawa Citizen*, 27 December 2004, p. A9.
8. Don Martin. "Sgro was right to step aside, given the air of scandal at the immigration department," *Ottawa Citizen*, 15 January 2005, p. A3.
9. Bernard Shapiro. "The Sgro Inquiry: Many Shades of Grey," Office of the Ethics Commissioner, Ottawa, June 2005, appendix IX-1. Original letter to Honourable Judy Sgro, M.P., 2 May 2005.
10. Simpson, "Does politics mean never having to say you're sorry?"
11. Ibid.
12. Susan Riley. "The ethics commissioner has some explaining to do," *Ottawa Citizen*, 11 May 2005, p. A18.
13. Shapiro, "The Sgro Inquiry," p. 19.
14. Ibid., pp. 18-19.
15. Ibid., p.19.
16. Ibid., pp. 19-20.
17. Ibid., p. 20.
18. Ibid.
19. Ibid.
20. Ibid., pp. 20-21.
21. Ibid., p. 23.
22. Ibid.
23. Ibid.
24. Ibid.
25. Ibid., p. 23.

26. Jack Aubry. "Ethics commissioner Bernard Shapiro admitted Tuesday the process he used to hire a Liberal-connected law firm to investigate a complaint against former Immigration minister Judy Sgro was inappropriate," *CanWest News*, Wire feed, 11 May 2005, p. 1.

27. Canadian Press. "Public insurance cheaper—report: Drivers pay far more for private-sector vehicle insurance, consumer study says," *Halifax Daily News*, 11 September 2003, p. 12.

28. Canadian Press. "Ontario motorists saddled with skyrocketing insurance: Consumer study finds that Toronto drivers can pay 500 per cent more than other regions," *Guardian* (Charlottetown), 11 September 2003, p. A11.

29. *Montreal Gazette.* "Insuring car can cost 6 times as much in TO," 11 September 2003, p. A14.

30. *The Province* (Vancouver). "Public auto insurance 'a big saver,'" 11 September 2003, p. A33.

31. Steve Erwin. "Toronto drivers pay up to 500% more for auto insurance: Consumer study," *National Post,* 11 September 2003, p. FP1.

32. Terry Corcoran. "Auto insurance failure," *National Post,* 11 September 2003, p. FP13.

33. Michael Kane. "Auto insurance '30% more' in Alberta," *Vancouver Sun,* 8 July 2005, p. A11.

34. Author interview with Insurance Bureau of Canada, 2 December 2003.

35. Author interview with Theresa Courneyea, 2 December 2003. Excerpts of interview printed in Mark Milke, "Insurance fraud," *National Post,* 4 December 2003, p. FP13.

36. Dan Bellerose. "Ontario drivers pay through roof: Insurance $1,000 more than in B.C., study says," *North Bay Nugget,* 20 July 2005, p. A1.

37. Peter Kennedy. "Auto insurance cheaper in B.C. than Alberta," *Globe and Mail,* 8 July 2005, p. S3.

38. Cathy Gulli. "'Outrageous' costs hammer Ontario drivers," *National Post,* 20 July 2005, p. A5.

39. Kate Gauntlett. "Albertans pay more, consumer study finds: Some rates are 50% higher than in Saskatchewan," *Calgary Herald,* 8 July 2005, p. B1.

40. *Victoria Times Colonist.* "B.C. drivers pay less than Albertans for car insurance," 8 July 2005, p. C8.

41. Ashley Ford. "ICBC fairest in the land: Study gives public auto coverage top grade," *The Province* (Vancouver), 8 July 2005, p. A39.

42. Ibid.

43. Karen Kleiss. "City drivers pay more for auto insurance, consumer survey confirms," *Edmonton Journal,* 8 July 2005, p. B1.

44. Gulli, "'Outrageous' costs hammer Ontario drivers."

45. Author interview with Insurance Bureau of Canada, 21 July 2005.

46. Bruce Cran. "Junk opinion," published on the Consumers' Association of Canada website, August 2005, www.consumer.ca/pdfs/junk_opinionaug_05_(2)2.pdf.
47. Author interview with Doug Henderson, Media Relations Division, Insurance Corporation of British Columbia, 24 August 2005.
48. Author interview with Theresa Courneyea, 2 December 2003. Excerpts of interview printed in Mark Milke, "Insurance Fraud."
49. Theresa Courneyea. "Re: Auto relief, too little, too late?" *Globe and Mail*, 31 October 2003.
50. Editorial. "Governments must get involved in insurance," *Sault Star*, 17 July 2005, p. A8.
51. Author interview with Jim Wahowich, 2 December 2003. Excerpts of interview printed in Mark Milke, "Insurance Fraud."
52. Michael Kane. "Auto insurance '30% more' in Alberta."
53. 1989-2003 estimates from Canadian Taxpayers Federation, Access to Information results from Industry Canada 2001. Other: Industry Canada 2004-05 project contributions: http://strategis.ic.gc.ca/epic/Internet/inoca-bc.nsf/en/ca02068e.html
Industry Canada 2004-05 project contributions: http://strategis.ic.gc.ca/epic/Internet/inoca-bc.nsf/en/ca02123e.html
54. Cran, "Junk opinion."
55. Ibid.
56. Author interview with Bruce Cran, 8 July 2005. Excerpt printed in Mark Milke, "Junk auto insurance statistics," *National Post*, 22 July 2005, p. FP19.
57. *The National*. Canadian Broadcasting Corporation, 17 May 2005. Time: 22:00 EDT. Network: CBC Television.
58. Ibid.
59. Paul Volcker. *Manipulation of the Oil-for-Food Programme by the Iraqi Regime*. Independent Inquiry Committee into the United Nations Oil-For-Food Programme, 27 October 2005, p. 79. Available at http://www.iic-offp.org/documents/IIC%20Final%20Report%2027Oct2005.pdf.
60. Christopher Hitchens. "Unmitigated Galloway," *The Weekly Standard*, 30 May 2005, Vol. 10, No. 35, pp. 23-24.
61. Obtained by and reprinted in the *National Post*, 19 July 2005, p. A16.

Chapter 12

1. Hugh L. Keenleyside. *Canada and the United States: Some Aspects of the Republic and the Dominion*. New York: Alfred A. Knopf Inc., 1929, p. 49.
2. Ibid., p. 42.
3. John Bartlett Brebner. *North Atlantic Triangle: The Interplay of Canada, the United States and Great Britain*. New Haven: Yale University Press, 1945, p. 6.

4. Ibid., p. 6.
5. Keenleyside, pp. 5-6.
6. Ibid., pp. 4-7.
7. Brebner, pp. 42-43.
8. Ibid., p. 51.
9. Ibid., p. 51.
10. Ibid., p. 51.
11. Keenleyside, pp. 16-17.
12. Ibid., p. 27.
13. Ibid., p. 41.
14. Ibid., p. 45.
15. Ibid., p. 42.
16. Ibid., p. 47.
17. Ibid., p. 49.
18. Brebner, *North Atlantic Triangle*, p. 88.
19. Northrop Frye. *The Bush Garden*. Toronto: Anansi, 1971, p. ii.
20. Margaret Atwood. *Survival*. Toronto: Anansi, 1972, pp. 31-32.
21. Frye, *The Bush Garden*, ii.
22. Ibid.
23. Ibid.
24. Charles Doran and James Sewell. "Anti-Americanism in Canada?" *Anti-Americanism: Origins and Context*, Thomas Perry Thornton, ed., *The Annals of the American Academy of Political and Social Science*, Vol. 497. Washington, D.C.: School of Advanced International Studies, Johns Hopkins University, 1988, p. 107.
25. Paul Hollander. *Anti-Americanism: Critiques at Home and Abroad, 1965-1990*. New York: Oxford University Press, 1992, p. 415.
26. J.L. Granatstein and Norman Hillmer. *For Better or Worse: Canada and the United States to the 1990s*. Toronto: Copp, Clark, Pittman Ltd., 1991, p. 89.
27. Ibid., p. 89.
28. Gord McIntosh. "Copps vows to push magazine legislation," *Vancouver Sun*, 14 April 1999, p. A14.
29. John Holmes. "Crises in Canadian–American relations: A Canadian perspective," Lansing Lamont and J. Duncan Edwards, eds. *Friends So Different: Essays on Canada and the United States in the 1980s*. Ottawa: University of Ottawa Press, 1989, p. 18.
30. Ibid., p. 26.
31. Ibid., p. 22.
32. Ibid., pp. 26-27.
33. Ibid., p. 27.

Chapter 13

1. In I.W. Gillespie. *Tax, Borrow and Spend: Financing Federal Spending in Canada, 1867-1990*. Ottawa: Carleton University Press, 1991, p. 48.
2. Charles Adams. *For Good and Evil: The Impact of Taxes on the Course of Civilization*. Lanham, MD: Madison Books, 1993, p. 2.
3. Alan Duncan and Dominic Hobson. *Saturn's Children: How the State Devours Liberty, Prosperity and Virtue*. Cited in Niall Ferguson, *The Cash Nexus: Money and Power in the Modern World*. New York: Basic Books, 2001, p. 67.
4. Adams, *For Good and Evil*, p. 169.
5. J.H. Perry. *Taxation in Canada, Canadian Tax Paper No. 89*. Toronto: Canadian Tax Foundation, 1990, p. 17.
6. J.H. Perry lists the various taxes in pre- and post-Confederation Canada in the now out-of-print book: *Taxes, Tariffs, and Subsidies, Volumes 1 & 2*. University of Toronto Press, 1955, pp. 575-616.
7. Ibid., pp. 35-36.
8. Ibid., pp. 33-34.
9. Ibid., p. 75.
10. Ibid., pp. 33-34.
11. M.C. Urquhart and K.A.H. Buckley, eds. *Historical Statistics of Canada*, series G1-25. Toronto: MacMillan Canada, 1965, pp. 197-200.
12. Ibid., pp. 201-03.
13. J.H. Perry. *Taxation in Canada, 3rd edition*. Toronto: University of Toronto Press, 1961, p. 14.
14. Perry, *Taxes, Tariffs, and Subsidies*, pp. 51-52.
15. Ibid., p. 61.
16. Sir Richard Cartwright, cited in Gillespie, *Tax, Borrow and Spend*, p. 48.
17. Quoted in John Duffy, *Fights of Our Lives*. Toronto: HarperCollins, 2002, pp. 48-49.
18. Gillespie, *Tax, Borrow and Spend*, p. 51.
19. Ibid., p. 56.
20. Ibid., p. 59.
21. Information on past health care taxes from J.H. Perry, *A Fiscal History of Canada: The Postwar Years, Canadian Tax Paper No. 85*, Canadian Tax Foundation, 1989, pp. 653-55.
22. Bryden, "PM hints tax hike on offing."
23. Doug Fischer. "Eves and McGuinty sign pledge not to raise taxes," *Ottawa Citizen*, 12 September 2003, p. A1.
24. April Lindgren. "Biggest tax increase in decade," *Ottawa Citizen*, 19 May 2004, p. A1.
25. Duffy, *Flights of Our Lives*, pp. 48-49.
26. Perry, *Taxes, Tariffs, and Subsidies*, p. 153.
27. Ibid., p. 157.

28. J.L. Granatstein and Norman Hillmer. *Prime Ministers: Ranking Canada's Leaders.* Toronto: HarperCollins, 1999, p. 110.
29. Quoted in John Robert Colombo, *New Canadian Quotations.* Edmonton: Hurtig Publishers, p. 350. Original quotation in Dale C. Thompson, *Louis St Laurent,* 1967.
30. Thad McIllroy. *Diefenbaker: Remembering the Chief.* Toronto: Doubleday, 1984, p. 56.
31. Quoted in Colombo, *New Canadian Quotations,* p. 110.
32. Quoted in Colombo, *New Canadian Quotations,* p. 138.
33. Wendy Warburton and Stephen Bindman. "Report proves country broke," *Ottawa Citizen,* 6 September 1985, p. A1.
34. Joan Bryden. "PM hints tax hike on offing," *National Post,* 2 October 2002, p. A1.
35. Opening campaign statement by Prime Minister Paul Martin, Leader of the Liberal party, Canwest News Service, 30 November 2005.
36. Stephen Harper. Speech to the Council for National Policy, Montreal, June 1997, downloaded 15 December 2005, www.theglobeandmail.com/servlet/story/RTGAM.20051214.wtext1214/BNStory/specialDecision2006.

Chapter 14

1. John Bartlett Brebner. *North Atlantic Triangle: The Interplay of Canada, the United States and Great Britain.* New Haven: Yale University Press, 1945, p. vii.
2. J.H. Perry. *Taxation in Canada, 3rd edition.* Toronto: University of Toronto Press, 1961, p. 10.
3. J.H. Perry. *Taxes, Tariffs, and Subsidies, Volumes 1 & 2.* Toronto: University of Toronto Press, 1955, pp. 110-11.
4. Ibid., pp. 110-11.
5. Ibid., pp. 150-51.
6. Ibid., p. 147.
7. Ibid., p. 153.
8. Ibid., p. 154.
9. Perry, *Taxation in Canada,* p. 10.
10. Perry, *Taxes, Tariffs, and Subsidies,* p. 157.
11. Ibid., p. 711.
12. Ibid., p. 228.
13. Revenue figures from *Taxes, Tariffs, and Subsidies,* pp. 640-66.
14. A.M. Moore and J.H. Perry. *Financing Canadian Federation, Canadian Tax Papers No. 6.* Toronto: Canadian Tax Foundation, March 1953, p. 15.
15. I.W. Gillespie. *Tax, Borrow and Spend: Financing Federal Spending in Canada, 1867-1990.* Ottawa: Carleton University Press, 1991, p. 154.

16. "Taxes and society," United States Department of the Treasury, www. ustreas.gov/education/faq/taxes/taxes-society.html.
17. Richard M. Bird. *The Growth of Government Spending in Canada, Canadian Tax Papers No. 51.* Toronto: Canadian Tax Foundation, July 1970, p. 266.

Chapter 15

1. Letter to Len Crispino from David MacKinnon, study author, in Ontario Chamber of Commerce, *Fairness in Confederation—Fiscal Imbalance: A Roadmap to Recovery*, November 2005.
2. Len Crispino. Ontario Chamber of Commerce news release, 9 November 2005.
3. Ontario Chamber of Commerce, *Fairness in Confederation*, p. 2.
4. Ibid.
5. Ibid.
6. Letter to Len Crispino from David MacKinnon.
7. Susan Delacourt. "Ottawa handout hike upsets rich provinces: Ontario, Alberta dig in their heels. McGuinty seeks 'fairer' share of cash. First ministers tackle transfers," *Toronto Star*, 26 October 2004, p. AO1.
8. Editorial. "Ontario's fiscal high-wire act," *Toronto Star*, 26 March 2005, p. FO6.
9. Ibid.
10. Canadian Taxpayers Federation, news release, 12 October 2004, www.taxpayer.com.

Index

A

Index

About the Author

Mark Milke is a former director of the Canadian Taxpayers Federation, where he served as a spokesman first in Alberta and then in British Columbia. Educated at the University of Alberta, he is originally from Kelowna and has lived in the United States and Japan. A columnist and writer, his work on taxes, politics and government has appeared in newspapers such as *The Vancouver Sun* and *National Post*, and he is a regular contributor to the *Calgary Herald*. His first book on BC politics, *Barbarians in the Garden City— The BC NDP in Power*, was received with critical acclaim. He is an avid hiker and nature photographer.